The Prostitution of Sexuality

The Prostitution of Sexuality

Kathleen Barry

New York University Press
New York and London

NEW YORK UNIVERSITY PRESS
New York and London

Library of Congress Cataloging-in-Publication Data
Barry, Kathleen.
The prostitution of sexuality / Kathleen Barry.
p.   cm.
Includes bibliographical references (p.   ) and index.
ISBN 0-8147-1217-7 (cloth : acid-free paper)
1. Prostitution—Moral and ethical aspects.   2. Sex oriented
businesses.   3. Sex crimes.   4. Women—Crimes against.   5. Feminist
theory.   I. Title.
HQ117.B37   1995
306.74—dc20   94-27897
CIP

New York University Press books are printed on acid-free paper,
and their binding materials are chosen for strength and durability.

Manufactured in the United States of America

10   9   8   7   6   5   4   3   2   1

Contents

The Prostitution of Sexuality *is a culmination of nearly 2 decades of my scholarly research and feminist activism. It originated in* Female Sexual Slavery, *published in 1979 and issued in paperback by New York University Press in 1983.* Female Sexual Slavery *launched international movements on the issues it addressed, and this fact, along with the dramatic changes in the conditions I described in my original work, have occasioned this essentially new book.*

Introduction

Sexual exploitation objectifies women by reducing them to sex; sex that incites violence against women and that reduces women to commodities for market exchange. Sexual exploitation is the foundation of women's oppression socially normalized. This is a difficult and painful subject to study. I tried to back away from this painfulness when I wrote *Female Sexual Slavery*. I said then:

When a friend first suggested that I write a book on what I was describing to her as female sexual slavery, I resisted the idea. I had gone through the shock and horror of learning about it in the late 1960s when I discovered a few paternalistically written books documenting present-day practices. During that same period I found a biography of Josephine Butler, who single-handedly raised a national and then international movement against forced prostitution in the nineteenth century but who is now virtually unknown. I realized that Josephine Butler's current obscurity was directly connected to the invisibility of sex slavery today. And so I wrote a few short pieces on the subject and incorporated my limited information into the curriculum of the women's studies classes that I taught.

But to write a book on the subject—to spend 2 or 3 years researching, studying female slavery—that was out of the question. I instinctively withdrew from the suggestion; I couldn't face that. But as the idea settled over the next few weeks, I realized that my reaction was typical of women's response: even with some knowledge of the facts, I was moving from fear to paralysis to hiding. It was then that I realized, both for myself personally and for all the rest of us, that the only way we can come out of hiding, break through our paralyzing defenses, is to know the full extent of sexual violence and domination of women. It is knowledge from which we have pulled back, as well as knowledge that has been withheld from us. In *knowing*, in facing directly, we can learn how to chart our course out of this oppression, by envisioning and creating a world which will preclude female sexual slavery. In knowing the extent of our oppression we will have to discover some of the ways to begin immediately breaking the deadly cycle of fear, denial-through-hiding, and slavery.

Far from being the project I feared facing, the research, study, and writing of this book *[Female Sexual Slavery]* have given me knowledge that forces me to think beyond confinement of women's oppression. Understanding the scope and depth of female sexual slavery makes it intolerable to passively live with it any longer. I had to realistically visualize a world that would preclude this enslavement by projecting some ways out of it. Reading about sexual slavery makes hope and vision necessary.

That was 1979.

Because I found it painful to write about this fact of women's lives, for the next decade, the 1980s, I tried to shift some of my work into other areas. In 1980, just after my book *Female Sexual Slavery* was published, I conducted meetings on this issue at the 1980 Mid–Decade of Women Conference in Copenhagen, from which came an international feminist meeting held in Rotterdam in 1983. I am grateful to Barbara Good for her networking that led now Senator Barbara Mikulski to initiate a resolution we drafted on prostitution that was adopted in the 1980 U.N. Conference in Copenhagen, a significant boost to this work. But launching international feminist political action to confront sexual exploitation also brought out the proprostitution lobby— organizations and individuals who actively promote prostitution—who made me and my lectures the focus of their attack and disruption and hate campaigns for several years.

I returned to the United States to find that our own feminist movement against pornography which I was part of launching in the 1970s had escalated with the most important legal approach to have come out of our movement to that point, the feminist civil rights antipornography law, "the Dworkin-MacKinnon Ordinance," as we have come to call it. Political radical feminism more and more was directing its energies to the struggle against pornography, challenging sexual liberals and just plain liberals for their promotion of sexual abuse and exploitation. This brought out the "sexual outlaws"; lesbian sadomasochists and heterosexual women hiding behind their private pornographic sexual lives joined forces to form the "Feminist" Anti-Censorship Task Force. Radical feminism was under siege as it had been a century earlier. We barely noticed the shift that was occurring in the women's movement, the shift to a one-issue movement. We had already learned that single-issue movements do not survive because they are disconnected from the totality of women's oppression.

I found myself in the ironic position of building an international movement only to come home to my own movement to find I was out there alone on the issue of female sexual slavery. I lectured on prostitution as a condition of sexual exploitation. But it was treated by the movement as an "add-on," an issue tacked on to the work against pornography or sexual violence simply to be sure that all the bases were covered.

After organizing an international meeting in Rotterdam on female sexual slavery in 1983, exhausted and depressed from repeated undermining and personal attack on my radical feminism by the proprostitution lobby and by Western liberals there, I announced to several feminist friends including Robin Morgan, whose support has been more than sustaining, that I had gone as far as I could on this issue. I explained that even after organizing an international meeting, I was still alone and I was withdrawing.

But they had other plans. They were excited about how the international network I had been developing could begin a new wave of NGOs, nongovernmental organizations in consultative status with the United Nations. (I actually moaned aloud in the restaurant when Robin proposed this over dinner.) Having worked with many human-rights NGOs internationally, I could see the potential for global feminist consciousness raising. The international networking I had been developing on the issue of traffic in women would qualify our coalition for human rights (Category II) status with the United Nations.

However, I rejected then, as I do now, the idea of a one-woman movement. Although I could no longer be out there alone on this issue, especially among women from the West, I reluctantly initiated the application to the United Nations for NGO status. That work, along with demands for lectures and actions organized on behalf of victims, kept me going despite my personal decisions and even despite the toll it began to take on my health, not to mention the extreme costs to my professional career.

At last, by the mid 1980s something had changed. In the United States Evelina Giobbe announced the organization of WHISPER (Women Hurt in Systems of Prostitution Engaged in Revolt). Then Susan Hunter organized the Council for Prostitution Alternatives.

In the Asian region in particular women have mounted massive campaigns against sex industries and their consumers. I have had the privilege of working with dedicated women like Aurora Javate DeDios and the Philippines Organizing Team, Yayori Matsui in Japan, Jean D'Cunha in India, and Sigma Huda in Bangladesh who have brought deeply felt and powerful analysis to the issue of sexual exploitation of Asian women.

In 1987 I decided it was time, once and for all, to move on to other issues. At the New York Conference on Sexual Liberals and the Attack Against Feminism, I gave the issue back to our movement, challenging the audience of 1,500 feminists not to let this work on prostitution and traffic in women be reduced to a one-woman movement. I asked them to take up the issue, and I added emphatically, "do not call me." And no one did for almost a year. What I did not know was that during that time Dorchen Leidholdt, who had organized the 1987 conference and had been spearheading radical feminist actions through Women Against Pornography, had indeed taken up the issue. She and a group of women were organizing an international conference on traffic in women in 1988. Calls from Dorchen for information and clarification drew me back from my short hiatus, but this time things were different. From international feminism we launched The Coalition Against Trafficking in Women, organized based on my original work, *Female Sexual Slavery,* first published in 1979. By then the international work against traffic in women had become a feminist movement.

As we worked together and gained nongovernmental status with the United Nations, we found new avenues for addressing women's human rights. In 1986 I had been a rapporteur in a UNESCO meeting of experts on prostitution held in Madrid. In that meeting it was clear to me that present U.N. conventions could no longer address the problems of sexual exploitation. I remember telling Wassyla Tamzali in the Division of Human Rights and Peace Rights at UNESCO that that five-day meeting was the first time since I wrote *Female Sexual Slavery* that I had been challenged into new analysis of this issue. Seven years was a long time to wait. Those new ideas led to a collaboration with UNESCO in a meeting I held at Penn State in the spring of 1991, which has led to the development of a new model for an international human rights law, the Convention Against Sexual Exploitation. Such momentum internationally and with feminists in the United States in 1992 formed the basis of a Plan of Action for networking on the part of the Coalition Against Trafficking in Women and UNESCO. The plan as Wassyla Tamzali and I developed it called for joint action to create an international network to confront sexual exploitation, especially in prostitution as a violation of women's human rights. The work and support of

Twiss Butler and Marie Jose Regab, of the National Organization for Women has provided encouragement and networking.

Despite the overwhelming prostitution of women's sexuality, the unbridled trafficking in women worldwide, and the sex-industry-supported proprostitution lobby, I have seen many important changes since the mid 1970s when I was researching and writing *Female Sexual Slavery*. Back then, prostitution and traffic in women were as disconnected from the women's movement as they were silenced. In Europe Denise Pouillon Falco, Renée Bridel, Suzanne Képès, and Anima Basak sustained long-standing movements and actions on this issue when it was silenced elsewhere. They provided hope, support, and friendship. But in research, prostitution, treated as a form of female deviance and an area of criminology, was considered inevitable but controllable. Traffic in women had been made invisible after the campaigns of Josephine Butler in the nineteenth century. But in 1986 sitting in a conference organized by Cookie Teer in North Carolina when Evelina Giobbe described her new organization WHISPER, with tears in my eyes, I realized that it had all been worth it.

In the beginning of our women's movement, in the late 1960s and early 1970s, in thirst of our history and in search of our theories, we voraciously read of our feminist past. We were struck by the most glaring political mistake of our foremothers—an error not at all evident to them during the first wave of feminism. After more than 20 years of radical feminist struggle against the widest and deepest range of exploitations and violations against women, that first wave of the U.S. women's movement made the tactical error of focusing primarily on one issue above all others—suffrage. The reasoning was sound, the practicality clear: that without political power women would not be able to gain for themselves their other demands.

But that strategic shift, from radical feminist confrontation against *oppression* to single-issue movements emphasizing legalistic reform, was the beginning of the end. By the time women achieved their goal of suffrage, the women's movement had died. It would take at least another 70 years for women to use their vote for women.

Twenty-five years ago, launching this second wave of the movement, we radical feminists promised ourselves that we would *never,* ever concede our radical movement by reducing it to a single strategy, that we would never retreat from the interconnections among all issues confronting women. To do so would be to concede our revolution and reduce our struggle to individual personalities and to legal reform. But it has happened.

Not only have issues of sexual exploitation been reduced to a single-issue movement; they have been configured only (or at least primarily) in terms of legal change. But patriarchy will never make itself illegal. Long before new laws are enacted or ever actually protect women, the struggle for them is where and when feminists set new standards. Our struggle must go beyond law and reform to their roots in the experience of female oppression. I consider legal change to be an important aspect of our movement and struggle. That is why since the beginning I have supported and promoted the civil rights antipornography legal proposals, and I have promoted the development of new international law. But law, attractive as it is to a captivated American audience, is only one part of radical change. What ultimately matters is that male behavior change.

In the 1990s we have found that in the United States women's issues have become so dissociated from each other that there are separate movements for abortion rights under the euphemism of "choice" while at the same time the euphemism "choice" is turned into the rallying call for the promotion of sexual exploitation through pornography and prostitution as fostered by sexual liberals and the proprostitution lobby, who ask, don't women "choose" prostitution? pornography? (as if this question made an ounce of difference to the customer-, i.e., male-driven market). Meanwhile our movement has become so deconstructed that issues like teenage pregnancy and prochoice, which means girls' right to abortion, are dissociated from the very conditions that have produced a crisis in teenage pregnancy: sexual exploitation—the wholesale sexualization of society and promotion of early sex through pornography and the legitimization of prostitution.

Feminist programs have suffered with the fragmentation of issues. There has been the reduction of some feminist programs we launched, such as rape-crisis programs initiated in the early 1970s to social-work programs of the 1980s. This has further deconstructed the political commitment of feminism to revolutionary change. And consequent to this, we radical feminists have been isolated, made into targets of the sexual liberals and proprostitution lobby because we insist on confronting sexual exploitation as a condition of *oppression*.

How did pornography come to be taken up as a feminist action dissociated from other issues—especially prostitution, especially rape, especially sexual harassment? As feminist political action against pornography escalated, it separated into a particular movement of its own. The separation was forced, in large part, by the attacks from sexual liberals. In this near-deadly struggle, radical feminism began to turn more and more exclusively to antipornography because we were embattled and fighting to survive, as was true with Susan B. Anthony when she desperately turned to focus on a single issue, suffrage, in the nineteenth century.

The civil rights, anti-pornography ordinance developed by Andrea Dworkin and Catharine MacKinnon defined pornography as "sexually explicit subordination of women." This definition was a key to inclusiveness, to widening the girth of the movement, for it refers to a collective female class condition. Oppression. Domination. And so revolutionary struggle has been inherent in this anti-pornography work, even if the movement has lost focus on the fullest, widest range of issues and, most importantly, their interconnections—for it is in their interconnections that we find revealed the complex web of patriarchal domination of women as a class. The history of feminism is a warning to us against turning from one single issue to the next. When we open up a "new" issue, last year's issue goes to therapy or social work—possibly important but apolitically individualized.

When in the second half of the 1970s I was writing *Female Sexual Slavery,* I did not consider that I was writing a book on prostitution. Nor, as I've already established, was I trying to break open the next "new" feminist issue. My effort then and since has been to integrate the violation of women by prostitution into the feminist struggle and to move it, as one of several connected issues, into the forefront of the feminist agenda. I have approached this struggle by understanding prostitute women not as a group set apart, which is a misogynist construction, but as women whose experience of sexual exploitation is consonant with that of all women's experience of sexual exploitation.

What I was doing in *Female Sexual Slavery* was writing about the use of sex/sexuality as power—to dominate—as a condition of oppression. I am concerned with a *class* condition. My study of sex as power then and now inevitably, continually, unrelentingly returns me to prostitution. I knew then that one cannot mobilize against a class condition of oppression unless one knows its fullest dimensions. Thus my work has been to study and expose sexual power in its most severe, global, institutionalized, and crystallized forms. I reasoned that we could know the parts because we would know the whole. From 1970 I had been involved in initiating radical feminist action against rape, but until I learned of the traffic in women and explored the pimping strategies in prostitution, I did not fully grasp how utterly without value female life is under male domination. Women as expendables. Women as throwaways. Prostitution—the cornerstone of all sexual exploitation.

To confront the whole, the female class condition, strategically and politically, I launched action in an international arena of human rights because sex is power over all women. As the female condition is a class condition, sex power must be addressed as a global issue, inclusive of all of its occurrences in the subordination of women. To do that prostitution must be centered in this struggle.

I have chosen to focus my militancy and strategizing against oppression on *human rights*. While promoting individual civil rights, I believe that human rights can be taken further. Expanded to the human condition, it has been used to recognize that peoples—such as those under apartheid, and those under any form of colonization—have a right to self-determination. The appeal of human rights to me is its ability to protect the class, collective condition—and this is a protection not yet available to women. However, the decolonization of the sexually exploited female class has not yet begun. In 1970 I participated in issuing the Fourth World Manifesto, written in response to socialists who tried to coopt the women's movement to serve the left as if men were not imperialists of sex. In that manifesto we established the colonization of women as a condition of patriarchy. Where the United Nations will protect the "sovereign [read independent] rights of all peoples and their territorial integrity,"[1] in our present human rights work, I intend to see that women, as a territory sexually colonized, are granted that protection. With the struggle of our movement, we will one day see to it that, according to U.N. human-rights standards established for other groups, sexual exploitation is treated as a class condition that is *a crime against humanity* as much as it is a crime against any individual human being.

Thus, in studying sex as power in *Female Sexual Slavery,* I found the class condition of all women to be fully revealed in prostitution. That finding led me into almost two decades of work on developing an international human-rights approach to confronting that class condition globally.

But to get to that point in our struggle we must go back to the original premise of radical *political* feminism: that the personal is political and therefore, the separation of them—the "whores"—and us—the "women"—is utterly false, a patriarchal lie. And that means that we must talk about sex. The sexuality of today.

Not only in pornography. Not only when it is explicitly "against our will."

In this work, I am shifting from my previous work on the sexuality of prostitution to my new work on the prostitution of sexuality. I am taking prostitution as the model, the most extreme and most crystallized form of all sexual exploitation. Sexual exploitation is a political condition, the foundation of women's subordination and the base from which discrimination against women is constructed and enacted.

The feminist international approach of this study recognizes that there are worldwide commonalities to women's subordination and that therefore there must be a commonality to power arrangements across races, classes, and state boundaries. The word "gender," intended by feminists to refer to the social basis of sex ascription and thus to reveal sexual politics, has been neutralized by academics so that it now simply refers to biological differences between the sexes. "Gender" has become an apolitical term, a word that makes it possible to not have to specifically designate "woman." "Gender" makes patriarchy, the historical and political context of power, disappear. That is the context in which female sexuality is prostituted worldwide today in order to secure the domination of women.

The facts of women's subordination and patriarchy do not disappear because language is depoliticized and neutralized. In this work I am studying prostitution as institutionalized and industrialized sexual exploitation of women, developed from patriarchal feudalism. Theoretically, I have developed a macro-level analysis of the global condition of women that is lodged in the micro-level analysis of human interaction and personal experience. Sociologically, this work explores sexual exploitation by bridging the "macro-micro" gap, which has been noted as a problem whenever research is confined to one level or the other. From a feminist perspective, this is the bridge from the personal to the political. It recognizes that sexual exploitation is a condition that includes all women in prostitution. As prostitution has become industrialized and a global economy has come to shape international relations, it is more important than ever to feminist research and activism that these different levels of analysis be joined.

For the study of prostitution, traditional measures are not available. Beyond general estimates of prostitution populations, there are no reliable statistics on prostitution because it is by and large illegal. Even where prostitution is legalized, greater percentages of it remain illegal, and it is controlled by organized crime and therefore inaccessible for measurement. And prostitute women are not counted in the development of demographic data and trends in research on women in development.

The most reliable knowledge and documentation of trafficking in women and children come primarily from three sources: (1) human-rights organizations, which are primarily concerned with children and operate from a distinction between "free" and "forced" prostitution in a context of severe poverty, (2) AIDS activists, researchers, and foundations who in the last 5 years have begun to address prostitution, considering it central to the spread of AIDS and being concerned with it from that standpoint, and (3) feminist organizations concerned with women's rights and human rights, which address the concerns of the other two groups in their particular focus on women. Only feminist/human-rights organizations and activists are addressing the full range of conditions that promote trafficking and sex industrialization because only they are concerned with women (and therefore children and AIDS and poverty). Therefore, research on this subject draws both from first-hand observations and from the documentation and statistics produced primarily by these groups. In the case of prostitution, sex trafficking, and sex industrialization, the reports, statistics, and estimates from state governments are the *least* reliable. Frequently, local police and border guards are either involved in the trafficking or taking bribes. In fact, some national government officials have made the point that human-rights workers give the government a bad name by exposing cases of trafficking.

A combination of qualitative methods is the best approach to exposing practices that are otherwise inaccessible, especially because they sustain exploitation.[2] The approaches I have taken to the study of sexual exploitation are

1. to document the dimensions of prostitution and traffic in women globally and to trace them historically in order to identify macro/global patterns and trends and to determine the impact of the West and its global economic dominance on the developing world;
2. to adopt a symbolic-interaction approach to interpretation in studying the individual experience of sexual exploitation, particularly prostitution;
3. to analyze the interaction of the macro/global condition with micro-individual/interactive experience in terms of international human-rights law, and to identify projects and programs that did not exist when I was writing *Female Sexual Slavery* but that now are some of the best examples of success in confronting sexual exploitation, particularly in prostitution; and
4. theoretically to consider sexual exploitation as a condition of oppression in terms of sexual relations of power.

Adopting global, theoretical, individual/interpretive, and programmatic-policy and legal approaches, one could argue, is too large an undertaking. Surely such a work risks overgeneralization. However, because sexuality has not been dealt with comprehensively but rather is typically disaggregated in sexological and criminological research, an overall study of the interlocking forces of male domination is required in order to locate women in prostitution within the class conditions of women under patriarchal domination. In order not to reduce women in prostitution and women who are subjected to the prostitution of sexuality to biologically sexed beings or to deviants and criminals, it is necessary to risk some overgeneralization in the process of bringing together the forces that shape sexual exploitation of women today.

My research in this book has developed over two decades. During that time, through my work with women on all the continents, I have had repeated opportunities to present my analysis, confirm my findings, and reassess my assumptions so as to achieve their present refinements. In order to study global macro trends in the absence of concrete statistical data, I have turned to a variety of sources: my own original research in documenting specific cases of female sexual slavery, as well as cases documented and brought before the United Nations, court proceedings, and newspaper accounts. Through the international network and the number of international meetings I have organized, I have been able to confirm cases. From many divergent sources, I have drawn together a range of material that has made it possible to identify new patterns and practices.

To study the interactional effects of the individual experiences of sexual exploitation, I have drawn from my own interviews with prostitute women that began in 1977 and have continued as I have worked with women in different world regions. With these interviews and those from recent research, I explore the interactive dimensions of sexual exploitation.

Symbolic interaction is the study of the interpretation of gestures in human interaction.[3] It posits that in interpreting the meaning of the other, we approximate our understanding of the other's meaning by putting ourselves in the place of the person with whom we are interacting. Not only does symbolic interaction provide an intense approach to the interpretation of meaning of subjects in experience; for me it also establishes the point of view of the researcher.

For the researcher in symbolic interaction, the meaning of a situation is derived by interpreting that meaning from the point of view of the person in the situation. That is, all that is taken in by the persons engaged in interpreting each other's gestures constitutes the interpretation and the situation. Interpretation is then what produces social reality and is the source of social facts.[4] For the feminist researcher studying women's experiences that are violations of human rights, one step further is required in order effectively to interpret interaction. Engagement with one's subject involves taking on the meaning of the other by putting oneself in her place, by asking "What would I have done?" and "What meaning would I have interpreted if I were in that situation?" This feminist approach, combined with symbolic interaction, is what makes it possible to break the silences surrounding sexual exploitation.

As a research approach, the significance of symbolic interaction is that it is neither intraindividual nor deterministic. It recognizes not only that interaction takes place in a situation (what some psychologists prefer to call "context") but also that interaction is the situation. It is the part and it is the whole. To conduct research from this approach it is necessary to reconstruct the situations of sexual exploitation in order to determine their meaning—meaning that is both individual and social. The situations are both the interpretative interaction and all that surrounds the individuals, including the individuals that are taken into account in the interpretation. But the situation in which interpretation takes place stretches far beyond the immediacy of interaction to include the geographic, economic, and political landscape from which meaning is drawn in interpretation. Therefore, global conditions and private life intersect in interpretation. In analyzing conditions of sexual exploitation, this is how macro and micro are brought together. In this sense interpretation produces social facts that are neither reducible to the individual, nor to intraindividual phenomena, nor to dissociated personal interaction.

Some things stay the same as much as they change and that is why I began this work only as a revision of *Female Sexual Slavery*. But two years into the "revisions" I was back to doing original research and developing new theory. Revision proved to be an impossible project because too much has changed since 1979. I am grateful to Donna Ballock and Brenda Seery for assistance with entering revisions into the manuscript and for their willingness to do that over and over again long after I would declare that I had finished but I had not. I deeply appreciate Rosemary Gido's reading of earlier drafts, Polly Connelly's reading of the final manuscript, and Colin Jones, Director of New York University Press for his suggestions and patience with the rewrites.

Prostitution of Sexuality, as the title of the work reveals, indicates the direction of the changes in prostitution toward its normalization in nonprostitute sexual exchanges. This book presents new theory and analysis that explore in depth the effects of prostitution on women and the implication for women's human rights. All that remains in this work from the original *Female Sexual Slavery* are some of the original cases and analysis that I have included now for the purpose of comparison with the present situation. I have documented the major practices in trafficking today and left those cases from the earlier work that reflect the connections and comparisons between trafficking then and now. Moreover, it is now possible politically to theorize about this issue beyond the ways that were just beginning to be possible in the 1970s.

Prostitution and sexual exploitation have grown dramatically and changed significantly since I wrote *Female Sexual Slavery*. As I compared then with now, the *Prostitution of Sexuality,* much more than a revision of *Female Sexual Slavery,* became a new work. As I sifted through the new knowledge we have gained, the revisions became rewrites and eventually new chapters. Through the meetings, work, organizing, and campaigning of the 1980s and the 1990s with feminists around the world and within the United Nations and UNESCO, my theories and analysis have grown, changed, and developed. This has led to entirely new chapters on "Prostitution of Sexuality," "Sexual Power," "Industrialization of Sex," "Traffic in Women," and "Human Rights and Global Feminist Action."

I have retained my historical study of Josephine Butler, who, for decades, has been a model for me. However, today I probably understand better why. Her passionate commitment to fighting state-regulated prostitution was deeply connected to her direct work with women victimized by it. When I first wrote *Female Sexual Slavery*, I was particularly concerned to give a feminist-historical base to this work and to analyze her struggle against regulated prostitution. In the last decade, as the proprostitution lobby and the sexual liberals have promoted prostitution as free sex and a viable profession for women, I now know that Butler was not only an important but also a problematic historical figure for me—because of the issues she challenged, and because of those she *did not challenge*. When I reread this chapter from *Female Sexual Slavery* and began to revise it, I was surprised to see the extent to which I had *not* explored the underlying bases of abolition, the foundations for abolitionist distinctions between "free" and "forced" prostitution. Challenging that distinction and showing it to be compromised is central to my work today, and so I was forced to reconsider the position I had taken on it in *Female Sexual Slavery*. Thus this work represents not only a revision of my previous thinking but also, to some extent, a reversal—or rather, not exactly a reversal but a new theory and policy orientation that I discuss in the last chapter.

The chapter on pimping has been revised, but not as dramatically as the others. Changes in pimping have taken place not so much in terms of practices as in terms of new approaches by the proprostitution lobby to have prostitution decriminalized and legitimized. However, with the normalization of prostitution in both the Third World and the West, I have significantly revised and expanded my study of state laws on pimping, all of which are still reducible to the idea of the "state as pimp." This book has been written while I have been directing the Coalition Against Trafficking in Women and we have been developing a new international human-rights law against sexual exploitation. Working on this law with Janice Raymond, Dorchen Leidholdt, and Elizabeth DeFeis in the Coalition and human-rights advocates, especially Wassyla Tamzali at UNESCO and others at the United Nations, has enriched this work as much as this new research was brought to bear on the development of this international law. Elke Lassan's translations of German reports and interviews have been invaluable to the international scope of this work.

I have slightly revised the chapter on Patricia Hearst, to explain why, personally and politically, her case was important in my study then and is still important to consider now. Furthermore, I have been able to expand upon the method of symbolic interaction that led to my original interpretive understanding of her case, an important approach to revealing the silences in women's lives. However, there is another important reason for retaining this chapter. Many feminists, workers in rape-crisis and sexual-abuse programs, and victims of prostitution have frequently told me of the importance of this chapter and the chapter on the befriending and love strategies of pimps in explaining what Susan Hunter called "terror bonding." Indeed, these are central chapters, describing elements of what Dee Graham in her important new work, *Loving to Survive,* refers to as a societal Stockholm Syndrome that likens women's loving in patriarchy to the captivity of hostages.

It is my hope that with this book I have theoretically advanced the work against sexual exploitation and especially prostitution. I am not treating theory as an abstraction from reality. Feminist theory is theory only if it is rooted in women's realities and from there reveals and explains women's class condition.

The other new dimension of this work, which was not possible in my first book because it did not exist in the 1970s, appears in the last chapter, in which I have brought together a sampling of strategies—personal, local, regional, and international—for individual survival and international action—strategies that have been developing throughout the movement and around the world since the early 1980s—strategies that were not yet known when I was stuck in my isolation writing *Female Sexual Slavery*—strategies that reveal a world of feminist action, global commitments to confront patriarchy. For me these strategies, and the people behind them, represent not only effective actions but an interconnected movement, a struggle, a love of as much as a thirst for our liberation. To them this book is dedicated.

1

Prostitution of Sexuality

"What is a woman? Ans: Support system for a pussy." That sign, nailed to a post on the street of an outdoor bar, summarized the sex industries, not only there in Angeles in the Philippines, but everywhere. The next sign, "Protect yourself from AIDS, use condoms," made it appear that under these conditions, aids was the only risk to women. This was only one scene that I thought about in 1993 as I was sitting on a panel in Manila, in a legal forum organized to address the question, "Are women's rights human rights?" Listening to my colleagues on the panel, I thought of the women trafficked from Bangladesh to Pakistan, of the women trafficked from Latin America to the United States and Europe, of the bar women in Olongapo, Subic, and Angeles I had met and talked to during the previous several days. Most of them still had the naiveté of many of the women who migrate from the distant rural countryside, some previously victimized sexually by incest abuse and rape, others without any knowledge or sexual experience, many not even fully comprehending what is happening to them, many still believing that their American "boyfriends" who left when the United States withdrew its bases from the

Philippines are still coming back for them, some gagging into towels after each blow job, and others, those in the cheapest bars (as if these hell holes made for and usually run by American and Australian men could be distinguished between cheap and cheapest), who are known as "three holers" because no orifice of the human body is protected from sale and customer intrusion.[1]

On this typically hot (95°), Philippine summer day, as we sat coolly in an air-conditioned room that was unaffected by the Manila "brownouts," my mind wandered back to the women from the bars I had met, some of whom I had come to know even during my too-short visits. I found my head swimming and my stomach clenched as my colleagues attempted to answer the question, "Are women's rights human rights?" Given the realities I had just seen and had seen over and over again for the previous 15 years, I knew again how easy it is to become distanced, a distancing that oftentimes leads either to academic pretense of objectivity or to legal liberalism with its pretense of neutrality.[2]

The intense concern among the human-rights activists and lawyers gathered in this comfortable room was blurred for me by the reality of the days preceding. I was reminded of my walks through the areas of the *maisons d'abattage* in Paris 15 years earlier. The utter disregard for women's humanity, as I saw it then and now, in Paris, in the Philippines, in Thailand, in brothels, on streets, and in storefront windows provokes a more direct but unasked question that must be placed before men, governments, their policies, and their institutions: "Are women human beings?"

When society becomes sexually saturated, sex is equated with the female body—where it is gotten, had, taken. In the sexualization of society, woman is sexed body. Sexualization of society constructs femaleness as an "essence" and as acquisition that is sex. As sexed body, woman is made universal, and women, accessible for sex, are made to be indistinguishable from each other. That is sexual essentialism.

By contrast, men may need sex, they may pursue it, they get it, have it, and frequently misuse it, and sometimes they may even be used for it. But men are not the objects of sexualization; neither as a collectivity nor in their individuality are they sex, sexed body. In fact, *men are not reduced to their bodies* or their biology or their drives. While male sexuality has been treated as driven by an imperative, however imperative their sexual drives are cultivated to be, men's identities are formed by what they do in the world, not by functions attributed to their bodies.

While sexual identities are *socially ascribed* to women, men *achieve* their identities as acting beings. Sexualization of society genders inequality. Sexual essentialism goes beyond promoting inequality to producing oppression. Patriarchal domination makes women undifferentiated among and from each other and makes them known, in the first instance, as different from men, and therefore lesser.

There are no biological givens about sex that are not social and political constructions. In that sense society precedes biology. Sexual "drives" are built into interactions as needs or necessities. Sex, accessible to men through the female body, is a social product of culture, a political product of gender hierarchy, and these are the conditions of male power. Sexualization is conveyed into society through body images of women in the media, in pornography, and in the "scientific" construction of sex through sexology, which reduces sex to its physicality.[3] Further, the construction of sexuality that reduces sex to a thing and woman to an object is a *public* condition which affects private life but has a public reality of its own. The public construction of sex as a social fact of male power sexualizes women as a public fact. The fullest patriarchal reduction of woman to sexed body is prostitution.

The everyday practice of equating female with sex is typified in the way Melinda entered prostitution. She had been a prostitute in the United States for several years when I met and interviewed her. She told me about her experience as a teenager coming home from the movies with her girlfriend one afternoon. She was waiting for a bus when a man approached her and told her he'd pay her $50 for a date. Being female and on the street was all that was required for her to be taken as a prostitute. But she was a naive 15-year-old who believed that he really wanted to take her out on a date. She talked with him for a few minutes and accepted his offer. With no idea that he had actually solicited her as a prostitute, she went to his hotel room, where she learned that being a "date" meant that he was buying her for sex. By the time she realized she actually had been picked up as a prostitute, she could not leave. Faced with the expectation that she provide sex, she reasoned, "Why not?" She thought, "It will be over quickly. I'll get out of here." At 15 she was picked up as a sex thing and "turned out" for prostitution. Once begun, she couldn't get away. Afterward, prostitution kept coming back to her.

In many cases like Melinda's, prior sexual abuse, particularly when it has been sustained over time, as in incest assault, has already predisposed women, made them particularly vulnerable to other sexual exploitations and to not fighting back. In exploring Melinda's story with her, I learned that it was not only the trick who picked her up on the street that had taken her for sex, so had her stepfather. What made her a prostitute to each of these males is that she was a female, and therefore could be taken as a body for them to use for sex.

When the human being is reduced to a body, objectified to sexually service another, whether or not there is consent, violation of the human being has taken place. The human being is the bodied self that human rights is meant to protect and human development is intended to support. However, in the American legal context, consent has become the defining factor in determining whether violation has occurred. In this way, the fullness of human experience and the human self is reduced to will, intent or consent, as if that is all that is involved in violation. Human will is the cornerstone of liberal theory and law, which makes the individual central and singular in the Western concept of rights. In this way, liberal legal theory does not consider oppression, the condition of class domination which is so pervasive that it actually invokes consent, collusion or some form of cooperation from the oppressed. Prostitution is structured to invoke women's consent, as is marriage, as is socially constructed sexuality.

In this work I am shifting from the nearly singular standard of consent or force in the determination of violation to its full human, interactive bodied experience, to span the range of oppression from individualized coercion to class domination. In the fullness of human experience, when women are reduced to their bodies, and in the case of sexual exploitation to sexed bodies, they are treated as lesser, as other, and thereby subordinated. This is sexual exploitation and it violates women's human rights to dignity and equality. Therefore, while pornographic media are the means of sexually saturating society, while rape is paradigmatic of sexual exploitation, prostitution, with or without a woman's consent, is the institutional, economic, and sexual model for women's oppression.

To the oppressor, sexual differences and racial differences are visible evidence that all women and people of color, being unlike whites and men, are the "other," the lesser. That is the significance of reducing woman to sexed body in the sexual saturation of society. It is how she is known, no matter what else she does, or who she is. In "otherness" time is made to stand still for the oppressed. By representing the oppressed as biologically or culturally different, by reducing them by means of their difference to "others," patriarchal power dismembers women from their history. That is how human beings are deprived of their humanity. The making/doing of history is the way in which human social action takes place over time. In violating contrast, oppression is a historical condition in which, for the oppressed, time is shrunk to the moment; for that is what it means to be ahistorical, outside of time, immanent and therefore not transcendent. This is the most ancient and contemporary form of subjugation in the world. These are the ideological justifications that underpin relations of power in racism, apartheid, and colonialism.

Sexual oppression, through its biological determinisms, halts women's forward movement and thereby attempts to annihilate the possibilities of their progress, change, growth, and development. Sexually subjugated women cease to be treated as if they exist in time, and to varying degrees they internalize atemporality contained by immanence. These are the conditions by which the subordinated are effectively deprived of the fullness and potential of their humanity. Men make themselves historical at the cost of those whom they have physically differentiated from themselves by race and by gender, those whom they have reduced to "other." To them, women are not just a different body, but sexed body. It is therefore not coincidental that when women begin to claim their own history—indeed, to enter into history because they are making it—men reinvoke woman as sexed body with a vengeance. That vengeance saturates the society with pornography and enters women's bodies through sexual exploitation.

Domination by sex, race, and culture is encoded in human beings.[4] The body is our connection as human beings to both our personal inner world and the social outer world, our self and society, and the body is the material location of differentiation, the connection to the world outside of oneself through which one knows oneself as a separate and distinct human being. The body both encases human experience and transcends itself as humanness is achieved and sustained in interaction with others and with and in the world. "Body image extends beyond the borders of the body,"[5] as Morris Berman points out. He quotes Paul Schilder: "In the construction of the body-image there is a continual testing to discover what could be incorporated into the body. . . . The body is a social phenomenon." Therefore to influence a person in terms of image "is to have an impact on that person somatically."[6] The body cannot be taken as a discrete object, separate from its interactive moorings, for as Berman and others have pointed out, "I am" also means "I am not." Interaction in the world and with others is simultaneously the source of one's differentiation as an individual self and the means by which the world and our interpretations of it are brought into the body. The self "has no other root than a visceral one." [7] Yet it has humanity because it is social.

Simultaneously and artificially, racism and sexism etch inferiority or superiority onto, and socially construct human life through, social interaction. Interaction is the most specifically personal means for encoding domination in human beings, onto human life, in the human condition. When domination is encoded through social interaction, it dehumanizes in each instance. Racism invokes the body, with the use of physically differentiated racial characteristics to claim the superiority of one group through the domination of another. In different historical moments those physical differences are attributed to biology or to culture. The effect is the same—the reification of difference to dominate. Likewise, sexism invokes the body in power relations of domination in that physically differentiated sex/gender characteristics are used by men to sustain their subordination of women. Sexual saturation of society is a political accomplishment of male domination. With sexism, domination is brought into the female body through sexual interaction. When sex is objectified and human beings are reduced to vehicles for acquiring it, sexual domination enters into and is anchored in the body. This is the foundation of prostitution and its normalization in the prostitution of sexuality.

Sex, an embodied dimension of the self, is *not* a preexisting physical or physiological fact, not an already-shaped fact of human experience that merely realizes itself when it is stimulated. "Drives" or impulses that are engaged in initiating sexual desire dictate neither the nature nor the quality of the sexual experience. Rather, sex is socially constructed. In patriarchy, it is a political fact of subordination.

If in human experience, sexual interaction is dehumanized and exploited, then violation of the self occurs. Indeed, we do not know the self as separate from social interaction in which it is being produced. But that is not all. Oppression essentializes human life and determines those it subordinates. Biological and cultural determinisms theorize the essentialisms, such as that woman is sexed body, that produce subordination by constructing domination as intellectual truth.

French physician Suzanne Képès has carefully considered the body in relation to human rights and particularly in terms of the violation of prostitution. She identifies "human" as "the condition of existing in the world with a body which is a source of energy and a mind, a psyche, closely linked to that body, depending on and reflecting everything that happens in that body." Understanding the body as a source of energy, "of different energies serving the motor, affective, intellectual, instinctive and sexual functions," Dr. Képès points out that health requires that these multiple, human energies be balanced through self-awareness and self-acceptance. For the body/self to negotiate in a world that supports its existence and also threatens it, self-awareness and self-acceptance are necessary to derive introspective knowledge that only comes "from the feeling of being present with oneself."[8]

Pursuing the duality of the individual and society, Dr. Képès distinguishes between the outer world, "that of everyday tasks, of joys and sorrows," and the inner world, "a permanent fabric of sensations, emotions, ideas, images, imagined or imaginary actions" that become known as the ego, or personality, or self.[9] Dr. Képès presents a "conventional medical view" of how the body responds to and interacts with its own energy:

The sympathetic and parasympathetic systems are connected in the hypothalamus, the oldest, instinctive part of the brain, and then in the thalamus, where the image of the body is formed. In the thalamus, which is itself connected to the limbic emotional centre and the regulatory matter known as reticulate, are stored actions, all the acts of our unconscious which will be released at a suitable moment. These are no stereotyped actions but actions which respect and reveal the original and specific structure of each individual, in a word: "true" actions. If these actions, which come from the depths of ourselves, are frustrated or corrupted, they block our energy.[10]

Dr. Képès's medical approach to the body physically reiterates the foundation of human rights, which recognizes each human being as a distinct person whose personhood has the inalienable claim to human dignity and rights. Violation occurring on the body, oppression absorbing the self, violates human rights because it segments human beings, separating them from their bodies.

When one loses contact with one's body, one dissociates from " 'the only thing in the world which we can feel both inside and out,' and which is therefore the channel through which we are able to get inside of everything." [11] The human need for "somatic anchoring" is disrupted. "If you are out of your body . . . you need a substitute for the feeling of being grounded." [12] Sexual exploitation, an objectification, is a disruption to the continuity of human experience, the undermining of sexual development for the subordination of women.

Human beings are incredibly resilient in the security of their bodied location just as they are fragile in the development of a self. In constructing the self, they are constantly negotiating their relationship to that which is not in their body. In the tension between inner and outer, the interaction between self and other, human beings negotiate their world and construct their identities. Violation is bodied—whether it is psychological and emotional, sexual, or physical. Violation occurs in exploiting those tensions between what is the self and what is outside of it. Distorting them destroys human experience. Following R. D. Laing's formulation, "*If our experience is destroyed, our behavior will be destructive. If our experience is destroyed, we have lost our own selves.*" [13]

The Social Construction of Sexuality: Stages of Dehumanization

Under male domination today, when sex is not explicitly treated as a genuine human interaction, it dehumanizes experience and thereby dominates women. The meaning that is the product of interaction can reveal how sex is experienced as an enhancement of human development or how sexual interaction destroys human experience. This study joins feminism with human rights to explore how meaning is produced in the experience of sex. Feminist theory exposes power and domination, but it goes further. It posits a reality above and beyond the present exploited condition from the conviction and commitment that power can be deconstructed and socially reconstructed into human and egalitarian relations.

Were it not for the groundbreaking feminist research over the last two decades that has revealed the personal harm and human cost of sexual exploitation, especially the work of Evelina Giobbe and WHISPER, of the Council for Prostitution Alternatives, and of Hanna Olsson in Sweden, of Liv Finstad and Cecilie Hoigard in Norway, and the work on incest abuse of Judith Herman, Florence Rush, Louise Armstrong, and Sandra Butler in the United States, were it not for the courage of women who have dared to speak their experiences of sexual exploitation, were it not for the unfailing feminist confrontation against the sex industries, particularly by Asian women's organizations and feminist activists against pornography worldwide—were it not for all of these women, their efforts and more, my understanding of how sex, a human activity, is turned into harm, a dehumanization, a human-rights violation, would not be possible.

On the other hand, were it not for the exploitation of women in prostitution, were it not for the transformation of the sexuality of prostitution into the prostitution of sexuality, were it not for the normalization of prostitution, accompanied by the silence of women who cannot or will not give voice and visibility to their private sexual exploitation, this study would not be necessary.

From all the above research and activism, from my own 20 years of work on this issue, from the women I interviewed when I wrote *Female Sexual Slavery* and since then, I have identified four stages in which prostitution socially constructs the sexual exploitation of women: (1) distancing, (2) disengagement, (3) dissociation, and (4) disembodiment. Prostitution is sexual exploitation sustained over time. Commodification is one of the most severe forms of objectification; in prostitution it separates sex from the human being through marketing. Sexual objectification dissociates women from their bodies and therefore their selves. By examining the social interaction of prostitution sex, we see more closely the harms of prostitution and of prostitution normalized.

1. *Distancing.* Prostitution sex, the act of prostitution, begins for women with distancing strategies in which they separate their sense of themselves—that is, their own, human, personal identity, how they know who they are—from the act of prostitution. Separation in prostitution begins with geographic relocation and extends to psychological dissociation. Once a woman has "turned a trick," she knows herself as an outcast (or in some few cases, namely, those women who promote prostitution, outcast takes the form of outlaw). Distancing begins with separation of self from family, home, and worlds of social legitimacy. When women are "turned out" for prostitution, they usually take a new name and get forged identity papers, which is frequently necessary in order to falsify one's age. As extreme and as violating as this appears, it is not unlike the separations women make from their family of origin, their own friends, and their own name when they marry. Even when women are not evidently coerced into prostitution, they begin by changing their name ("Lolita," etc.), an act that is central to their dissociation from their old or previous identity. These are acts of distancing from one's real identity and real self; they intensify the dissociation produced in the act of prostitution itself.

At the same time, distancing is a survival strategy for women in prostitution, who are able to stand away from themselves in the world and in the exchange of prostitution. They do not associate who they are in prostitution with who they are apart from being a prostitute. Distancing is an interrelated part of a complex web of other damaging, harmful effects of prostitution on women and girls. It causes women to become estranged from themselves in order to save themselves.

At a simplistic level, proprostitution groups argue that if prostitution were accepted as normal work for women, prostitute women would no longer be marginalized. But the reality of prostitution as a sex commodification is not that simple. Normalizing the sexual exploitation of women will not make it less sexually exploitative, it will only make it more available. In fact, if women are encouraged to incorporate within themselves, into their identities, the knowledge of themselves as socially acceptable sex objects, the damage of prostitution, of any sexual objectification, is intensified. However, distancing is only the first step toward the construction of woman as prostitute. Alone, it is not sufficient to ensure that women will survive prostitution or any other form of sexual exploitation. Distancing sets the stage for disengagement.

2. *Disengagement.* Disengagement is the up-front strategy of women in prostitution. Women engaged in the sex acts of prostitution report establishing emotional distance by dissociating themselves from the commodity exchange in which their bodies and sexuality are involved. Again, this is not different from what female teenagers, lovers, and wives report in the experience of objectified sex. As with rape victims, repeatedly they report that they are "not there." They are disengaged.

Disengagement is conscious and intentional action. It is central to the sex act of prostitution. Because sex is interactive, for it to be mechanically reproduced as commodity, sex requires that the women be there and "perform." For the women's part, they are "not there" when it is done in, on, with, or through them. Not being there is how they are engaged in the prostitution power relations invoked by customers.

In a recent Norwegian study of prostitution by Cecilie Hoigard and Liv Finstad, prostitutes report their dissociation from the sexual exchange men buy from them. Pia says, "I have to be a little stoned before I go through with it. I have to shove my emotions completely to the side. I get talkative and don't give a shit." Elisabeth reports, "You switch off your feelings, you have to do it." And Jane reports, "I've taught myself to switch off, to shove my feelings away. I don't give a damn, as long as there's money. It doesn't have anything to do with feelings."[14] In many accounts from different countries women report becoming icicles. And they view their customers with contempt even as they fawn over and dote upon them as the "prostitution contract," the implicit agreement with the customer, requires that they do.

Because the sexual relations of power involve women's bodies and their actions through their bodies with men who assume the right to buy that, disengagement gives a woman the emotional distance to be able to distinguish her real self from that of her self that is being used for sex as a commodity.

Prostitute women construct barriers. Through disengagement, prostitute women establish limits for customers in terms of what of their bodies and their selves can and cannot be used. These are limits that they enforce. Parts of the self cannot be accessed for use, which means that certain acts cannot be employed, certain parts of the body are off limits; often prostitutes refuse kissing or require the use of condoms as barriers demarcating the self. Certain things are kept for one's real self; as one French prostitute reported, "Never, never will he lie on *my* bed. He'll lie on a special sheet, on a blanket, but not on the bed that's my own bed."[15] In making these kinds of distinctions, women mark off parts of themselves that are real, personal—parts that they can, if they choose, engage for lovemaking that is not prostitution. Most frequently, however, prostitute women report being turned off to sex in their own intimate lives.

Differentiating parts of the self for sexual commodity is both vital to women's mere survival of prostitution, and destructive of women's humanity. It segments the self. But in fact, the self cannot be segmented. There are not separate parts of a self that can be taken as separate from the self. Some body parts, some physical acts cannot be relegated for sale while others are protected. Yet that is what is done and is why and how violation to the self occurs. When the self is segmented, which it cannot be, it is separated and its parts are used as separated fragments.

Segmentation of the self is distortion and produces dehumanization. Sex is an integral dimension of the human being, of the self. When it is treated as a thing to be taken, the human being is rendered into a thing, an objectification that not only violates human rights but also destroys human dignity, which is a fundamental precondition to human rights.

Can women choose to do prostitution? As much as they can choose any other context of sexual objectification and dehumanization of the self. Following from distancing, disengagement invokes harm, harm that takes the form of forcing distinctions between what are essentially nonchoices. This is how *women actually do not consent to prostitution* or any other condition of sexual exploitation—in rape, in marriage, in the office, in the factory, and so on.

At the same time, appearing to choose is an element of survival. Agreeing to go with a customer, taking his money, and agreeing to and performing specific acts appear to be choices. The appearance of choice is especially necessary for prostitute women for without it they could, in this stage of prostitution, lose their selves entirely. In this sense, to choose simply means *to act,* a fundamental aspect of being alive. And so women become engaged in establishing the terms of their own commodification. This is the prostitution contract, which "protects" women by involving them, invoking their self-acceptance in what is essentially the terms of their objectification, thus intensifying the harm and abuse of prostitution.[16] In the disengagement that follows from distancing, sex is made available in the prostitution exchange. Doing prostitution involves women in the dissociation of their own selves from their prostitution, over and over and over again. In the market exchange, if a woman stays in prostitution an average of 9 years and takes an average of 5 customers a day, 6 days a week, she will have sold sex in, on, and through her body 9,540 times to different men in anonymous contacts. This is a conservative estimate.

3. *Dissociation*. From her research and study of Swedish prostitution Hanna Olsson has described the male sexuality in prostitution as "male masturbation in a female body," [17] wherein the customer may demand, and in some cases may have to negotiate, where that takes place, either in the vagina, the anus, the mouth or all three. As Ulla points out, "They do it to empty themselves. That's all." [18] But that is not all; although sex is reduced to this act of male masturbation that has nothing to do with the woman as a human being, customers generally require that prostitutes act as if they are engaged with the customer emotionally, psychically, and affectively by entering into a fantasy or by feigning the role of a lover. Either the prostitute is to *act* like a whore or she is to *act* like an affectionate lover. On one hand, themes of perversion abound, particularly acting out "piss and shit" fantasies by which customers associate sex with filth, dirt, excrement. On the other hand, prostitutes are expected to act out submissive, subservient, docile, and fawning sexual behaviors. As numerous studies report, the customers, like the by now well-known profile of the average rapist, are "average men who want average sexual satisfaction." [19]

Men buy not a self but a body that performs as a self, and it is a self that conforms to the most harmful, damaging, racist and sexist concepts of women. Western men, particularly more "liberal" ones, often require from Western women an *enactment* that is sexually active and responsive as well as emotionally engaged. By contrast, traditional Western and Asian men may require of Asian prostitutes sexual behavior that is *enacted* with passivity, submissiveness, and slavishness.

In prostitution, customer demand includes specification of color and cultural characteristics, which are advertised and sold. Racism, which like sexual exploitation is an objectification that dehumanizes, is a foundation of the prostitution industry. A woman of color in prostitution is expected to sell not only a sexed body but a "colored" one also—from which she must also dissociate as that, too, is part of herself that she exchanges. Race is that which is bought with sex. And so it goes through different cultures; whatever the cultural context, prostitution in the sex exchange itself invokes and plays out the most reactionary racist and sexist stereotypes while segmenting women into buyable parts.

4. *Disembodiment and Dissembling.* In prostitution, what men expect from women is the *semblance* of emotional, sexual involvement, the appearance of pleasure and consent, a *semblance that they can treat as if it is real* in the moment of the commodity exchange. In this sense, they want prostitutes to behave like non-prostitutes—wives, lovers, and girlfriends. In other words, in the disembodiment of the self, which the prostitute constructs to protect her*self* from dissociation, we find the beginnings of the reconstruction of the subordinated, dehumanized self, which must *act* as if it is embodied by acting affectionate, by acting interested in the customer (for whom the women often have contempt), by acting sexual, by acting as if one is feeling sexual and *wants* to feel sexual, by trying to distinguish between acting as if one is feeling sexual and sometimes actually feeling sexual because one has inadvertently sexually responded, and then, by acting as if the racism and sexism in the act are a woman's self-chosen definition—all in all, by acting as if one is not the icicle that one already has become internally in order to protect one's self.

Distancing one's self in order to become disembodied and then acting as if the experience is embodied produces sex in prostitution. In this sense women become interchangeable with the life-size plastic dolls complete with orifices for penetration and ejaculation sold in pornography shops, but those dolls do not affect or dissemble a "response." Response is the differentiating factor because consistent with legalistic values of liberalism with the compulsive focus on will, response is considered an indicator of choice. That women respond in the sexual acts that dehumanize them is testimony to patriarchal construction of normal sexuality.

In women's experience, this is what prostitution is, including all of the acting and all of the physical and sexual behaviors in an anonymous commodity exchange. It is the sex of all sexual exploitations, institutionalized, systematized, and increasingly validated.

What Then Is Rape?

Beating, rape, and even murder are generally considered merely "occupational hazards" of prostitution. The Council for Prostitution Alternatives in Portland, Oregon, reported that of 179 women in their program who left prostitution in 1990–91, "seventy-eight percent of the survivors were the victims of rape, a class A felony. Almost half (48%) were raped by pimps an average of 16 times per year and more than three-quarters (79%) were raped by johns an average of 33 times per year.[20]

In the prostitution world, the payment of money is the distinguishing factor that differentiates rape sex from prostitution sex. In women's lives and experiences there is little distinction. In her WHISPER oral history project, Evelina Giobbe found that the prostitute woman "defined rape as a situation in which a customer had sex with her and then refused to pay or took back their money after the act."[21] Likewise in their study of 200 women and girls in prostitution in San Francisco, of the 73% who reported being raped while being prostitutes, Silbert and Pines found that in 19% of the cases the women tried to stop the rapist by telling him that she was a prostitute. By trying to return sex to economic exchange, the prostitute woman, rather than causing the rapist to withdraw, found that he escalated his attack. "They became furious at hearing the woman say she was a prostitute. Most started demanding she take back what she had said, insisting on taking her by force. In order to reassert their control, assailants then became extremely violent."[22]

Silbert and Pines pointed out that "when the victim told the assailant she was a prostitute and offered him sexual gratification, she was trying to assert some control over the situation." In comparison to those who did not tell, these women (12%) were subjected to more violent abuse. The rapists indicated in their behavior and words that they were directly involved with pornography.

In an effort to reduce accompanying beatings, the prostitute women offered sex that could be treated as if it were consensual, meaning sex to which they would not resist. The women distinguished rape sex from prostitution sex, not by the act, but by the payment of money. In the act of making the offer for prostitution exchange, the women behaved like bodied human beings who would willingly subordinate themselves to exploitation. This is the same condition that rape victims are in when they fight back and are told by their attacker to accept it or they will be hurt more or killed. As Silbert and Pines noted, the prostitute women were trying to assert control. But prostitution is sex bought on men's terms. Rape is sex taken on men's terms. The sex men buy in prostitution is the same sex that they take in rape—sex that is disembodied, enacted on the bodies of women who, for the men, do not exist as human beings. Men decide whether it is sex they pay for, or sex they take by force or with consent.

Rape of prostitute women has been a social enigma—not because prostitute women are not raped, for indeed they are, but because the experience of disembodied sex (in both rape and prostitution) has been reduced to issues of consent or of force. The prostitute women who offered consensual sex assumed that because they were sex, the commodity, by virtue of being prostitutes, offering sex would reduce the force. But both prostitution sex and rape sex are constructions of sex power. The prostitution of sexuality is the continuous reconfiguring of sex "on men's terms" to sustain women's subordination. In actuality, when a prostitute woman tries to assert sex divorced from rape, she defies one instance of sexual power—rape—to be subordinated in another instance—prostitution. That is why experientially rape and prostitution sex are undifferentiated for the women who are its vehicles. As one woman reported to Evelina Giobbe in her oral history project on women in prostitution,

Prostitution is like rape. It's like when I was 15 years old and I was raped. I used to experience leaving my body. I mean that's what I did when that man raped me. I looked up at the ceiling and I went to the ceiling and I numbed myself . . . because I didn't want to feel what I was feeling. I was very frightened. And while I was a prostitute I used to do that all the time. I would numb my feelings. I wouldn't even feel like I was in my body. I would actually leave my body and go somewhere else with my thoughts and with my feelings until he got off as it was over with. I don't know how else to explain it except that it felt like rape. It was rape to me.[23]

The Sexual Secret

Although often represented as sexually liberating, prostitution, fitted to male customer expectations, is a reactionary, regressive, and repressive sexual act. The market is driven by secrecy. Customers require anonymity and secrecy, and therefore prostitutes' protection from exposing their identities. Secret sex is what they buy. The origins of sexual repression can be found in the secreted buying of women's bodies. Marginalization of women in prostitution stems from this protection of the customer's secret sex, his requirement of anonymity and secrecy. He requires that she be the "other," the outsider, marginalized to sustain his secret. Secrecy is a foundation to sexual power in prostitution as sex industries display women on printed pages, in cages, on billboards, in storefront windows, but men, the customers, carry out their sex purchases in secret. The clandestine character of prostitution is part of the sexual experience and excitement customers buy. When we reach a time, as we surely will if feminism does not vigorously intervene, when prostitution is so normalized that men do not invoke secrecy to sustain their purchase of sex, we will have reached the dystopia of Margaret Atwood's *Handmaid's Tale* where prostituting women is the only sex.

In the first instance and the final analysis, prostitution is not about women at all. The fact is that whether women claim prostitution as a right or condemn it as an exploitation of them is irrelevant to the promotion and continuation of prostitution. Prostitution and traffic in women are not perpetuated based on whether or not women want to do prostitution or are forced into it. Women are in prostitution because men buy them for sex; men buy children for sex, and men buy other men for sex. Sometimes society is concerned about buying of children. Sometimes society is preoccupied with men being bought for prostitution. Rarely does anyone question men buying women for sex, despite the fact that in some countries women in prostitution are no longer counted in the thousands but in the millions.

Prostitution is a male consumer market. The intense public focus on women's will, her choice or her "right to prostitute," deflects attention from the primary fact that prostitution exists first because of male customer demand. Sex industries are in place—from trafficking to brothels—to provide female bodies to satisfy that market demand. What matters in terms of the ·prostitution market and male demand is that there are female bodies provided for sex exchange. How or why they get there is irrelevant to the market.

Beyond Limits

Distancing one's self in order to become disembodied to do prostitution is an effort to set limits and establish barriers with customers, to mark off oneself from the commodity constructed from oneself. Although setting limits creates a false sense of control, it is at least an effort to sustain some control in order to sustain one's self. When limits are quantifiably dropped, the self is abandoned. As rape denies women the opportunity to set limits on or establish the terms of exploitation, prostitution without barriers or limits is the merging of rape sex with prostitution sex.

Domenica, an older German prostitute woman and a leader in the movement for prostitute rights in Germany, worries about the younger generation of women in prostitution. In an interview with Alice Schwarzer, editor of *Emma* magazine, Domenica reflected on the changes she sees in prostitution today, describing it as like a "market fair" where the streets are flooded with women from all classes who do prostitution with no limits:[24] there is no bottom line to what customers are allowed to do, there is no bottom price, there is no separation of women from their lived experience as sexual objects—and they therefore must become them.

There are hierarchies that have structured the world of prostitution, stratifying women from high-class call girls to the lowest class of street walkers. In the last decade this structure has bottomed out and given way to prostitution without limits. In contrast to her generation of women, who learned to set rules and establish limits that enabled their survival of (and in her case survival *in*) prostitution, Domenica points out,

My room is no dumpster. I am not a crap heap. We senior whores have our laws. We only do it with condoms, have always done so. We don't allow kissing, because this is what you can only do at home, of course. Anally—nothing doing. But the young girls who usually get drugs from a pimp and are then sent on the street, they do everything. They cannot care less. They are so broken in spirit and body, they don't have the strength to take care of themselves. . . . Today they are rather isolated, they completely surrender to their pimp.[25]

In other words, the construction of prostitution through the stages I have identified above is collapsed; the self is not distinguishable to these prostitute women or girls, because they do not set limits that define their own selves. This younger generation of women and girls in prostitution is not composed of women who stand behind the banners of a proprostitution movement to promote the idea that "all women are whores" and that "sex work" is a viable economic alternative for women. These are the teenage girls and young women who have experienced prior sexual abuse, poverty, and homelessness and have become the prostitutes without limits, selves that are synonymous with prostitution. Therefore the severity of the effect of prostitution on them personally also has no limits. In other words, the prostitution of sexuality through distancing, disengagement, dissociation, and dissembling, which has allowed women in prostitution to sustain some aspect of their selves and to keep a self apart from that which is sold, has collapsed in street prostitution in the 1990s.

Drugs play a different role in the debasement of women in prostitution than they did a decade or two ago. In the 1970s one could find ample evidence of drug use among prostitutes. Pimps often dealt in drugs as well as women. Women often reported needing something "to get through with it" as they turned one trick after another. But generally both pimps and prostitutes knew that a woman strung out on drugs would not generate much income and eventually would be useless on the streets. On a more casual or occasional level of prostitution, some women with drug habits would turn tricks just as they would steal to support their habits. But many never really entered prostitution because the drugs pulled them off in another destructive direction.

Criminologists Lisa Maher and R. Curtis have studied women into crack cocaine and street prostitution in New York City. They have found that "the widespread use of crack in many poor urban minority neighborhoods has increased the number of women participating in street-level sex markets."[26] Their study supports Domenica's observation in Germany that there is increased isolation of women in prostitution, particularly in the heightened hostility prostitutes have for each other. A Detroit director of a clinic for addicts, Dwight Vaughter, explained crack cocaine in terms that are increasingly synonymous with street prostitution today: "It overwhelms every other human instinct. Crack comes first; something to eat and a safe place to stay means nothing in comparison. The instinct to protect your body, the instinct for life itself, is overwhelmed."[27]

Maher and Curtis have shown that "crack-induced increases in the number of women sex workers" has caused a shift in the nature of prostitution "from vaginal intercourse to blow jobs, indoor to outdoor," which has "deflated the going rates for sexual exchanges."[28] The fall in prices, combined with the virtual "anything goes" access customers have to women, reflects the latest changes in prostitution, the bottoming out of it. This is what Domenica meant by "they do everything," and doing it for next to nothing ($3 for a blow job, $5 for a fuck) has made street life in prostitution a rougher place to be. It has increased customer violence—beatings and torture have become a taken-for-granted part of the prostitution exchange—along with the violation that is the prostitution of sexuality.

Norwegian sociologists Liv Finstad and Cecilie Hoigard have found that while prices in prostitution vary over time, there has been a minimum to which women have held. "The system of minimum prices is an exact parallel to the internal solidarity employees exhibit when it comes to the question of pay. Personal interests coincide with common interest. If someone sells herself cheap, it affects all the others. Prices fall."[29] And that sets women more intensely against each other.

Hoigard and Finstad found that in Sweden prostitution prices are set by the price of smack. "The women who see themselves as hooked have their daily routines, shifting between shots and tricks."[30] This direct relationship between drug costs on the street and the price of a trick was also found in Oslo, Stockholm, Hamburg, London, and New York. The price of a trick is not only related to the daily expenditure on drugs but is also directly related to the marginalization of women in the labor force and the homelessness forced on women through domestic violence and poverty.

Maher and Curtis's research exposes the life of homeless, addicted, often pimp-controlled women on the streets, for whom prostitution becomes one of the very few "opportunities for revenue generation that are available in the informal economy."[31] This study found that women did prostitution while men in the same neighborhoods stripped cars. "Men still very much control the informal economy in these neighborhoods and the street drug scene in which social and occupational relations are increasingly embedded."[32]

Maher and Curtis's findings reveal a pattern different from what we saw in the 1970s in relation to drug abuse. Crack-cocaine prostitution evokes a deeper desperation and reveals an abandoned self. Drugs become a reason for doing prostitution when there seems to be little reason to exist. Trespassing certain boundaries in which a self can be kept intact means giving up on survival. In homelessness, desperation reaches new extremes. By contrast the effort to survive, to keep oneself together even within prostitution by finding ways to try to protect oneself, reveals human beings who are somehow still engaged with themselves, still fighting for survival. Even if they are despairing of the present moment, they are surviving for a future moment when things might be different.

But, for many immigrant women, for women coming from prior sexual slavery and drugs, all of this—their efforts to survive—seems to have bottomed out. They have given way to deeper levels of deprivation wherein prostitution becomes the means by which they give up having a self. The possibility of being a whole person is thrown away in the despair of it all. Even that fact of desperation is trivialized in the superficial assumption that in bottoming out of prostitution, one does prostitution for the money for drugs. Bottoming out means that human agency is not there. Giving up on one's survival becomes possible when there are no social conditions to support and promote survival. When the world of prostitution hits a new bottom, women become socially confused within a reality in which their survival is of no significance.

In both the Maher and Curtis research and that of Hoigard and Finstad, early childhood sexual abuse figured largely in the backgrounds of the women crack and smack addicts on the street. They had experienced the prostitution of their sexuality in incest assault, from which they, like every child subjected to it, learned to dissociate. They now do a prostitution from which they are disembodied, taking drugs through which they further dissociate from themselves. The desperation of homelessness and poverty added to the destruction from early childhood sexual abuse leaves young women and girls approaching prostitution without limits— there is nothing of the self left to save for survival. Trespassing those limits, where harm is contained, reduces the self to the sexually exploited thing that one is doing. The price is cheap because fast money is needed for another fix. But the price is also cheap because there is almost nothing of value left. Women are existing in their most severe conditions of dehumanization ever, for unlike the slave master who sold the body of another for a cheap price, these women sell themselves. There is not much of life left for them. Unlike women who distance themselves from prostitution, these women have little or no social space in which to be other than prostituted.

Murder

Systematic sexual exploitation reduces the value of female life to that of "throwaway women" who are like no-deposit, no-return bottles or cartons disposed and unaccounted for. When I first began my research in the late 1970s, I was shown some photos of prostitution homicides taken by the police. One file puzzled and horrified me. It contained a photo of a huge trash barrel in the basement of an old building. I peered at this photo for a few moments before I realized that a dead girl's body had been stuffed into the barrel. Only her arm, circled above her head, was showing. In New York City alone in 1975, official police statistics documented 71 prostitution homicides. At least 54 of them were committed by pimps or tricks.[33] This figure is undoubtedly conservative.

Maher and Curtis found that in 2 neighborhoods in New York City, at least 4 women in prostitution were killed during the time they were doing research: "One woman was hurled into a parking meter from a van being chased by the police; another was murdered and her decapitated body, minus her breasts, was found over by the railway tracks. Another woman . . . was beaten to death by a date." [34]

The fate of prostituted immigrant women rarely surfaces. Mariscris Sioson was one of the many of the 80,000 Filipino women who immigrated to Japan for jobs and in the hands of the Yakuza, the Japanese mafia, were turned into bar women. When Sioson's body was returned to the Philippines for burial, the Japanese medical determination of organ failure as the cause of death did not stand up to the evidence on her body of extreme brutality. The unexplained brutality, evidenced in severe head wounds and slashes on her legs and other parts of her body, would have been left unexplained had Sioson's parents not taken the medical photographs to the press. However, after President Aquino dispatched an investigator to Japan for a fact-finding mission, reports began to equivocate on the charges of wrongdoing. [35]

Whether foreign immigrants or local runaways, it is difficult to determine the incidence of murders and suicides of prostitute women. No one counts. Prostitute women's disengagement from former friends, family, and "straight" society makes them anonymous, then invisible. No one knows. Within the prostitution world, no one cares.

But when a prostitute kills a trick, the john, it is as if the world might come to an end. In 1992, Aileen Carol Wuornos was convicted and sentenced to death in the killing of a trick who may very well have been a serial murderer of prostitutes, as her story, reported by Phyllis Chesler, who has championed her case, suggests:

I said I would not [have sex with him]. He said, yes, you are, bitch. You're going to do everything I tell you. If you don't I'm going to kill you and [have sex with you] after you're dead, just like the other sluts. It doesn't matter, your body will still be warm. He tied my wrists to the steering wheel, and screwed me in the ass. . . . Eventually he untied me, put a stereo wire around my neck and tried to rape me again. . . . Then I thought, well, this dirty bastard deserves to die because of what he was tryin' to do to me. We struggled. I reached for my gun. I shot him.[36]

In all, Wuornos killed 6 violent tricks. A woman serial killer. Chesler points out that "serial killers are mainly white male drifters, obsessed with pornography and woman-hatred, who sexually use their victims, either before or after killing them, and who were themselves *paternally* abused children."[37] They do not claim self-defense, nor are they threatened with beating, rape, and murder, as was Aileen Carol Wuornos.[38] After being convicted in the first trial, she was convinced by her attorneys to plead guilty or no contest to the other charges.

As a woman serial killer *of men,* the Wuornos case has generated dramatic media attention and her acts have incited the full wrath of Florida justice. She has been sentenced to death 5 times, and given the state's fury over the death of male tricks, it would seem, as Chesler points out, that "if the state of Florida could, it would electrocute Wuornos once for each man she's accused of killing."[39] The murder of women is one of the occupational hazards of prostitution, clearly demonstrated in the court trial and treatment of her case, which was dissociated from the context in which she was prostituted and reduced to sex to be used at the will of her customers, which includes his will to kill, apparently.

In Rochester, New York, Arthur Shawcross was on parole from a manslaughter conviction when he killed 11 women between 1988 and 1989. Most of the women were prostitutes. He was sentenced to life imprisonment. During a "cleanup" or sweep of prostitutes that involved arresting more than 12,000 women in 1992, 10 more prostitute murders occurred.[40] None of these murders has evoked the wrath that Wuornos's killing in self-defense provoked.

Serial murders of prostitute women are periodically reported. From late 1977 to early 1978 a Los Angeles strangler brutally raped and murdered several women; most of his victims were prostitutes. During the same period many street walkers in northern England were victims of a "ripper's" mutilation murders. Serial murders of prostitutes have continued, and in 1992, 9 prostitute women in Detroit, all crack cocaine users, were strangled and left in empty buildings. Their bodies were nude, and they were bound and gagged. Some bodies when found were badly decomposed, having been in the abandoned buildings at least 6 months.[41]

Meg Baldwin summarized prostitution murders, giving a sense of their scope:

Forty-eight women, mainly prostitutes, were killed by the Green River Killer; up to thirty-one women murdered in Miami over a three-year period, most of them prostitutes; fourteen in Denver; twenty-nine in Los Angeles; seven in Oakland. Forty-three in San Diego; fourteen in Rochester; eight in Arlington, Virginia; nine in New Bedford, Massachusetts, seventeen in Alaska, ten in Tampa. . . . Three prostitutes were reported dead in Spokane, Washington, in 1990, leading some to speculate that the "Green River" murderer of forty-eight women and girls had once again become "active."[42]

As Jane Caputi points out, "serial sexual murder is not some inexplicable explosion/epidemic of an extrinsic evil or the domain of the mysterious psychopath. On the contrary such murder is an eminently logical step in the procession of patriarchal roles, values, needs, and rule of force."[43]

Murder, bottoming out, rape, and prostitution itself are consequences of dehumanized sexuality, a condition of oppression. When liberal legal constructions of human will are invoked to determine if, when, and where violation occurs, the dehumanized sexuality of patriarchal oppression is dissociated from the individual violations. Cause and consequence are dissociated. Domination prevails.

As I found in *Female Sexual Slavery,* the agents of that power are men who may function individually or in concert with each other, considering the numbers of men who are pimps, procurers, members of syndicate and free-lance slavery gangs, operators of brothels and massage parlors, connected with sexual exploitation entertainment, pornography purveyors, wife beaters, child molesters, incest perpetrators, johns (tricks) and rapists, one cannot help but be momentarily stunned by the enormous male population participating in female sexual slavery. The huge number of men engaged in these practices should be cause for declaration of a national and international emergency, a crisis in sexual violence.

To this list should be added the sexual liberals who promote pornography as free speech and prostitution as consenting sex.

The emergency I identified in *Female Sexual Slavery* has not yet been recognized. By the end of the twentieth century masculinist society has found the answer in the normalization of prostitution in the prostitution of sexuality. Women's human rights violations are becoming conditions of normal sex, confirmed in women's consent and answering the question posed by the Marquis de Sade in the eighteenth century, "But where is one to find free slaves?"

Sexual Power

Lisa Mamac, born in a rural farming village in the Philippines, tried to escape the inevitability of marrying there and raising her own family in the poverty in which she grew up. Like many women moving from rural to urban areas as their country is industrializing, Lisa left her village for a large city with plans to go to school. Rural to urban migration socially dislocates women and girls as patriarchal power in traditional societies provides almost no possibilities for women outside of marriage or their family. Under these conditions women are made particularly vulnerable to sexual exploitation. Away from home and on her own, Lisa fell in love and then became pregnant, only to learn that the man she was involved with was already married. He left her and she struggled alone with her infant, who died at 8 months. She tried to go back to school but did not have the money. Finally she became involved with a man who said he would put her through school. But he didn't. In October 1981, Lisa met a man who was a chief prosecutor in the court of justice of the region in which she lived. He told her of a high-paying position as a receptionist in a 5-star hotel in the Netherlands. He arranged for her to have the job. As women are marginalized from the developing economies of their industrializing countries, emigration often appears to be the only way to survive.

Most women trafficked into prostitution are from rural areas and have been in brief marriages or liaisons with men who abandon them.[1] When Lisa arrived in the Netherlands, she was put into a brothel. Like many women trafficked into prostitution, Lisa's only chance for help was to appeal to customers to help her escape. In 1983, one customer listened to Lisa's story and agreed to help her. But it was 2 years before police investigations led to a police raid on the brothel. Once she was free, with the support of Philippine groups in the Netherlands, women's organizations there, and women's groups in the Philippines, in 1985 Lisa Mamac began the struggle to win justice in her case. In 1988 Jan Schoemann was expelled from the Philippines and was convicted in Dutch courts of trafficking and sentenced to serve two and a half years in prison. His Philippine counterpart, Nestoria Placer, a former government official, was freed by the Philippine court in 1991. The judge in the case turned the blame back on Lisa Mamac and "her glaring immoral conduct manifested by her unusual inclination for illicit sex" in contrast to Placer, whose "character is beyond reproach and whose public life remains unblemished."[2] In 1993, the case was on appeal.

Lisa Mamac, caught in the vulnerability of women migrating from rural poverty, was trafficked into prostitution. At the same time, prostitution was being industrialized in her own country. Sex industrialization had been set in motion to service the military, particularly of the U.S. Subic Naval Base and Clark Air Force Base. Furthermore, Lisa was trafficked from the Philippines to the Netherlands, one of the Western countries that has taken the lead among post-industrial nations in legalizing and normalizing prostitution. Lisa Mamac's exploitation in prostitution encapsulated all of the stages of sexual exploitation that I have identified in this work: (1) trafficking in women, (2) military prostitution, (3) sex industrialization, and (4) normalization of prostitution.

Historical Stages in the Deployment of
Sexual Exploitation

Patriarchal power is singular in its reduction of women to sex, but varied in its political and economic strategies for deploying sexual subordination. Sexual exploitation is differentially shaped according to the economic development of each region, which determines how sex is constructed and deployed to subordinate women. Therefore, there is no one strategy of patriarchal power and sexual politics.[3] While each of these 4 stages of sexual exploitation are found in any historical period or in any stage of a country's economic development, they also constitute progression, one leading to another with economic development and prosperity.

1. *Trafficking in women* prevails especially in pre-industrial and feudal societies that are primarily agricultural, where women are excluded from the public sphere. Women's reduction to sex is a fact of their status as the property of their husbands. Under such conditions women are governed by marital relations of power through the exploitation of their unpaid labor in the home, their reproduction, and their sexuality. They are privatized by marriage, and their labor outside of the home is confined within the informal economic sector, not counted in the public economy. Sexual subordination and economic dependency resulting from women's status as the property of their husbands is *marital feudalism*. In feudalism men may sexually exploit their wives, take concubines, and buy prostitutes with impunity as the privilege of male domination that services their promiscuity. By contrast, as women are sexual property of men, any sexual act outside of their marriage, including rape and forced prostitution, is usually considered infidelity and the victims are severely punished. There is little or no social space for women outside of the private patriarchal sector. However, prostitution prevails for men. In the private patriarchal sector, women and girls are supplied to

brothels primarily through brutal trafficking and forced prostitution.

2. *Military prostitution* in war and in many areas where there is a massive military presence provides for soldiers' rest and recreation, R & R. Increasingly wars are being fought primarily in Third World countries, or in somewhat more developed areas such as Eastern Europe was when much of it was reverted to underdevelopment by war. Likewise, military prostitution proliferates in the areas where women's vulnerabilities from war, because of rape in war, in economic underdevelopment from war, and in the patriarchal traditionalism of the society where the war is waged, makes them accessible to be prostituted as sex commodities for soldiers who are usually foreign men—either aggressors or occupiers.

3. *Sex industrialization* accompanies economic development. With industrialization and the development of a public economic sector, larger numbers of women leave the privatized household in search of jobs in the public economy, usually in urban areas. As industrializing economies shift from domestic to export-oriented production, Western-originated sex industries work with local and regional traffickers to build sex industries. Women migrating from rural to urban areas constitute a ready pool for procurers. Their labor, having been unpaid and exploited at home, is devalued in the public economy, and they are marginalized from it. Exploitation in the family leads to exploitation of labor in the public economy. As industrialization accelerates, sex industries buy women's sexual exchange at a higher rate than most women can earn in export processing labor. Sex industries prostitute significant proportions of the female population, which can no longer be spoken of only as forced prostitution in terms of trafficking in women. In this phase, the primary emphasis of sexual exploitation shifts from trafficking in women to sex industrialization that is usually not characterized by physical coercion or slavery. Rather, economic destitution in the displacement of women from rural to urban areas and the absence of work oppor-

tunities close down the world of possibilities for women. As sex industrialization develops, for some women it has the appeal of fast money in an increasingly commercialized world of commodities that are available primarily to men.

4. *Normalization of prostitution* takes place with higher levels of economic development in post-industrial societies. In post-industrial, developed societies, when women achieve the potential for economic independence, men are threatened with loss of control over women as their legal and economic property in marriage. To regain control, patriarchal domination reconfigures around sex by producing a *social* and public condition of sexual subordination that follows women into the public world. Sexual exploitation is individualized to fit the domination of economically independent women. Sexual saturation of society through pornography promoted by sexology sustains individualized sexual exploitation in the public domain. By contrast, public images of the sexual subordination of women are not necessary under feudal conditions, wherein sex is a fact of privatized property arrangements of marriage and there is no economic or social alternative to marriage for women. Nor is the issue of women's consent important or even relevant when they are legal property of their husbands. But in the sexual saturation of society through pornography, when women are reduced publicly to sex, women's sexual consent becomes paramount in importance to sustain their subordination. Pursuing work in industrialized sectors, women are removed from men's control of them in the family. The social control of women is reinforced in the public world by invoking women's consent to the prostitution of sexuality. Economic development and the potential for women's economic equality produce a new public, social exploitation, which is built from the prior, privatized sexual exploitation of women in marriage. When single, economically independent, emotionally autonomous women evade sexual reductionism and become historical reality, publicly institutionalized sexual exploitation reverts them back to sex.

That was the experience of Anita Hill, a prominent African-

American lawyer, when she reported her experience of Clarence Thomas's sexual harassment of her to the congressional committee that would confirm Thomas to the U.S. Supreme Court in 1991. When Hill testified before the congressional committee, the committee saw in this African-American woman her refusal to be sexed body, reduced to sex. Her refusal to be sex deeply challenged the sexual power of racism and the historical reduction of African-American women in slavery to sexual property, that is, to the sexual ownership of their white masters.[4]

The committee's interrogation of Anita Hill, especially the threats from Pennsylvania Senator Specter, were more than a reaction against one woman. The all-male congressional committee made of Anita Hill a nationally televised lesson to all women— and their message to U.S. women was to withdraw, to retreat. As she bravely and unswervingly stood up to that day of grilling, of intensive cross-examination, of unrelenting efforts to find a modicum of motivation, other than justice, for her allegations, women throughout the United States became aware, as many had never been aware before, of the reality that if a woman of Anita Hill's character cannot be believed, none of us will be believed. That was the message from the congressional male bonding, racist as it was, that enveloped Clarence Thomas within its protective cover. Hill's case acquired such prominence because she became paradigmatic of the woman who refuses to be reduced to body, sexist body, racist body, and the fact that she is African-American made her refusal to be sexed body an ultimate act of defiance.

Culture of Sex and Construction of Sexuality

Sexual power is a political condition of women's lives that is either privatized and feudalistic or public and industrial, or both. In each historical period, under each set of economic conditions from marital feudalism to sex industrialization and normalized prostitution, sexuality is socially constructed, shaped in the society by social norms and values to fit to the particular conditions of patriarchy. Society (not biology, not drives, not needs, and not desires) precedes sexuality, giving structure and context to the individual experience of it.

As society socially constructs sexuality, acts of sexual exchange are where domination is produced and, in turn, they give shape and form to physiological sexual impulses, drives, or needs. It does not work the other way around, as sexologists would have it. That is, the sex drive does not manifest itself as some innate reality that then determines sexual behaviors. Christine Delphy has pointed out that "it is oppression which creates gender" and that "gender in its turn created anatomical sex, in the sense that the hierarchal division of homogeneity into two transforms an anatomical difference (which is itself devoid of social implication) into a relevant distinction for social practice."[5]

In the industrialized world, the social, cultural production of "sexuality," the sexuality of normalized prostitution, has developed and been deployed through the science of sex, sexology, and its counterpart, pornography, the graphic representation of prostitution sex. Foucault poses the question "whether, since the nineteenth century, the *scientia sexualis* . . . has not functioned, at least to a certain extent, as an *ars erotica.*"[6] The public and social deployment of sex as *sexuality,* "proliferating, innovating, annexing, creating, and penetrating bodies in an increasingly detailed way, and . . . controlling populations in an increasingly comprehensive way,"[7] created "discourses" through which sex, which has no pre-social definition or meaning, became sexuality, a condition of sexist power.

A century of development of public, social sexual preoccupation in the West in liberal areas has shifted the social expectation of coupling away from marriage and its privatization of women under one male authority, the husband, toward sex and the public colonization of women for male sexual servicing. Conservative areas of post-industrial society demonstrate the effort to reconfine women within the family, under reproductive and sexual control.

A sexual imperative looms over *coupling*. It signifies for the late twentieth century what *marriage* had meant for previous centuries in terms of control of women. As women are no longer necessarily identified as wives, they are expected to be known through their sexual connection to another. Coupling has become a social signification that women are sexually connected to another—therefore under control, a control of women that marriage no longer assures. The imperative that women be/are sexual is a historically recent social force constituted to sustain male domination when women cannot be controlled by marriage or in economic dependency.

The 1960s sexual revolution took as its bibles the works of sexologists and pornographers, both of which groups, as Sheila Jeffries pointed out, were hostile to women's liberation in the 1960s and 1970s.[8] Finally, by the 1980s, they had reduced the meaning and significance of women's "liberation" to pornography where "liberation" means trespassing *traditional masculinist* sexual norms to replace them with *modern, public masculinist* norms that reduce woman to sex. The culture of sexual liberation, developed in the twin discourses of sexology and pornography, produces sex as an objectified "thing" to be gotten, taken, had. That "thing" has been reified in the orgasm. As Stephen Heath points out, orgasm is "the key manoeuvre in the sexual fix":

As long as orgasm holds the centre of the stage, we will never get out of the sexual norm, a redirection of the sexual, the realization of sex as a commodity with men and women placed and held essentially, as their "nature," male and female, the difference, as the agents of that exchange.[9]

In a century-long development of a masculinist culture of sex in the West, sexuality has been made compulsive, and it is compulsively treated as if compulsive sex is "normal" sex. The deployment of sexuality generally follows the progression of pornography, which emerged for massive distribution in the early 1960s. As legal control of pornography was lifted, its subject matter escalated from pictures of nude women to more provocative poses. By 1967 more sexual explicitness was expected by consumers,[10] which finally led to hard-core, violent, humiliating, degrading sex and the snuff films in which women were murdered in the sexual fix.

Today male domination is sustained in large part by the failure of society to distinguish between sex that is exploitation and sex that is positive human experience, enhancing rather than destroying human lives. Feminism has intervened in the patriarchal construction of sex. In their civil rights approach to pornography, Andrea Dworkin and Catharine MacKinnon redefined pornography to be "a systematic practice of exploitation and subordination based on sex which differentially harms women."[11] Dworkin and MacKinnon defined pornography as harm not only because it is violent—because it presents women being penetrated by objects or animals, because it presents women injured, bleeding, bruised in pornographic sex—but at its core pornography is violating because "women are presented as dehumanized sexual objects, things or commodities."[12]

Legally, Dworkin and MacKinnon have identified the subject matter of pornography as *"graphic,* sexually explicit presentation that produces a subordination of women through *pictures and/or words"* (emphasis added). Prostitution is the *enacted* version of pornography, where the graphic representation of the subordination of women comes to life. The normalization of prostitution is the pornographic deployment of that subordination into private lives and personal relationships. Now, not only is it the daily, subjective experience of a class of women, identified by their commercial availability to service men sexually, but of women as a class through the prostitution of sexuality.

In defense of male domination, sexual liberals, those who have promoted sex as a form of freedom and as a matter only of individual choice without regard to whether that sex enhances or harms human experience, have moved to censor the civil rights approach to pornography. By the 1990s the progression and escalation of pornography has become the masculinist culture of sex in which prostitution is the normative model for sexual behavior. It does not stop there. This Western masculinist construction of sex, this colonization of women's bodies, is a major dimension of Western hegemony as American, European, and Australian men, in the military, in businesses, and as tourists, impose that sex in the form of market demand on women in Third World countries. The U.S., U.N., or other occupying military forces have not just discovered sex for the first time when they rape and prostitute women of Third World countries, nor is that the end of it when they return home to lovers or wives.

In each historical condition of sexualization—feudalism, industrialization, and post-industrial society—the subordination of women is accomplished through (1) the sexualization that reduces women to biology, locating women in a class condition where they are expropriated bodies to be fetishized, which treats sex and women's lives as *essential* rather than *social* reality; (2) the reduction of human beings to bodily functions, driving women out of history; and (3) atemporality in which women cease to exist in time. In sexual exploitation, women are universalized and therefore not historical, biologized and therefore not social.

By contrast, Catharine MacKinnon summarizes the legal and social reality that would obtain if sex were not the condition of subordination:

If the sexes were equal, women would not be sexually subjugated. Sexual force would be exceptional, consent to sex could be commonly real, and sexually violated women would be believed. If the sexes were equal, women would not be economically subjected, their desperation and marginality cultivated, their enforced dependency exploited sexually or economically.[13]

Prostitution of Sexuality

When prostitution is normalized it is no longer the exchange of money and the anonymity in the fact that she has known this guy maybe 10 minutes that differentiates how women in prostitution experience the night from how many women, teenagers, and young girls around the world experience it. By the 1990s, sex that is bought in the act of prostitution and promoted in pornography does not look significantly different from the sex that is taken in rape, pressured in teenage dating, and apparently given in many private relationships. This leads to the conclusion that, in the West, normatively the lines between rape, prostitution, and private sex have blurred.

The legacy to women of the sexual liberation movement and the legitimization of pornography of the 1960s has not been women's liberation but rather the prostitution of sexuality. By the 1990s, the video cassette recorder has done more than bring pornography home into the bedroom and private sexual relations. With the camcorder, it has made the bedroom—or wherever pornography that is prostituted sex is done—the location for making pornography. It has been reported that about one-third of the approximately 75 new adult videos each month are made by amateurs at home.[14] And as husbands and lovers see a market value to film their private, intimate moments at home, women are reporting that the sex scenes are becoming more and more torturous. Diana Russell in her study of rape found that 10% of the 930 women she interviewed had experienced pornography being brought into their sex lives:

Ms. C: He was a lover. He'd go to porno movies, then he'd come home and say, "I saw this in a movie. Let's try it." I felt really exploited, like I was being put in a mold.

Ms. D: I was staying at this guy's house. He tried to make me have oral sex with him. He said he'd seen far-out stuff in movies, and that it would be fun to mentally and physically torture a woman.

Ms. F: He'd read something in a pornographic book, and then he wanted to live it out. It was too violent for me to do something like that. It was basically getting dressed up and spanking. Him spanking me. I refused to do it.

Ms. H: This couple who had just read a porno book wanted to try the groupie number with four people. They tried to persuade my boyfriend to persuade me. They were running around naked, and I felt really uncomfortable.

Ms. I: It was S & M stuff. I was asked if I would participate in being beaten up. It was a proposition, it never happened. I didn't like the idea of it.

Interviewer: Did anything else upset you?

Ms. I: Anal intercourse. I have been asked to do that, but I didn't enjoy it at all. I have *had* to do it, *very* occasionally.

Ms. M: Anal sex. First he attempted gentle persuasion, I guess. He was somebody I'd been dating a while and we'd gone to bed a few times. Once he tried to persuade me to go along with anal sex, first verbally, then by touching me. When I said "No," he did it anyway—much to my pain. It hurt like hell.[15]

In their early 1980s study of 12,000 heterosexual and homosexual couples, sociologists Philip Blumstein and Pepper Schwartz found that married people were having more sex and more regularly. While sexual activity was increasing in the home, sexualities have configured around gender rather than sexual preference/ orientation. Sexually speaking, "husbands and male cohabitors are more like gay men than they are like wives or female cohabitors. Lesbians are more like heterosexual women than either is like gay or heterosexual men."[16] Their conclusion was based in significant part on preferences for sexual practices in relation to power and control. In the gendering of sexuality, often men consider their genitals the main focus of the sex act. Generally, more sex has led to more sexual objectification that dissociates sex from an interactive experience with another. This is the sexuality that was set in motion by pornography, particularly *Deep Throat*, made by Linda Lovelace while she was sexually enslaved by the pimp/pornographer Chuck Traynor.

Sex that is not mutually interactive and is dissociated from one's partner will eventually invoke women in disengagement, dissociation, and disembodiment. It is not surprising then that for women reciprocity was important in their sexual relations. In the couples study, heterosexual women expressed preference for intercourse because it involves mutual participation; it was more central to their sexual satisfaction. But, as Andrea Dworkin points out:

women have wanted intercourse to be, for women, an experience of equality and passion, sensuality and intimacy. Women have a vision of love that includes men as human too; and women want the human in men including in the act of intercourse. Even without the dignity of equal power, women have believed in the redeeming potential of love.[17]

Women and men have arrived at different places to participate in the sexualization of society and the intensification of sexual exploitation in private life. Continuing with Dworkin, "these visions of a humane sensuality based in equality are in the aspirations of women; and even the nightmare of sexual inferiority does not seem to kill them."[18] By choice and desire, male sexuality configures around disengaged sex, sex for the sake of itself, separate from the human experience and interaction that it actually is, thereby destroying sexual interaction in favor of sex that is objectifying, the origins of the prostitution of sexuality. This is socially constructed sex, the conditions that prevail when sexuality is made an element of power relations of sexism.

If the prostitution of sexuality, the reduction of oneself to sexual object, is increasingly demanded of adult women, it is an even more pressing requirement of teenagers. With the sexualization of society, first sex is occurring at earlier ages, in the teenage years. Sexual norms in high school and college dating are expressed now in the language of prostitution: "hooking up" identifies dating for the purposes of having sex. In 1981, 19% of unmarried girls had had intercourse by the age of 15. By 1988 that figure increased to 27%. In 1991, 50% of unmarried females and 60% of unmarried males between the ages of 15 and 19 have had sexual intercourse. Not surprisingly, 1 in 5 girls age 15 to 19 who are sexually active become pregnant.[19]

The fear of AIDS and the crisis in teenage pregnancy has led to new programs in the mid 1990s that promote sexual abstinence among teenagers. Their approach teaches girls how to resist pressure for sex and "hooking up." It is similar to drug prevention programs that teach young people how to resist pressure to take drugs. They are taught to turn away from pressures to have sex by asserting their own goals. These initiatives are being promoted especially by the African-American communities and by organizations such as the Urban League. These programs may lead teenagers to increased sexual autonomy and sexual self-determination. But they do not directly confront the harm of early sex to human development. Abstinence or virginity projects are frequently dismissed as moralistic, representative of repressive "family values" promoted under the Bush-Quayle administration. And indeed some of them use the fear of AIDS and the crisis in teenage pregnancy to reinvoke sexual repression. However, programs focused on sexual and personal autonomy through controlling sexual activity until developmentally mature hold the potential of challenging sexual power relations that frequently undermine teenage female development.

While there have been racial differences in frequency of early sexual intercourse, according to the Alan Guttmacher Institute, "most of the increase in female sexual activity in the 1980s was among white teenagers and those in higher income families." [20] This trend reflects the normalization of early sexual behavior by the bourgeois and upper classes in their exploitation of women and girls, which sets the standards that eventually produce that exploitation among the working classes and the poor. In a 1993 survey of high school seniors in a private girls preparatory school on the East Coast, (with a total of 67 from 108 responding) 40.3% had had sexual intercourse, 92.5% of them having had first intercourse between ages 15 and 17. The pattern of sexual behavior in 1993 for high- and middle-income, mostly white teenage girls in this school follows the pattern that Blumstein and Schwartz found in 1983 among adults. The study found that 63.2% had stimulated a boy to orgasm while 50.7% had been stimulated to orgasm by a boy; 45.6% had performed fellatio on boys while 36.8% had experienced cunnilingus.

Research is beginning to make the connections that feminists established a long time ago. "A substantial proportion of young adolescents who are sexually active are active only because they have been coerced," according to Bruce Ambuel and Julian Rappaport who cite research that reports that "although 7% of White and 9% of African-American 14-year-old girls have experienced intercourse, only 2% of White and 6% of African-American 14-year-olds participated voluntarily."[21] This is the sexual socialization into the prostitution of sexuality where coercion becomes a normalized dimension of sexual life. These are the conditions under which coerced sex becomes chosen sex. As a recent study conducted by the American Association of University Women establishes, these are the conditions for producing educational, economic, and political subordination because these are the conditions that diminish achievement far beyond the experience of sex. In the AAUW study, 81% of all students in grades 8–11 say they have experienced unwelcome sexual behavior at school. Seventy-six percent of the girls and 56% of the boys in the study reported receiving sexual comments or looks while 65% of the girls and 42% of the boys were touched, grabbed, or pinched in a sexual way. These figures indicate how sexual development of teenagers initiates female sexual subordination in the early years and cuts off female potential for development. The negative effects of present normative teenage sexual behaviors overwhelmingly impact on girls' experience of and success in school. Thirty-three percent of girls and 12% of boys subjected to sexualization do not want to go to school, and 32% of girls and 13% of boys do not want to talk in class because of their experiences. Other effects disproportionately impacting girls are that after being sexually harassed many find it hard to pay attention in school and difficult to study. Twenty percent of the girls' grades have dropped and 17% are thinking about changing schools.[22]

Every year, Ed Donnellan, a high school teacher, conducts a survey with female students who range in age from 14 to 17.[23] Donnellan uses this survey for consciousness raising about sexual exploitation. In 1992, of 70 students surveyed, 17% reported that they had been subjected to intercourse against their will. And 57% reported being kissed against their will while 25% indicated that their genitals had been touched against their will. In 1993, 9% had intercourse against their will while 78% had been touched in their thigh or crotch against their will.

Donnellan's survey produced other responses from students. One 14-year-old told him privately that she had sex with 13 boys in the previous 9 months and "I don't even like it." The widespread sexualization of women through pornography and the media has intensified teenage male expectations of sex and female teenagers' experience of social pressure to be sexually active, believing that they can't say no.

When I spoke to Donnellan's class, some students asked what they should do if they find pornography when they are babysitting. I suggested that they call a friend or trusted family member to come over, stay with them and accompany them home, but not to remain alone in the company of a potential sexual exploiter. Some of the girls feared that such protection would appear to be too extreme a response, making them appear weak or uptight, a fear that extends to pressures for sexual relations.

There is little evidence of the effect of early sex on identity development in adolescence. But as coercion is increasingly normalized, the roots of female dependency can be found here. Rather than in some natural or essential design of femaleness, here is where the foundations are for girls' and women's difficulty in marking separate identities of their own, the basis for autonomy, independence, and, of course, equality. Here are the contemporary foundations of sexual subordination and gender inequality.

On one hand, those who promote sexual exploitation emphasize women's choice to prostitute and to engage in pornography. On the other hand, campaigns against sexual violence make women's consent the primary issue. Both approaches separate the sexual power of male domination from the system of patriarchal *oppression* by which men as a class subordinate women and thus reduce them to a sex class. Consent—either its willed assurance or its denial—does not determine, identify, or cause *oppression*. When violence is separated from oppression, violation of consent must be established in order to establish a woman's victimization. Such legalistic construction of victimization, which fails to recognize patriarchal political oppression, incessantly places women and girls in the position of claiming sexual violation from an increasingly passive, non-interactive role—as beings acted upon by brute force and therefore violated. Yet subjection to that kind of force is part of a continuum of sexual exploition and oppression, and it is not necessarily the most frequently occurring element. Consent to violation is a fact of oppression. Any oppression. All oppression.

Sex as Labor?

The prostitution exchange is the most systematic institutionalized reduction of woman to sex. It is the foundation of all sexual exploitation of women. It is the prototype, the model from which all other sexual exploitation can be understood. Put another way, if this practice is not recognized as sexual exploitation and as a model for the sexual subordination of women, then all other forms of sexual exploitation will be ineffectively addressed, many going fully unrecognized as sexual exploitation.

In the normalization of the prostitution of sexuality, it is not surprising to find that prostitution is increasingly considered to be merely another form of labor. Considering prostitution as merely another form of labor raises the question, what kind of labor? Slave labor or exploited labor of feudalism or class exploitation of capitalism?

Slave labor is condemned universally because it deprives human beings of freedom and of the gains from their labor, and child labor is considered to be work that not only denies freedom but is developmentally premature. If, for example, consent was the criterion for determining whether or not slavery is a violation of human dignity and rights, slavery would not have been recognized as a violation because an important element of slavery is the acceptance of their condition by many slaves. So deeply is the self-hatred of racism and sexism encoded.

Various theories of labor and analyses of labor markets treat capitalist labor as the exploitation of surplus value, revealing inequalities and dual labor markets. Consider labor in the production of the commodity of human services. In between unremunerated, exploited domestic labor that includes emotional labor and private sex exchange exists a range of personal services that are marketed—psychological therapy, counseling, and physical therapies, including massage. Human services begin with distinctions and differentiations—demarcations of what is saleable. Psychological therapy and massage each identifies appropriate treatments for particular conditions that are provided for a price. They may be meant to improve emotional and personal life, and the purchaser may receive emotional and/or personal satisfaction and even pleasure from them. But the therapist is not selling emotions, desires, drives or other aspects of their person. The difference from prostitution is that these services do not invoke sex; in fact, professional ethics in these fields require of the service providers that all protections against sexualizing the services be accorded their clients or customers.

The question of whether paid sexual exchange is exploited as labor does not fully address the question of whether certain experiences and actions should be conditions of labor at all. Dangerously, feminism has not yet asked about sex what marxists and socialists have asked about labor. Marxists ultimately envision labor freed from capitalist exploitation and laborers owning their own labor power. Can feminism, without contradicting its commitment to liberation, envision women as free sexual laborers sometime in the future? As prostitution becomes the model for patriarchal sexual relations of power, the unasked, unexplored, and seemingly hopelessly mired question surfaces: What do we as women want sex to be? How shall we socially construct sexuality as a condition of our liberation?

The recent research on women's unpaid domestic labor that addresses that part of it that is emotional labor[24] has confounded this issue and the answers to these questions, as it tends to adopt the terms "sexual labor" or "sex work." The terms "sex work" and "sexual labor" imply that sex, if it were not exploited by traffickers, pimps, and industries, *should be* labor, or a condition of laboring, work that anyone should be able to engage in at a fair wage with full benefits of social services. In the absence of political consciousness of the exploitation of labor by capitalists and by husbands, the term "sex work" becomes imbued with a sense of normalcy.

There is an even larger question beneath this debate: Is emotional labor exploited because it is unremunerated, or is it exploited because emotional and sexual life have been reduced to mere servicing, to a labor that sustains gender power relations? Women's subordination in general and sexual exploitation in particular raises the question asked earlier: What in the range of human experience should be considered as labor? And how do we achieve a condition of unexploited labor?

And beyond reducing the human experience of sex to labor, the promotion of "sex work" is specifically gendered: services are bought by men, provided for men—services that are not only the privilege of male domination, but the cause. With economic development and advancement, as material conditions improve for communities, families, and individuals, more emphasis is placed on inner life, emotions, and the personal. The self begins to be understood and developed in relation to inner life and emotions.[25] Emotions, inner life, and the personal are gendered; they have distinctly different meanings for women and for men. Emotional work and sexual service become part of what men require from women. Men's emotional disengagement and sexual requirements are not merely a matter of masculinist socialization.

Rather, male underdeveloped emotional life and objectified sexual life are produced in power arrangements. In those power arrangements, emotions and sex are reduced to labor that is exploitation of women.

When sex is a requirement in the line of domestic duties, it is made into a form of labor and a dimension of sexual power in marriage. When sex is accepted as another form of labor, human beings cannot be protected from the destruction of that human sexual experience. Given that the human body is the location of ourselves, its fragility and vulnerabilities require protections. The body is extended into realities beyond it through social interaction, from the inner to the outer world, from self to other, and in this location of the body in the human condition, there is fragility. Then what do we constitute as the norms for its (our) protection? Patriarchal domination of women and capitalist markets that are now internationally interdependent have brought us to fundamental questions of human existence: Not can, but should emotions, sex, and reproduction be rendered into saleable commodities?

The principle that guides my work is that in confronting prostitution as an exploitation of women, we are also concerned with freeing women from being reduced to sex and reproduction as acts of labor and of market exchange. Janice Raymond has critiqued the marketing of reproduction in *Women as Wombs*.[26] If feminism is to win women's liberation, then sex and reproduction must be treated as experiences that protect rather than violate human fragility and vulnerability while supporting women as sexual and reproductive beings of their own choosing. I would suggest that the minimum conditions for sexual consent are in sex that is a human experience of personal dignity and one that is enjoyed with respect and pleasure. Neither marriage nor prostitution, as structures of patriarchal domination, institutionally provide for them. Therefore, although women and men may experience sex that does not violate human dignity and personal respect, their experiences are not because of but external to structured patriarchal power. And those experiences do not obviate the fact of women's *class* oppression produced in the prostitution of sexuality.

The logic of the present study, and all of the suppositions of the women's movements against violence against women and against pornography, assume a new possibility—that sex, when it is a condition of our liberation, will be experienced in the human condition as a human experience, a personal interaction of pleasure, of attachment and affection, of human wholeness, and, for those who choose, for reproduction.

Proprostitution

In the small but highly vocal proprostitution movement, some few women are treating their prostitution affirmatively, as "sex work," as experiences of unrepressed sex that they control. Theirs is not unlike some heterosexual women's and lesbians' defense of sadomasochism as an enactment of sexual desire for women; in the movement to promote pornography this group is led by F.A.C.T. and its views are promoted in works like Carol Vance's.[27] Many women actively promote pornographic sexuality as a chosen dimension of their lives while many other women actively claim and positively assert a "prostitution identity." Are they dehumanized by these dissociations, or are they only claiming a self-chosen identity? If women actively choose pornographic, prostituted sex, can we consider that sex as harmless because it is chosen? These questions collapse the experience of harm into the act of consent, rendering invisible the harm of the prostitution exchange, dissociating it from the fullness of lived experience, and locating it only in human will. This is a variant of liberal ideology, which drives economic markets by elevating individual choice in order to maximize consumerism. In this way, the sex of prostitution is reduced from being a class condition of women to a personal choice of the individual. Under the decadence that elevates individual choice above the common good, chosen patriarchal violation serves capitalist market exchange.

A feminist analysis of sexual exploitation requires analyzing the class condition of women in relation to actual, lived experience. Developing a feminist human-rights perspective refocuses the question back to the act, to lived experience, to the conditions under which sex takes place, and asks whether or not that constitutes violation. In human rights, the determination of harm must rest on the act, the experience and its representations, not only individually but collectively in women's class condition. If the act exploits, it is in itself destructive of human life, well-being, integrity, and dignity. That is violation. And when it is gendered, repeated over and over in and on woman after woman, that is oppression.

But some women in prostitution promote their own sexual exploitation and treat it as a condition of women's freedom or self-determination. Erich Goode points out, "For most of us to find the behavior attractive, something we would want to participate in, we must 'neutralize' the negative status of the behavior or nullify our feeling about participating in it"[28] because "most of us find despising ourselves as too painful."[29] Therefore, to neutralize not only the deviant status of prostitution but also the actual harm it produces, to treat that harm as sexy, fun, and a kick, is to valorize it and to promote it. In prostitution that means actively incorporating dehumanization into one's identity—to live it, embrace it, and ultimately to promote it. What is dehumanized sex, if it is not sex in which one has become disembodied? To actively accept this, to live dehumanization as if it were an original human condition, the act of an intact self, is to live one's fragmentation, that which kills the human self, as an actively chosen option, as wholeness, as fun, as pleasure.

Ultimately, the only way to promote such dehumanization for oneself is to promote it for others, assuming that doing so will neutralize its social stigma. Hence a proprostitution movement.

Hence the validation of pornographic sex in marriage and intimate coupling. Hence the promotion of lesbian sadomasochism. But promotion of prostitution is not only about trying to change social stigma. Proprostitution lobbying has become increasingly validated in a general climate of dehumanization of sexual relations, what I now consider to be the prostitution of sexuality.

Promoting prostitution publicly is *not* the way prostitution will be neutralized and destigmatized. The sexual relations of power constitute the political context for proprostitution movements that publicly affirm the use of sex to exploit women. To "embrace" prostitution sex as one's self-chosen identity is to be actively engaged in promoting women's oppression in behalf of oneself. It means that the sex that customers buy, which is an objectified sex that dehumanizes, is what a woman in prostitution promotes when she chooses it as her own identity.

For women who promote prostitution, neutralization of it requires internalization of all that women who simply survive prostitution have distanced themselves from, have dissociated from themselves, going through each of the steps—from distancing to disembodiment—and then internalizing their opposite, treating the sex as their own spontaneous experience of it. It is the embodiment of prostitution sex even as prostitute women are disembodied while doing it. Women who experience everything from distancing to disembodiment are not rejecting that which for some few women in prostitution is accepted. As prostitution is sexual exploitation, it harms the human self and destroys through sex, dehumanizing women. In other words, to promote the sexual servicing of others through the use of oneself, *one must re-embody that which has been disembodied* of the original developing self.

It does not work the other way around. There is not an original, essential, embodied prostitution. To treat prostitution as if it is not sexual exploitation is to assume that sexual dehumanization is the original human condition.

Typically the proprostitution lobby, fronting for the international sex industry, has been credited with neutralizing the negative status of prostitution by promoting legal and social acceptance of it. If, then, accepting one's prostitution and incorporating it into one's identity requires only "deviance neutralization," it is because prostitution is identified as "deviant" instead of as the human-rights violation and dehumanization that it is. Prostitute organizations are absolutely right in wanting that deviant label removed: as long as prostitute women are the deviants, all of the women who accept sexually objectified sex and incorporate it into their identities are protected from having to incorporate into their identities the recognition of themselves as prostitutes.

In the sexual objectification of women, the problem is more complex than the theory of "deviance neutralization" suggests, for this theory requires that what one does be understood as deviant in the society. Prostitution has been considered deviant, but through the prostitution of sexuality it is losing its deviant label because it is increasingly the normalized experience of sex. Therefore, when women in prostitution defend and promote their activity as work, it is not that they are merely trying to neutralize a deviant category that has been assigned to them. They are requiring that their sex exchange for money be treated merely as sex. When they achieve their goal, then *equal acceptance of every form of sexual objectification and dehumanization that goes under the overall designation of "sex"* will achieve the prostitution of sexuality. This is how the sex of prostitution is normalized.

In the normalization of pornography, and the prostitution of sexuality, the experience of sex is no longer relevant in determining whether sexual enhancement or sexual degradation has taken place. Normalized prostitution is a product of liberal individualism where free will or consent prevail.

In the prostitution of sexuality we can find the basis for the developing support for the proprostitution movement from many women who are not prostitutes. Nonprostitute women's promotion of prostitution is about something other than destigmatizing prostitution. The wider support for prostitution from nonprostitute women has to do with reinforcing the distinction between prostitute and nonprostitute women, especially as it becomes indistinguishable in the sexual acts through the prostitution of sexuality. In other words, *as prostitution sex becomes recognized as the prostitution of "normal" sexuality, the only way nonprostitute women know that they indeed are not whores is by insuring that some women are sustained in a separate category, whether they call it prostitute, or they call it "sex work."* Through non-prostitute women's promotion of prostitution, the separation of prostitute and nonprostitute is maintained. Knowing those women who do "sex between consenting adults" as "sex workers" protects other women from being seen as whores when they are doing that same sex in their marriages, in dating, or in anonymous, unpaid liaisons.

Sexual Relations of Power

To locate all of sexual exploitation within the real, lived experience of patriarchal oppression is to speak about power. In his search for a theory of sexual power, Foucault came close in his *History of Sexuality*. Establishing that the term "sexuality" originated in the nineteenth century, he located sexual power in history rather than ahistorical biology. He rejected the marxist tendency to identify power only as an overarching power of the state or as a general class condition, in other words, to identify power only as public and social. He theorized on sexual power at a level of analysis that invokes the personal, private, social domains that have been ignored by earlier theorists of sexuality.

Sex as power, Foucault told us, is ubiquitous—it is everywhere at once "not because it has the privilege of consolidating everything under its invincible unity, but because it is produced from one moment to the next, at every point, or rather in every relation from one point to another." [30] Foucault gave us a middle ground of theory in which the sex relations of power can be recognized as "a multiplicity of force relations immanent in the sphere in which they operate and which constitute their own organization."[31] Consequently, he found that the domain of sex and power is not driven but rather constitutes

an especially dense transfer point for relations of power: between men and women, young people and old people, parents and offspring, teachers and students, priests and laity, an administration and a population. Sexuality is not the most intractable element in power relations, but rather one of those endowed with the greatest instrumentality; useful for the greatest number of maneuvers and capable of serving as a point of support, as a linchpin, for the most varied strategies.[32]

Yet, in order to understand how sex is constructed into power, we need to get at it where it operates without becoming lost in its individualized components. The problem with Foucault's theory is that in seeking to elucidate sexual power at the micro level, he abandons attention to the collectivized conditions that produce classes of power.[33] Sexual power operates at all levels. It is constantly being reproduced in sexual relations that are at once private and coupled and at the same time collective, institutional, and public. Important to Foucault's contribution is his recognition that in sexual relations "power is everywhere, not because it embraces everything, but because it comes from everywhere." But he eliminates structure, and by doing so, he dissolves the hierarchy of power, making power amorphous. In defining power, he makes it undefinable and his theory diminishes responsibility for power.

As Foucault tells us, sexual power is everywhere and comes from everything, but its agency is secreted in its ubiquity. For Foucault, "there is no subject"; the agents of oppression elude identification. What is important about Foucault's definition of power is that he reveals the difficulty in exposing sexual power as it is constantly "produced from one moment to the next" in the intertangled web of the "multiplicity of force relations." However, because Foucault does not directly confront power as gender-structured hierarchal relations, in the context of sex in marriage, in prostitution, in structured inequality, his theory achieves what he sought to avoid. His definition of power merely reinforces masculinist theories of power that obscure that privatization and personalization of patriarchal power by considering power primarily at the level of the state.

However, Foucault is correct that there "is no binary and all-encompassing opposition between ruler and ruled" in the sense that such oppositions suggest that the one who has power is acting, thus making the oppressed who is acted upon a passive figure. But there is interaction and reciprocity in the relations of power. Power is produced through interaction, and that interaction includes the participation of both the "ruler" and the "ruled," the oppressed who are acting, historical, and temporal, even though the ruler thinks and behaves as if they are not. Exploring interaction makes it possible to reveal power, and this is particularly true in the sexual relations of power. In women's shelters, as women recount the interactions of privatized abuse, consciousness exposes and makes public previously obscured power relations.

Power is not exclusively enacted among opposites, by one gender on the other, as men and boys are not excluded from sexual exploitation as individuals. The evidence that men and boys are in some cases sexually exploited is not a negation of sexual power that is a *female class condition*. Rigid adherence to false binary oppositions (individual men and boys versus individual women and girls) conveys the contrary (that men and boys are not equally exploited) and then makes the exception, the sexual exploitation of boys, into the rule.

However, Foucault's rejection of binary oppositions are not based on the same assumptions as those of the feminist theory I am presenting here, which looks beyond oppositions to understand the complexities of sexual relations of power. For Foucault and his followers, rejecting binary oppositions provided him (and them) with the opportunity to deflect attention away from the agency and social location of domination, the dyad, the couple wherein sexual power is constantly constructed. In destructuring power, he made the relations of power disappear because he made their agents invisible. In trying to connect sex and power, Foucault dismantled the dyad, the nexus wherein sexualized human relations become dialectically hierarchical sexual power relations. But a theorist's denial of reality does not change that reality; it only hides it. It is impossible to eliminate from the social landscape that which constructed it, the institutional and individual power structure. Without an analysis of power, Foucault's "multiplicity of force relations" becomes mired in its own diversity. Domination becomes particularized into and unidentifiable among these multiple lines of power. For Foucault, individualized sexual relations of power, operational in dyads, are not collectivized to form systematic domination, because in his definition of sexual power he has eliminated class conditions, the referent for interpersonal, gendered relations of power. Sexual power would lose its interpersonal enforcement if there were no class-based, institutional, systematized, and state-based domination beyond and distinct from its individual manifestations.

Foucault relativizes sexuality to each instance of it. The idea that sexuality is used to "serve the most varied strategies" and is "endowed with the greatest instrumentality" goes nowhere. There is no overall pattern, no consistency from one unit or one sexual relation to another.

Power is relational. It actively engages oppressor and oppressed. In its "multiplicity of force relations," power operates between classes—economic classes, the capitalist and proletariat; race classes, whites and people of color; and sex classes, men and women. Hegel's description of the reciprocity of master and slave and Marx's analysis of the economic relations of the capitalist and working classes identify power relations dialectically constructed into power hierarchies that are sustained by the advantages gained by oppressors in their exploitation of the oppressed. The power of oppression is as diffuse as it is direct. Direct violence, then, is only one aspect of oppression in the subordination of the "other."

Laborers go to work voluntarily and take a wage for their work that does not represent the full value of their labor; the difference between the value of their labor and the wage paid constitutes the profits of the capitalist. The relations of power between them are sustained in the wage-profit calculation. That is fundamental to the interaction in domination; it is the foundation of the relationship between oppressor and oppressed. A relational theory of power identifies the way subordination is frequently held in place through the active participation of the subordinated without blaming them for their oppression. Hegelian and marxist theories of power reveal dynamics of oppression that account for the interactive relational force that keeps oppression in place.

The relational power of male domination reaches into the private, into and onto the body, through interactive sexual relations that are rendered into sexual exploitation by the power that forges the economic relations of women under patriarchy. Considering sexual exploitation as lived experience, identifying it in sexual acts, whether or not they involve consent, and analyzing sexual exploitation in terms of institutions that promote it, namely prostitution and marriage, gives oppression a substantive context and identifies it as a sex-class condition.

Among the collective conditions of domination, only in the subordination of women are class relations of power simultaneously personal relations, where interactions that are as intimate as sexual relations are also the relations of power. Sexism and sexual exploitation of women as a class by men as a class are class relations that operate as individual interactions. A feminist relational theory of power, of the subordinated female gender class, must reveal power in personal interactions, in physical and emotional relations that operate at the most private and intimate levels of human existence.

Patriarchy superimposes class conditions of power relations upon sex/gender relations between men and women, interpersonally establishing a near-perfect fit between the class relations of power and gendered interpersonal relations. This has created a particularity to women's oppression, making it unique in that it is constructed in gendered interpersonal relations that invoke sex. It is highly public, visible, and structural, and yet simultaneously it is personal—hidden, secreted, and bodily, physically, and emotionally internalized.

Gender relations of sexual power are institutionalized and simultaneously individualized in prostitution, pornography, and marriage. Sex is a relational power that is realized in human relations that take place in private, usually hidden from view. In the French history of private life this is referred to as "the secret."[34] As sexual relations are usually unseen and often unspoken, except in group sex and/or gang rape, power relations are structurally privatized and yet commercialized.

When private interactive sexual power relations are made invisible, so is power in sex industries denied. As sex becomes industrialized, not only in business but also through multinational conglomerates, the use of sex in the power relations in which the United States dominates the Third World is made invisible. Consequently, the individual unit of interaction in the sexual relations of power is both realized and sustained by state policies and the industrial development of sex industries that commodify and exchange women.

In the context of these sexual relations of power—the privatized, sexualized location of women's oppression—when women leave home—as runaways in Western countries, as migrants in the Third World, in the absence of feminist political refuge or of viable economic alternatives—they are most frequently reduced to the public, political institution of sex: prostitution. Again, the power relations of racism and Western hegemony that close down economic alternatives for women of color invoke prostitution as a normative condition for women in poverty.

Power is gain; it produces advantage and superior status by and for the dominating class through the subordination of the "other." Because sexual exploitation actively harms women, the gain that men derive from it does not merely advance men. Sexual exploitation also forces women backward, regresses women into the harms it conveys, thereby thwarting women's ability to achieve, to move forward, to grow and to develop.

Feminist Political Consciousness vs. Ideology

Over the last decade, as I have listened to women's responses to my first book, *Female Sexual Slavery*, I have heard from some women that they found the book "too painful to read" or "depressing," while others were "empowered" by it because their experiences had been revealed as exploitation and slavery, or simply because domination had been named and explored.

Yet another reaction has been to classify this work as "victim feminism," or "male bashing." In the United States this is more than backlash. This highly vocal, media-hyped assault on feminism as a *liberation* movement is aligned with conservatives and liberals, who both attack feminism for "political correctness" (p.c.). They silence social protest and political consciousness not only of sexism but racism, homophobia, and the environment by denying women's oppression. Anti-feminism in the form of women's defense of men is not new to the women's movement. But the alignment with right-wing anti—"political correctness" forces is new. Katie Roiphe typifies a dangerous women's movement collusion with both the right and the liberals against what they call the political correctness of feminism. With no data of her own, citing flawed critiques as her sources, Roiphe has challenged the existence of date rape and Mary Koss's date rape statistics that reveal that 1 in 4 women will be raped in college. Roiphe, raising a women's movement defense, is concerned that women are being seen only as victims, or "that men are lascivious, women are innocent." [35] Roiphe questions women's agency when rape takes place after a woman has been drinking or has taken drugs, as if the society is not gendered, is not patriarchal, and has no relationship to individual behavior.

Since the emergence of the U.S. women's movement in the

late 1960s, the political left has consistently tried to delegitimize feminism on the same terms that, today, Wendy Kaminer defended Roiphe in the *New York Times:* "protesting their sexual victimization enables privileged, heterosexual white women to claim their share of the high moral ground ceded to victims of racism, classism and homophobia."[36] Kaminer's support for Roiphe suggests the origins of the anti-feminist women's movement in the left. Right-wing accusations of political correctness build from the left wing's 25-year campaign to delegitimize independent feminism, denouncing it as privileged or bourgeois. Yet until now, until it became politically incorrect to indicate one has been raped, or that men oppress women, it had been impossible for the left wing to invalidate the women's movement, precisely because the movements against sexual exploitation raised feminism beyond only issues of economic class.

Roiphe is representative of some women who have come to the movement in a general apolitical climate and who have learned about women's issues from books, the media, lectures, and through women's studies. By and large, women's studies, having dissociated itself from feminist activism, is an increasingly apolitical study of women. Where feminism originated in the 1960s in consciousness raising that raised the personal to the political, many women replace feminist consciousness and political liberation with personal choice (the real p.c.). The movement, increasingly emptied of political consciousness, approaches issues in terms of personal choice, an inheritance from the earlier "me" generation that is almost a perfect fit with the ideology of American individualism. It treats issues as if they exist outside of, apart from, and indeed irrelevant to any social conditions and power arrangements in the immediate or distant environment, that is, anything that exists outside of their own conjuring.

In the 1990s we risk repeating history. By the 1890s the women's movement that had originated in the 1850s was emptied of political consciousness. The movement was rapidly reduced to apolitical reform that blindly supported prevailing national ideologies, ideologies which aside from the narrowed concept of women's rights then, were exploiting the rest of the world. That generation brought feminism to an end. It invoked the silencing of confrontation against sexism for over 60 years until the 1960s.

By the mid 1990s, it appears that the women's movement is going in the same directions, which intensifies the isolation of feminists whose commitments to women's liberation is framed from hard-won, difficultly achieved consciousness. And what is at the root of the reactionary positioning of the women's movement? Their term "male bashing" is more than accusatory; it is representational. First, it represents collusion between women who identify themselves as feminists and the most reactionary forces of the right wing, particularly Rush Limbaugh, who originated this term. Now, in a reactionary alignment between right-wing agitators and sexual liberals, some women are identifying their feminism as that which will protect men, racists, heterosexists, and polluters from being "bashed." The strategy is not direct nor is it straightforward. As sexual relations of power have surfaced through consciousness and in activism with other movements, presumably some men, some whites, some heterosexuals, some environmental polluters have become uncomfortable as their groups and some specific members are increasingly identified as perpetrators of injustices and exploitation. Rather than confronting sexual power, these women turn on women who are exposing oppression and confronting injustice and charge that we are reducing women to victims, a concept that could only create attention in the absence of political consciousness as consciousness recognizes victimization as other than passive. As Janice Raymond has put it,

Once upon a time, in the beginnings of this wave of feminism, there was a feminist consensus that women's choices were constructed, burdened, framed, impaired, constrained, limited, coerced, shaped by patriarchy. No one proposed that this mean women's choices were *determined*, or that women were passive or helpless victims of patriarchy. That was because many women believed in the power of feminism to change women's lives, and obviously, women could not change if they were socially determined in their roles or pliant putty in the hands of patri-archs.[37]

We are faced with a movement that is not only not remember-ing that history but is increasingly driven by women who were not there when consciousness ignited, and for the first time in decades of deadening silence, women created new possibilities for themselves which were possibilities for their class. The critiques of power relations that characterized the feminist movement in the late 1960s and early 1970s have been replaced by the apoliti-cal emphasis on the personal choice of hopelessly mired individu-alism. This is the sexual liberalism that Sheila Jeffreys defined as "a set of political beliefs and practices rooted in the assumption that sexual expression is inherently liberating and must be permit-ted to flourish unchecked, even when it entails the exploitation or brutalization of others."[38] It is now evident that neither "sexual liberalism" nor "backlash" are adequate terms to identify the nonconscious ideology of personal choice as it is interlinked with the agendas of the right wing as well as liberals.

Under these conditions, the women's movement is increasingly compelled to prove extreme force in order to charge rape, and to ignore how the sexual relations of power seep into daily life, shaping particularly male–female interaction in the society. Being laden with the burden of proving extreme force is a reversion to where we were in 1970 when we first launched the movement against rape in the United States. This is how the women's move-ment against sexual violence is placed on the defensive as it has been since the beginning of the Reagan administration's threat-ened cutback of social services and its censorship of social protest. Many rape crisis centers and wife abuse shelters began to limit their services or restrict the kinds of cases they took. Trying to look more like social service agencies, they hoped to protect the precious little funding they had. Roiphe and the vanguard of women who are intent on protecting men from supposed male bashing now perpetuate the self-imposed limitations initiated in the reactionary administration of Reagan and perpetuated by Bush. It is a curious and dangerous allegiance between the right-wing, fundamentalist, and political reactionary stance and these women who promote personal choice to treat rape as normal sex, to promote pornography, to treat racial hatred as a personal preference for a racially "pure" environment, to treat homophobia as the personal choice to live with and work outside of association with lesbians and gay men. Hyper-individualism and elevation of personal choice as the only and therefore ultimate condition of freedom, if it prevails over the feminist movement, will be its final deconstruction.

The harm of personal choice politics and campaigns against political correctness is intensified for oppressed groups as it is another manifestation of capitalist market liberal ideology that emphasizes individualism to serve market competition and promote consumerism. But more than that, it creates an ideological environment that elevates personal choice above *any* concept of a common good or collective well-being. The idea is that freedom is defined as personal choice in a context of structured, politically imposed inequality that ranges from male–female relations to the relationship between Western nations and the Third World. Ultimately the reduction of political consciousness to personal choice reverts all issues to the liberal construction of consent. At base this is how market economy ideology promotes patriarchal domination in post-industrial society.

While the slogan of the movement against sexual violence, "No Means No," firmly asserts that individual women refuse to be cajoled into sexual experiences they do not want with men they reject, it also suggests that *sexual* victimization of women takes place only when consent is not given, when women explicitly say no. It suggests that when women do not say no, when women actively consent, they are not violated. Defining rape in terms of violation of consent shifts the emphasis of political consciousness from the act of victimization, the use of sex to exploit, to individual will; it shifts oppression from a class condition of sexual exploitation to individual experiences of it. That is how women in prostitution are excluded from being recognized as sexually victimized. Prostitute women are made to be the "other"—the women for whom the act of abusive, violating, dehumanizing sex is meant—because their consent is established in the market exchange, where they take money for sex.

The patriarchal power of sexual liberalism has deployed ideologies that narrowly construe consent in context of social normalcy of impaired judgment. Patriarchal law can address individual conditions of coercion but it will not help women confront conditions of collective oppression. It is not a crime to oppress women through sexual exploitation where those lines blur. The law will not resolve women's subjection to sexual power. Nor will it correct its own liberal ideology that individualizes every case so that there is no recognizable collective condition. Only a collective liberation movement's struggle with analysis of oppression can do that.

The facts of women's subordination often lie in realities that are obscured in silence or normalized in acceptance but that nevertheless dehumanize and brutalize us as women even when we do not directly experience their most extreme manifestations—unless we bring to them consciousness of women's condition as a political reality.

Breaking silence and facing the brutal realities of sexual exploitation require feminist political consciousness. Consciousness transforms brutal facts and painful realities into new knowledge that exposes power and ignites action. Confronted with sexual exploitation, to move from not knowing to awareness without *political* consciousness of power relations leaves one confronted either with prevailing liberal ideology or raw pain, and therefore unable to know that because sexual exploitation is not inevitable and has been politically constructed, it can also be deconstructed—by women.

The common denominator in all sexual exploitation is the disruption of and violation of a woman's identity, that sense of "who I am" and "who I can be." Prostitution and incest abuse are twin acts—they are the terrorist models of female subordination in that they invoke girls' and women's splitting from their selves, segmentation of the unsegmentable, partitioning of human realities that can only be whole. Consciousness of sexual politics in confronting oppression restores the whole from its segmentation. It is the foundation for healing and action.

Feminist political consciousness moves feminism back and forth in a dialectical interaction between the personal and the political, the particular and the general, inevitably taking us from our own cultural and national specificity to the international community and global feminism, and back again. Political consciousness extends our awareness of our social location from our homes to our communities, from nation-states to the international economy and the global political order. International feminist activism leads us logically to analysis of patriarchal power.

Consciousness requires being able to see the conditions by which sex is exploited, and that requires considering what occurs in the sex exchange. Consciousness is not only an intellectual awareness; rather, political consciousness allows us to know women's experiences of *individual* exploitations and of *oppression,* not only as painful subordinations but also as potentialities for their transcendence. I am not speaking of transcendence in only spiritual or ephemeral terms. Feminist consciousness is knowledge of material, concrete conditions that, because it knows them in terms of domination that produces brutal realities, also knows of the possibility of revolutionizing those material conditions in confronting domination. Feminist consciousness recognizes the fuller terrain of male domination—oppression. Consciousness of *oppression* makes strategies clearer, vision fuller, and action deeper.

Popular criticism of feminism alleges that it reduces women to victims. But women's knowledge of themselves as victims, as "empowered," as oppressed, and/or as liberated is knowledge that is realistically accessible to women only through political consciousness. Due to fear of the potential of consciousness to produce change, this dynamic, powerful knowing has been reduced to "political correctness." But, in fact, the power of political consciousness is that it is personally liberating because it enables vision of the world of patriarchal domination as it is. Without consciousness, in the suppression of consciousness, prior to consciousness, knowledge is isolated to individuals and in that isolation it goes unnamed, unspoken. As knowledge is produced in interaction with others, isolation relativizes it and relegates it to intra-individual psychological conditions. While feminism is charged with reducing women to victims, women's isolated, suppressed anger and pain from domination is reduced to clinical conditions, material sources of the pain. Objective knowledge is located outside of, as well as within, the self. It can either function as an exterior determination of the self as it does in oppression or as the basis for collective action as it does in consciousness.

Personal empowerment that treats overcoming objective domination as an act of will, a psychological state, is an idealistic approach that traps knowledge of oppression within individualized, personal feelings and preferences.

Consciousness reframes personalized, isolated knowledge of objective conditions, recognizing them as political conditions. Reformulating knowledge redefines victimization, which is no longer recognized as an intra-individual experience and therefore is not a matter of consent or will of individuals.

Thus, the crucial difference involved in knowing the worst of patriarchal domination of women turns on political consciousness of women's oppression. Consciousness, as I am discussing it here, is a political knowing of the personal reality that is carried into action that not only confronts but also includes the knowledge and conviction that it can/will/must transform present realities. It is active knowledge, found and created in social action, surpassing the patriarchal limits of the possible to imagine and to know another reality as possibility.

Consciousness is the basis of activism, of project, of new

knowledge and political confrontation generated by the feminist movement against sexual exploitation. Because it is the consciousness of sexual politics and because it confronts the political and social realities of domination and oppression, that same consciousness is the foundation from which it is possible to find ways for women individually and collectively to heal from rape, prostitution, and all forms of sexual exploitation. Consciousness of sexual politics forms the supportive network that women find coming off the streets, running away from home, and/or going into therapy. That consciousness becomes constructed in political struggle and knowledge.

Most importantly, political consciousness is feminist only if it is multidimensional and inclusive. Therefore, if it is not global, it is not consciousness; if it does not embrace the range of conditions that constitute oppression, it is merely reform of patriarchy, to make it work better with modifications. Feminist consciousness is diminished if the movement confronts and effectively addresses only one issue, such as pornography in the West or trafficking in the Third World, without addressing the entire matrix of sexual exploitation. Therefore, single-issue feminism is a contradiction to feminist consciousness of oppression. So is missionary feminism, which occurs when Western women do not recognize that which exploits women in the Third World springs from their own experience of sexual politics. Likewise, precisely because of the power of prevailing misogynist ideologies, in the superabundance of poverty that appears impossible to see beyond, in the intense sexualization of women that seems to be all there is, feminist consciousness must see the possibility of a future that is the rejection of these present realities.

Consciousness is not a matter of having the correct political analysis or knowing the right answers. That is ideology. Ideology is a structured, preformed set of ideas that justify particular power arrangements. Ideology replaces political consciousness either with an embedded taken-for-grantedness of the present situation or with a prefabricated political analysis. Consciousness, on the other hand, exposes everyday realities as power relations, making it possible to see and identify that which is taken for granted as structured power. Consciousness is accessed through critical reflection, which reveals power, dominance, and subordination in the dailiness of life. Feminism must confront dominant ideologies not only in the state but also in the home, not only in public but also in bed. In the West, the liberal legalism that rationalizes the market economy and promotes individualism often remains unquestioned as feminists struggle for legal change for women. The first failure of consciousness occurs in feminism when one assumes that she can be immune from the influences of her national and cultural ideology.

Personally, I have had to confront the limits of legal liberalism many times in order to try to shed its ideology from my work. This is an ongoing condition of consciousness. In 1983 I met with Hanna Olssen, the Swedish researcher who was responsible for a major government study, *The Prostitution Report*. Hanna and I had previously had the opportunity to discuss our research on prostitution in Sweden in 1981. We had been struck with the fact that, in different parts of the globe, unknown to each other, we had not only researched the same subject but had come to very similar conclusions that were published at the same time. In *The Prostitution Report*, she spoke of the "loveless male society" while I discussed befriending and love (terror bonding) as pimp procuring strategies in *Female Sexual Slavery*. In 1983, getting away from the pressing business at hand in the international meeting I had convened, she candidly asked me, "My god, Kathy, why did you have to call it slavery?" Realizing that she knew very well why prostitution was enslaving and that was not the question, I mentally searched for the issue behind her question.

Of course. Unwittingly, I had fallen into the "free-force" dichotomization of women's choices, which had led me, in *Female Sexual Slavery*, to propose decriminalization as the appropriate legal strategy for confronting prostitution. At that moment, I felt refreshed, having been caught in what I now perceive to be the trap of the American mind, which must contend with a U.S. concept of rights limited and distorted by the individualism that promotes market exchange. Intense hyperindividualism narrows rights to individual rights and in so doing it instrumentalizes them. Under an individualism that promotes market economies, rights are reduced from being enhancements of the full human condition to serving the instrumental end of market economies and therefore promoting the competitive edge of individualism. Reducing human rights to individual consent instrumentalizes the meaning of rights as they serve the market economy. When instrumentalized, rights are not primarily concerned with the quality of human experience. In the extreme represented by U.S. sexual liberalism, rights are understood in market-economy terms, in terms of a deregulated human condition that emphasizes individual choice and human will over the quality and content of human experience.

According to the feminist human-rights concepts I am developing in this work, "consent" is not the indicator of freedom, nor is absence of consent the primary indicator of exploitation. The liberal construction of consent narrows the feminist analysis of oppression to individual wrongs and drowns feminism in the ethics of individualism. It confines sex to a matter of consent and will and does not consider how sex is used, how it is experienced, and how it is constructed into power.

Individually and institutionally, the lived experience of dehumanized sex harms women and sustains the gender class condition. It is oppression. Consent to oppression or an apparent "will" to be objectified is a condition of oppression. It is never a state of freedom. Sexual exploitation is oppression, and that means that it will be accepted and even promoted within the oppressed class. That is what oppression is! This is how every form of oppression is sustained. Violating consent may then be an aspect of exploitation, but it is not its defining feature. Therefore, freedom cannot be confined within a unidimensional concept of consent; it must expand to the full human condition—the female condition. It must be inclusive of the full range of exploitations visited upon women as a class. In that context the movement against sexual violence or violence against women is one challenge to a broad-based condition of sexual oppression that includes prostitution just as it includes sexual subordination of women in marriage and of teenagers in dating.

And thus I find that the issue of consent and the concept of force have falsely separated prostitution from rape, legally and socially. In marriage, in dating, and in rape, what women have to prove is not that they were abused but that they are not whores, that is, that they are not sexed bodies. In response, movements against sexual violence are increasingly confined within "no means no" campaigns that treat rape not as sex but as aggression, as if the two could not be considered together. That is too little for a liberation struggle to demand. Fully confronting sexual power will only take place when women are determined, as we have been, to win our full liberation.

Josephine Butler:
The First Wave of Protest

In 1798, two private physicians were given the task of examining Parisian prostitutes; they were required to report to the police any cases of infection. In 1802, a dispensary was established, and the police began registering all public prostitutes, who were required to submit to semiweekly examinations.[1] In 1871, at the International Medical Congress in Vienna, an international law was proposed to make regulation uniform throughout the world.[2] By the middle of the century, this system had developed into regulation—state-supported prostitution. The state-regulated brothel *(maison close)* made prostitution legitimate. Regulation was accepted by many as a social reform that improved the hygienic conditions of prostitution.

During the French Revolution venereal disease was so widespread that it often undermined military effectiveness. The chief concern was to find a way to prevent disease without inhibiting soldiers' access to prostitutes. The practice of regulation of brothels quickly spread from the military to the general public. From its institution in France and Germany, regulated prostitution began to spread across Europe. Officially, such regulation was seen as a mechanism for controlling venereal disease; unofficially, it legitimized prostitution and encouraged a widespread traffic in women.

Through regulation, official state sanction of prostitution in brothels accomplished three things of long-lasting impact: (1) it treated prostitution as normal and legitimate, (2) it covered up other abuses and the traffic in women, and (3) it introduced a new distinction between forced prostitution and "free" prostitution.

In the mid-nineteenth century, between 1864 and 1869, regulation was introduced into Great Britain through the Contagious Diseases Acts. When the Contagious Diseases Acts became law, one woman, Josephine Butler, dared to challenge them, and in doing so she created an international movement. In her campaigns against "forced prostitution," Josephine Butler changed the direction of nineteenth-century European prostitution. For that time she stemmed the mounting tide that in the late twentieth century has re-emerged and is directed toward complete legitimization of prostitution. Butler's motivations and politics were feminist—she not only helped protect women from prostitution, but she also wanted men held accountable for their sexual behaviors. Yet she and the abolitionist movement (the movement to abolish regulation) that she organized invoked a dangerous distinction by differentiating between free and forced prostitution. Regulation, having already legitimized prostitution, left the reformers in the position of confronting prostitution as violation only when it involved *other* victimizing practices such as pimping. To differentiate between freely chosen and forced prostitution was to imply that some prostitution is acceptable. Today it would be comparable to suggesting that drug abuse is acceptable when it is not forced, when people inject themselves without direct coercion from others. The liberal emphasis on consent, which, in Butler's time, was developing as an ideology of industrial capitalism, has become a superficial and technical distinction that obscures the harm of the act itself.

Before launching her campaigns against legalized prostitution,

Josephine Butler had personally been engaged in helping young girls and women get out of prostitution on the docks in Liverpool. She outraged her neighbors when she brought prostitute women home, nursed them to health, and helped them create new lives. She persisted with the support of her husband. Deeply affected by the economic and sexual degradation to which these women were subjected, she saw how quickly women responded to supportive care, immediately grasping at the opportunity to get out of prostitution.

The Contagious Diseases Acts were designed to protect the health of military men by subjecting any woman whom the special Morals Police identified as a prostitute to a "surgical examination," which involved the use of crude instruments for special vaginal examinations by often cruel doctors. The coarse brutality of doctors, men who had only recently taken over the work of midwives, and the arbitrary police identification of women as prostitutes, combined with Victorian morality to create an outrage among women against such examinations. "The examination was demeaning because of its public character. Streetwalking at night was one thing; being forced to attend examinations during the day often taunted by young boys . . . was another."[3] The acts were enforced in 11 garrison towns, military stations, and naval seaports. An amendment to the 1864 act required that all women identified by the Morals Police as prostitutes submit to a medical examination. If a woman was found to be free of venereal disease, she was then officially registered and issued a certificate identifying her as a clean prostitute. The state created the prostitution supply for customers.

The Percy case exemplifies the way in which regulation entrapped women. Mrs. Percy supported her family by working in a musical theater on a military base. Her 16-year-old daughter accompanied her each evening, and they were always escorted home by a military officer. One evening during their walk home, the police approached her and her daughter, identifying them both as public prostitutes and ordering them to report for the requisite medical examination. Mrs. Percy's daughter gave the following account to George Butler, Josephine's husband, when she was taken in by the Butlers after her mother's suicide:

They called the police and ordered my mother to go up to the Metropolitan Police Office and bring me with her. Mamma and I went. We there saw Inspector G———. He was in his room, and mamma was first called in alone. I cannot, therefore, tell what passed between mamma and the Inspector, because I was never the same person again after that hour. She told me that she assured Inspector G——— that she would rather sign her death warrant than the paper he gave her to sign. I was then called in. I shall never forget the moment when I stood before Inspector G— and he accused me. He said, "Do you know, girl, why you are here?" I replied, "No, sir, I do not." He said, "You are here because you are no better than you should be. You know what that means, I suppose?" I said, "No, sir, I do not." He laughed in a horrible way when I said this.[4]

The Contagious Diseases Acts not only regulated and controlled prostitutes but they also showed the rest of the women that to venture out of their homes was to risk being identified as a prostitute and thereby put into prostitution. Mrs. Percy refused to submit herself or her daughter to the surgical examination, and she made her anger known through a letter to the *Daily Telegraph*. The Morals Police were determined more than ever to make a lesson of Mrs. Percy and her daughter. Under pressure, the theater that employed Mrs. Percy fired her. She and her daughter moved out of town but were convinced by one of Mrs. Percy's coworkers to return to work under a false name.[5] The Morals Police unrelentingly pursued Mrs. Percy, warning lodging houses that if they took her in they would risk being cited for running a disorderly house. In desperation, with no place to live or work, Mrs. Percy threw herself into the Basingstoke Canal.

In 1869, after the final act passed, Josephine organized the Ladies National Association to campaign for the repeal of the acts. A statement from the association, summarizing its position, was published in the *Daily News* on December 31. It was accompanied by the names of 130 of the 2,000 women who had signed it; among the names were those of Josephine Butler, writer Harriet Martineau, and Florence Nightingale. The statement said, in part,

Unlike all other laws for the repression of contagious diseases, to which both men and women are liable, these two apply to women only, men being wholly exempt from their penalties. The law is ostensibly framed for a certain class of women, but in order to reach these, all women residing within the district where it is in force are brought under the provisions of the Acts. Any woman can be dragged into court, and required to prove that she is not a common prostitute. The magistrate can condemn her, if a policeman swears only that he "has good cause to believe" her to be one. . . . When condemned, the sentence is as follows: to have her person outraged by the periodical inspection of a surgeon, through a period of 12 months; or resisting that, to be imprisoned, with or without hard labour—first for a month, next for three months— such imprisonment to be renewed for her whole life unless she submit periodically to the brutal requirements of the law.

Victor Hugo was among the many who responded to this appeal; he encouraged the women to "Protest! resist! show your indignation!" and wrote, "I am with you to the fullest extent of my power. In reading your eloquent letter, I have felt a burning sympathy rise in me for the feeble, and a corresponding indignation against the oppressor."[6]

In organizing the Ladies National Association and in issuing their statement, Josephine began her political campaigns against prostitution and the acts behind them. While, as she believed, the injustices of the Contagious Diseases Acts would always be felt more keenly by women, she was acutely aware of the barriers that women activists had to confront even to summon the courage to speak in public, much less to challenge men's control of the government, the acts, the streets, and indeed even public thought. Josephine insisted on separate ladies' associations throughout her political career. She exhorted the women, "We must cease to 'recognize superior wisdom' in those who oppress us, and learn to abhor the despotism of a public opinion formed by men, which has so long, and with such calamitous results, aimed at holding in bondage even the inmost thoughts of women."[7]

The Contagious Diseases Acts to regulate prostitution initiated a sexual slavery of women. Josephine responded with a war against that tyranny, a campaign for destruction of the sexist double standard of morality, and a demand for the personal liberty of all women. She called for a return to "the mark of a common standard of purity, and an equal judgment of the sin of impurity for both sexes alike."[8]

In her speeches she pointed out the results of the double standard on men's behavior:

The language of men towards women is, and has ever been, far too much of this character. "You must make us good, and keep us good; you must continually pray for us, we having no time (nor inclination) to pray for ourselves or you; you must save our souls while you minister to our daily comfort; . . . and somehow or other you must, you *absolutely must,* get us into heaven at last. You know how! We leave it to you; but remember you are responsible for all this." I think I should be ashamed, were I a man, to throw such awful moral and spiritual responsibility upon women, while doing little for their souls in return.[9]

Butler believed that a social movement against legalized prostitution would not only protect women and girls from prostitution but would also help elevate the standards of sexual conduct. The campaigns to abolish state regulation of prostitution, focusing as they did on laws that actually promote prostitution and emphasizing the *extreme* cases wherein women and girls were trafficked, had the effect of historically overshadowing the larger and even more significant reality, the massive proliferation in prostitution itself.

With economic development, industrialization, and urbanization, in mid-nineteenth century United States and Europe, prostitution became highly visible and industrialized. Timothy Gilfoyle, in a history of prostitution in New York City, identifies the city as the "carnal showcase of the Western world" after 1820.[10] With industrialization came the commercialization of women as sexed bodies for hire. Business stood to profit from the rental of their properties for prostitution, and "illicit sex" increasingly became an "attractive form of capital investment."

Cities provided the condition of anonymity that customers require in prostitution. The earlier occasional or casual prostitution in mostly rural, preindustrial society gave way to pimps, who were initially hired by brothels to protect women from the mobs that formed in frequent brothel riots as the male citizenry reacted to the changing conditions.

With industrialization came a change in social mores. Commercialization emphasized public display of goods. "Never had so much been on show in the cities," Alain Corbain tells us of the growth of prostitution in France, where prostitute women showed and offered themselves publicly.[11] With urbanization and migration from rural to urban areas in Europe and the United States, women and girls found themselves at the bottom of the labor force. The developing sex industry siphoned women off the labor market—away from domestic labor, or work as servants, seamstresses, chambermaids, tailoresses, and milliners and into prostitution.[12] The new affluence of the business classes and the increased standard of living of men in general as a result of industrialization, along with the increase of male immigrants for labor in these industrializing economies, increased the market demand for prostitution.

Dr. William Sanger, a nineteenth-century scholar on prostitution, found that a substantial increase in prostitution in New York City accompanied the midcentury increase in immigration. Of 200 prostitutes in New York City in the 1850s, Sanger found that three-eighths were between the ages of 15 and 20 and another three-eighths were 21 to 25.[13] Gilfoyle, in his study of prostitution in New York City, summarized the situation through a remark of a police captain: " 'Startling as is the assertion,' remarked Police Captain Thomas Byrnes in 1886, 'it is nevertheless true, that the traffic in female virtue is as much a regular business, systematically carried on for gain, in the City of New York, as is the trade in boots and shoes, dry goods and groceries.' " [14]

In the United States by 1870, prostitution was developing into a multimillion-dollar industry.[15] Corbain shows a similar industrialization of prostitution in France[16] and associates the increased demand for prostitutes with social changes that are evident today in the expansion of prostitution in the developing world, namely, the increased wealth of certain bourgeois social groups, with businessmen experiencing a rapid increase in wealth; an increased mobility among men of this class, in France; the development of international tourism, bringing large numbers of foreigners to Paris; and a large rural-to-urban migration.[17]

Historian Judith Walkowitz pointed out that prostitution in English working-class communities had been fairly casual prior to the Contagious Diseases Acts. Before industrialization and regulation through these acts, prostitutes were not particularly identified as a special class and were thus allowed some opportunity for mobility out of prostitution. They were part of the community in which they grew up, and as women they were invisible in public because the private sphere still confined women's existence. They were invisible as women but could be bought as sex. With deprivatization, the deployment of sexuality, and the subsequent efforts to legitimize prostitution, the acts forced a distinct separation of prostitutes from their neighborhood. "They were designed to force prostitutes to accept their status as public women by destroying their private identities and associations with the poor working-class community."[18] Neighborhood women rallied to prostitutes' support in resisting the acts. "Women seem to have been the organizing force behind public demonstrations in the defense of registered women. In their response to the Contagious Disease Acts, they appear motivated by personal sympathy for the plight of a neighbor, as well as by hostility toward the metropolitan police as interlopers in their community."[19] Further, community women assisted prostitute women in escaping public identification by helping them get out of the area and into rescue homes in London.[20]

At the time, Butler was not only the first woman but also the most radical, in a feminist sense, to challenge prostitution. Rather than staying comfortably close to her rescue work of supporting individual women, Josephine Butler was distinguished from many of her contemporaries in that she attacked those who profited from prostitution: slaveholders, pimps, procurers, and the state (laws and corrupt governments and police). But like many feminists of her era who became preoccupied with "social housekeeping," her first goal was to purify the state on the assumption that if it were rid of corruption, if it were made morally responsible, and if its tyranny over women were toppled and its double standards abolished, then individual moral consciousness would follow.

The weakness of Butler's campaign lay not in her outrage nor in her organizing skills but in her strategy. Instead of campaigning against prostitution as customer abuse of women, Butler confined her campaigns to action against third-party coercion by pimps and state regulation. In opposing state regulation, she refrained from action in relation to "freely chosen" prostitution at a time when its industrialization made the women and the sex an ordinary commodity. Instead, by accepting the emerging concept of "forced prostitution," which referred to the young girls and women found on the street and forced to undergo medical exams only to be registered as prostitutes, Josephine Butler in her campaigns also had to implicitly accept that there was a prostitution that was not "forced." At that time, most of society considered prostitution to be harmful. Therefore, Butler's position likely seemed to be making inconsequential distinctions between free and forced prostitution in the 1860s, a century before Western society became so thoroughly sexualized through pornography and the media. However, social disapproval of prostitution did not prevent it from becoming a major industry in Europe and the United States.

In campaigns against the Contagious Diseases Acts, we can locate the emergence of the notion that prostitution is either "forced" or "free." This notion made invisible the ordinary, everyday business of industrial capitalism, a prostitution industry. What Butler did not and could not foresee was that by the late twentieth century, the false distinction between forced and free would become the basis of major international campaigns to legitimize all prostitution and to shift the definition of woman to that of prostitute through the prostitution of sexuality.

In 1870 Josephine began to travel throughout England, lecturing on the acts and organizing people for action against them. From the beginning, she made her appeal to the working classes, where she saw the most suffering from the effects of the acts and the greatest potential for political mobilization. Whereas she experienced a lack of pretense and a commitment to ethical standards among the working class, and thus a potential for change, she found these qualities absent in the delicacy and remoteness of society ladies of her own class.

As she analyzed it,

The position and wealth of men of the upper classes place the women belonging to them above any chance of being accused of prostitution. Ladies who ride in their carriages through the street at night are in no danger of being molested. But what about working women? What about the daughters, sisters, and wives of working men, out, it may be, on an errand of mercy, at night? And what, most of all, of that girl whose father, mother, friends are dead or far away, who is struggling hard, in a hard world, to live uprightly, and justly by the work of her own hands.[21]

Women "not only have been debarred from attempting to deal in any large sense with this evil, but they have been systematically drilled into silence on this topic."[22] She struggled on behalf of the most oppressed and exploited of women, but because she struggled institutionally only against state regulation of prostitution, she short-circuited the potential feminist revolution she had sparked. It would be another century before feminism could build on Butler's equality campaigns and focus on fundamental change in the sexual values and power that give men unlimited, unrestrained sexual access, including the purchase of women.

Butler, a careful organizer, built community outrage against the acts. This became the base upon which she built her campaign. But as she escalated her campaigns, public reaction escalated against her. In using the words "prostitutes" and "brothels," she defied the womanly codes of Victorian morality, and her direct language was considered abhorrent. She challenged male self-interest where it had been most protected and secreted. Mob violence began to accompany her speeches. During one campaign against a liberal who would not support repeal of the acts, mobs of men and young boys scuffling and throwing rocks forced her to hide in a hotel attic. The next day she was forced by the management to leave the hotel. Wearing a disguise, she sought refuge at another hotel, but the mob located her there also. Despite the threats, she insisted on addressing the women's rally as she had planned. A number of bodyguards, brought up from London by her supporters, enabled her to address the meeting, but afterward she had to run through streets and alleys to escape the mob. She eventually made it safely to the home of a supporter, who took her in and looked after her.[23]

As feared (or promised), regulation increased the traffic of women into prostitution. Meanwhile, everyday commercial prostitution expanded in the cities. But Butler's movement in England focused on the traffic of English girls to continental European brothels. Girls were often procured through newspaper advertisements offering positions of employment, usually for domestic work, or they were approached in railway stations, where young girls coming to the city from the country were easily identifiable.[24]

Josephine built her campaign from small-town organizations into a national and then international movement, with strategies that later would be employed by the suffragist Pankhursts in the Women's Social and Political Union campaigns. The strategy was to campaign against liberals who refused to introduce or support legislation to repeal the acts. As the movement grew, it attracted different interest groups. Historian Edward Bristow points out, "There was something of interest in the new abolitionism for every possible kind of libertarian and radical, as well as for the haters of sexual sin." [25]

However problematic Butler's distinction between "forced" and "free" would become to the work of twentieth-century radical feminists confronting sexual exploitation in prostitution, Butler's own kind of feminist radicalism (she didn't call it that) was evident in her confrontation against those who promoted prostitution and profited from it. She challenged the sexual double standards reflected in men who frequented prostitutes, and she insisted on a separate woman's organization to lead that struggle.

One of those who became actively involved in this movement was Alfred Dyer, a Quaker who published books on various religious and social questions, among them works by Josephine Butler. Concerned with child prostitution in England, he began to work with Butler and other abolitionists. They campaigned to raise the legal age of consent from 12 to 18, to make it easier to prosecute procurers of young girls for child or "forced" prostitution.

This marked the beginning of Butler's engagement in coalition organizing with men. Dyer learned of the traffic of young English girls to the continent, where they were forced into prostitution. A friend told him about a young English girl who was held in slavery in a Brussels brothel and was discovered by an Englishman who frequented the brothel. Although the Englishman was taken with her plight, he did not want to risk exposing his own identity by helping her escape, but he did relate the incident to a friend, who conveyed it to Dyer. Dyer methodically researched the story and, confirming details of the account, printed it: a 19-year-old girl "was courted in London by a man of gentlemanly exterior, who promised her marriage if she would accompany him for the purpose to Brussels." En route, at Calais, she was left with another man while her "lover" explained that he had to pawn a watch to get some money and would join her in Brussels. She never saw him again. Arriving in Brussels, she was taken to a closed brothel, the man with her was paid, and she was officially registered under a false name as a prostitute.[26]

Dyer correctly anticipated being charged with sensationalism when he published this story. The Brussels commissioner of police denied the alleged practices in a letter published in English newspapers. Dyer undertook his own investigation. In Brussels he visited several houses of prostitution, including one where he had heard that a young Englishwoman was being kept. He managed to buy time with her, and she told him her story of being seduced by a man in London who promised her a job in Brussels; when she accompanied him there, she said, she was brought to this house and officially registered by its proprietor as a prostitute under a false name. Her story was similar to that of the woman who had been taken to Brussels under the promise of marriage. According to Dyer, she wanted him to help her escape.

As Dyer reports it, he did not arrange for her escape himself but instead went to the authorities. Police corruption in regulated systems of prostitution was well known, so whether he went to the police in order to test their responsiveness or out of a sense of male bonding, we don't know. In any event, he was not successful. The commissioner of the police district performed a cursory investigation and reported that all was in order. Dyer returned to the house on his own and was denied access.

This incident and many other assertions regarding the traffic in women and girls for sexual slavery have been considered groundless by some contemporary historians who have blithely accepted the new but easily institutionalized distinction between "free" and "forced" prostitution imposed by the state regulation that encouraged trafficking. For example, Bristow argues that the woman allegedly held in the house was in fact a "professional prostitute," by which he means "a woman who has chosen the work of a prostitute and set herself up in business." The commercialization of prostitution—its ordinary, everyday sexual exploitation of women, which was not confronted by abolitionists unless it was "forced"—was endowed by researchers with the sense of a profession. More than that, Bristow's dismissal of such incidents followed from his casual disregard for the exploitation of women evidenced in his description of how, in the decade preceding Dyer's investigation, the British embassy had been responsible for returning home about 200 English girls. "While a few were innocent victims, most seem to have been professionals who did not know they would be kept in more severe circumstances than prevailed in the world of English vice."[27] This is an academic approach to research that reflects ideological acceptance of the position of regulation law, which was to treat all prostitution as normal and legitimate unless it was proven to have been coerced. In discussing prostitution in New York City, Gilfoyle reflects a similar male-liberal, proprostitution bias: "The willingness on the part of some women to choose prostitution over other forms of labor reflected an alternative attitude regarding their bodies."[28] Gilfoyle's academic nonchalance regarding sexual exploitation obscures the reality of nonchoice among poor female laborers. The sex industry—then in New York and Paris, now in Bangkok and Manila—compensates for the discriminatory wages that impoverished women in early industrialization.

Despite the economic impoverishment that industrialization caused for women, Dyer and those moral crusaders who flocked to Butler's campaigns emphasized the most extreme cases of "forced" prostitution. Specifically, the Dyer escapade revealed the changes in Butler's campaign strategies, the effect of abandoning her women-only organizing in favor of coalition with would-be supporters whose primary concern was not women. It is notable that not only did Dyer not free the woman who told him she wanted to escape; he may also have seriously threatened her life when the police informed the brothel of his report to them. When men entered the campaign against regulated prostitution, particularly in rescue work and investigations, one notes that consistently their behavior was dominated by righteous heroics in which the fate of the victim is secondary to the escapade they are performing. Distinguishing "free" from "forced" prostitution promoted such male heroics, which, marked by paternalism, allowed men who were acting from fatherly concern and care to play the hero. Further, it opened the space for treating the rest of prostitution not as exploitation but as a mere profession. Meanwhile, men's misguided concern for the plight of girls forced into prostitution created its own sensationalism, which in turn discredited the reports of the traffic in women. That was the cost paid by Josephine Butler and her movement when she welcomed the support and involvement of men like Dyer.

Dyer published his findings, and they were vehemently repudiated by Belgian authorities. Yet, with pressure from Josephine Butler, the British Home Secretary initiated an investigation. In 1880 he commissioned a London lawyer, T. W. Snagge, to inquire into the traffic of young English girls into prostitution in Brussels. Snagge had no prior connection with the abolitionist movement, with Butler, or with Dyer. His official report completely confirmed Dyer's allegations.[29] He found that English girls were being exported by systematic traffic to Belgium, France, and Holland for prostitution; that English girls were frequently induced by misrepresentation or false promises to leave England; that they ended up in prostitution houses; and that in those houses they were "detained by duress or subjected to cruelty and forced against their will to lead a life of prostitution."[30]

In May 1881, Snagge's findings led to an inquiry into legislation that would specifically curtail procuring and trafficking of English girls to other countries. Further inquiry into juvenile prostitution led to proposed legislation to raise the age of consent to 16. Strong opposition to the proposed legislation raising the age of consent and repealing the Contagious Diseases Acts resulted in its being compromised and stalled in committees.

Josephine Butler, desperate over the fate of this critical legislation, embarked on another paternalistic venture: the "heroic" plans of the famous English journalist W. T. Stead. Although Stead was by reputation a somewhat sensationalistic journalist, he was a first-rate writer and editor of the *Pall Mall Gazette*. His work and newspaper were known for their respectability and were solidly entrenched in the British middle classes. He joined the campaigns against the Contagious Diseases Acts when he heard the reports of abuse and torture in many of London's brothels. One brothel owner, Mrs. Jeffries, who specialized in providing virgin girls, was taken to court through Butler's efforts, only to leave after payment of a minimal fine.[31]

Neither the courts nor Parliament could be moved. The abolitionists had to rely on public opinion, which they would stir to outrage by exposing the exploitation and abuse in the brothels. Stead decided to look into allegations of child abuse in London brothels. As he learned of the atrocities, he is said to have forgotten his middle-class securities and given way to a personal agony and anger. He interviewed little girls as young as 4 years old who had been repeatedly raped in these brothels. He spent 6 weeks exploring and investigating the prostitution world of London's West End. But to publish a convincing argument, he needed final, unimpeachable evidence of the ease with which children could be purchased, examined for virginity, and turned over to brothels.

He proposed a plan, and Josephine concurred: he would find a procurer who would actually purchase a child and go through all the steps short of turning the child over to be sexually abused. A former female procurer, Rebecca Jarrett, who was under Josephine's care, was asked to carry out this project.

Rebecca Jarrett had entered prostitution at the age of 12 (the age of consent then), and after many years she had started her own brothels and procured young girls and women to work for her. She had tried to leave prostitution many times, but as long as she stayed in London she could not sever her connections from her former life. Finally, at age 36, she was taken in by Florence Booth, from the London-based Salvation Army, who sent her to Josephine.[32] In Winchester with Josephine, Rebecca severed her connections with prostitution and became actively involved in rescue work. Her knowledge of the world of brothels and prostitution made her almost fearless; she was able to go into many dangerous places and induce young women and girls to leave and come back to Winchester, where she took care of them.[33]

Rebecca agreed to help Stead. Under his direction she made her contacts and informed an old friend that she wanted to buy a child. The friend obliged and produced various children for Rebecca's inspection. Rebecca chose Eliza Armstrong, a 13-year-old girl. Stead gave Rebecca a £5 note for the purchase and told her that she must be absolutely sure that the parents were aware the child was being purchased for immoral purposes.[34] Mrs. Armstrong reportedly drank up her share of the money and was arrested that night for drunk and disorderly conduct.[35]

Without Josephine's knowledge, the child was taken by Rebecca and Stead to a midwife who was used by brothels to certify that young girls were virgins. So caught up was Stead in his own scheme that he never questioned the ethics of subjecting the girl to the very practices he was ostensibly condemning. Josephine was enraged when she learned of the extent to which he had carried his scheme. But he had the evidence he needed. The next day Eliza was taken to France and placed with the Salvation Army there.

With this final proof, on July 6, 1885, Stead launched his attack with the first in his series of articles entitled "The Maiden Tribute of Modern Babylon." Under the subheading "A Child of Thirteen Bought for £5," he published his first exposé describing the story of Eliza Armstrong and the conditions of prostitution.

The public's first reaction was stunned disbelief, followed by charges of sensationalism, followed by public indignation that led to near rioting. "The Home Secretary begged the editor to stop publication of the articles, fearing riots on a national scale. Stead replied that he would stop them the moment he received assurance that the Bill [raising the age of consent to 16, suppressing brothels, and protecting victims] would be carried through without delay."[36] The *Pall Mall Gazette* was banned by major news agents but sold out immediately on the streets. Hundreds of London

newsboys were arrested for selling the papers, but the charges
were dismissed. "It was on this day that George Bernard Shaw,
who was the reviewer on the *Pall Mall Gazette,* took a bundle of
papers out into the Strand and sold them."[37]

"Three days after the storm broke, Richard Cross, the new
Home Secretary, put the Criminal Law Amendment Bill through
its second reading."[38] It moved swiftly into law. Mass meetings
were held in London and elsewhere. Public indignation from the
Stead exposés had finally become a national concern. These gains
were not without cost, however.

The first cost was paid by the most immediate victims of Stead's
masquerade: Eliza Armstrong and Rebecca Jarrett. When the
Eliza Armstrong story hit the papers, Mrs. Armstrong's neighbors
were angry at her for selling her daughter and using the money to
get drunk. She defended herself by beginning a search for her
daughter. First, she reported to the police that Eliza was missing.
Eliza's father claimed that the child had been taken from him
without his consent. Stead, Rebecca Jarrett, and others were arrested, charged with abducting Eliza from her parents and inde-
cently assaulting and drugging her.[39] This turn of events gave
Stead's enemies, particularly those trying to thwart repeal of the
Contagious Disease Acts, an opportunity to try to discredit him.
Both Stead and Rebecca Jarrett were convicted and sentenced to
brief terms. Just as Eliza was used by Stead, so she then was used
by his opposition.

Imprisonment could only heighten Stead's personal and political sense of martyrdom in his battle. But for Rebecca, a recently
reformed prostitute, the trial and conviction meant having her
past dragged up before her and hearing herself publicly condemned. So harsh and abusive was the court that Josephine wrote
a tract in defense of Rebecca, blaming herself for having convinced the well-intentioned woman to work with Stead. In that
tract she wrote angrily of Stead's attitude after the trial: "He
speaks of having had a fair trial; compliments the prosecution;
confesses himself to have been to blame; hopes that nothing will

be done to reverse the sentence. . . . Perhaps Mr. Stead may think that he himself was courteously treated but what of the courtesy or even decent fairness shown in regard to Rebecca, upon whom the utmost of vituperation permissible in a Court of Law was vented?" [40]

The other costly result of the Stead exposé was political. Josephine Butler's movement was to be swept aside by the religious moralists who began en masse to take over the work after these exposés. Their righteous indignation was aroused over the issue of staining the purity of innocent English girls. They were preoccupied with protecting female virtue in order to preserve the family and contain women in the private sphere once again. In the beginning of her campaign the British churches had steadfastly refused to support Josephine; but once the issues caught the public's attention and created moral indignation, the church began to take an active role in the movement. By then the false distinction between free and forced prostitution had served to legitimize everyday street and brothel prostitution. Society began to look only at the trafficker as the social scourge and cause of the problem.

Josephine had made the tactical mistake of resorting to coalition politics with paternalistic men in order to build her movement. Inevitably this brought the purity crusaders in under her banner. She may have shared some similar convictions with them, but their political goals were decidedly different from hers. They played heroics, searched for the spotlight and attention, and strengthened the idea that women and girls needed to be protected by men. They intensified the sense of female dependence and emphasized female purity as the condition of women. What was wrong with prostitution, then, was that the originally pure were violated. Butler, on the other hand, not only campaigned for women's freedom, independence, and right to self-support; she also attacked men's sexual behaviors as the foundation of the double standard of sexual morality that produced the exploitation of women in prostitution.

Some men who worked with us at the beginning, shocked with the cruelty and illegality of the acts, fall off when they understand the thoroughness of our crusade, and that it is directed not only against cruel result of vice, *but against the tacit permission—the indisputable right as some have learned to regard it—granted to men to be impure at all.*[41]

She spoke of purity, but she meant something entirely different by it than did the purity crusaders. Her demand was for a purification of the state and of males' behavior. If that were attained, she was sure that protection of the individual liberty of women would follow. By contrast, the purity crusaders wanted to return women to the confines of repressive roles and Victorian morals by vigorously reasserting the traditional patriarchal distinction between "madonna" and "whore."

The issue of religious morality is a tricky one in relation to the sexual exploitation of women. On one hand, religious morality aimed at social purity was hypocritical, paternalistic, and elitist. On the other hand, Josephine Butler represented the kind of religious conviction that turned toward humanitarian relief and human rights. Of this kind of reformer David Pivar has pointed out, "Rather than appealing exclusively to religious institutions, they directed themselves toward the 'universal' religious sentiments common to all men."[42] Josephine was a deeply religious woman whose humanitarian work was inspired as much by her religious beliefs as by her commitment to human liberty. She brought her religious beliefs into her campaigns. She called upon them in her speeches, and her rescue work with prostitutes usually involved religious appeals for their conversion. But hers was a religious conviction that emphasized human dignity and liberty. When society has little to offer prostitutes as an alternative to the brothel or the street, when the condition and status of women is so low, the availability of social opportunities or employment for women so scarce, it is not surprising that, in her rescue work, Josephine's commitment, rescue work, and campaigns were welcomed as concrete support from women.

Because it was in part motivated by religious beliefs, Josephine's work, viewed from a historical perspective, now appears to have been a part of the social purity movement and has been reduced by historians to that. But the goals of the social purity movement were in direct opposition to those of Butler's feminist work. What in fact happened was that the social purity movement, by attaching itself to women's causes, was able to build a mass movement and to co-opt the work of feminist leaders like Josephine Butler.

By 1886, when the Contagious Diseases Acts were finally repealed, the conditions of prostitution had worsened. Under regulation, the international traffic in women had reached a peak. Prostitution had changed and solidified. The effect of the Contagious Diseases Acts was to transform neighborhood prostitution of working-class women "into a specially identified professional class. . . . The eventual isolation of prostitutes from general lower-class life was largely imposed from above, although it received the passive acquiescence of the poor themselves."[43] Separating women from their neighborhoods into distinct red-light districts and brothels identified the women as prostitutes more specifically and thereby made their ability to leave prostitution much more difficult. In the early years of the Contagious Diseases Acts, most prostitutes were young and single; by the late nineteenth century, the rigidifying of this social role resulted in women remaining in prostitution longer. Their social mobility had been effectively curtailed.[44] Undoubtedly other social factors facilitated the formalized categorization of women as prostitutes, but clearly the impact of the Contagious Diseases Acts was to create among women a distinct out-group in which women were socially if not physically trapped. In turn, this social and geographic isolation facilitated the criminal organization of prostitution, complete with pimps, procurers, and organized brothels.

To challenge the new conditions in all of their subtleties required the clear political vision Butler had brought to the earlier campaigns. Rather than combating prostitution per se, Butler fought organized prostitution, which she saw as incompatible with female emancipation and individual liberty. In one statement she asserted, "My principle has always been to let individuals alone, not to pursue them with any outward punishment, nor drive them out of any place so long as they behave decently, but to attack organized prostitution, that is, when a third party, activated by the desire of making money, sets up a house in which women are sold to men."[45] Butler believed that women's liberties could be achieved only by forcing the state to expose and break up rings of organized procurers and brothel keepers.

The problem is that what is violating, dehumanizing about the experience of prostitution is, first and foremost, the reduction of sex to exchange. Third-party control is another and different violation of women, and by focusing on the "third-party" pimps in prostitution, Butler strengthened the distinction between "free" and "forced" prostitution. Once prostitution had been differentiated in this way, campaigns against "forced" prostitution gave implicit acceptance to prostitution that is not imposed by a third party. Butler accepted prostitution. This was the fundamental weakness of her new campaign. In opening her movement to coalition politics, she narrowed its platform to forced prostitution and that became the foundation of the abolitionist movement. This opened the door to the rampant paternalism of the purity crusaders and religious moralists who began to dominate the movement. Social reform focused on the prostitute and the need to "uplift" her rather than on the customer and the objective of eliminating him. This led to the position of condemning all prostitutes except the innocent and pure victims, who could be saved and returned to their former state of innocence and purity, a reaffirmation of the madonna-whore standard.

One can only conjecture about the influence of Victorian male sexuality on the co-optation of the abolitionist goals and the redefinition of prostitution itself that resulted from these later purity crusaders. "Spending"—the Victorian euphemism for the emission of sperm—was seen as weakening, debilitating.[46] With extraordinary fervor, purity crusaders lectured that sexual containment was the ideal state.

In fact, Corbain points out that in the early years of regulation in France, the intent was to control or contain sexuality—"to repress, or at least to control, all forms of extramarital sexuality under the pretext of supervising prostitution."[47] Containment was supposed to allow men to store up their energies. And incontinence, besides being weakening, was morally wrong, sinful. Consequently, men were advised against masturbation and urged into marriage; as husbands they would not be expected to perform frequently, for it was widely believed that women had no sexual drive. The responsibility for sexual containment rested on women. While this was the creed of Victorian male sexuality, it was never assumed that men could live by the values of containment. The sexual double standard constructed male infidelity as inevitable. That infidelity was treated as a response to sexual repression as a rationalization for prostitution. As long as prostitutes were separate, isolated, and different from other women, Victorian men could secretly frequent them, taking care of their seemingly suppressed sexual desires, which could hardly be suppressed if they were seeking prostitutes, while maintaining a posture of containment in their daily lives.

As the purity crusades emerged into the twentieth century, they were dominated by two themes: the immoral destruction of innocent girls' virtue and sinful incontinence in men. Therefore their call was for purity and preservation of the family. Sensationalized accounts increased, describing sweet, innocent young things being chloroformed and dragged off to foreign brothels. Girls who resisted and fought to their death were seen as martyrs. The purity crusade included other reform issues, especially temperance. Often in their exhortations, leaders associated the evil of the traffic in women with the immoral debauchery of drink. Addressing the victimization of women became the means of attacking other behaviors that flouted religious principles—drunkenness, free love, and so on. And all of these issues, which had powerful implications for the conditions of women's lives (wife abuse, etc.), were distorted to serve the end of religious purity.

Sensationalism, derived from and spirited by the purity crusades, cast doubt on the actual accounts of the traffic in women and children. Sensationalistic writers and speakers dramatized their cause through horrifying and probably often fictionalized incidents of sex slavery. This created a separation between city/street prostitution and the traffic in women. Butler had been careful to focus on all exploitation of women involved in prostitution and had not separated her rescue work from her political campaigns, local prostitution from international traffic, one race from another. However, the sensationalism of the purity crusaders raised doubt as to whether traffic in women actually existed. Furthermore, street prostitution began to be treated as "free" in contrast to the "forced" prostitution associated with trafficking. This set the stage for the modern formulation of prostitution as mere "sex between consenting adults." Legitimization of prostitution was the final result of this campaign.

The regulationalist distinctions between free and forced prostitution accepted by Butler and the abolitionists defined exploitation: a woman had to be forced, and her character had to have been impeccable prior to her violation (as is required always in rape cases). The less sweet, innocent, and young she was, the less likely it was that she could be recognized as having been exploited.

As industrialization produced a public sexualization of women, the public reduction of woman to sex followed. Sex industries that burgeoned in this era normalized the public sexual exploitation of women.

It was in this climate that the term "white slavery" first came into common use. While the term rarely appears in Butler's writing or speeches, when she did use the term she used it to refer to the entire problem—regulation, prostitution, traffic in women. The term "white slavery" was formally used at the 1902 Paris conference, where representatives of several governments met to draft an international instrument for the suppression of the white-slave traffic (Le Traité des Blanches). While the term initially was intended to distinguish the practice from nineteenth-century Black slavery, it had immediate appeal to racists, who could and did conclude that the antitrafficking efforts were directed against an international traffic in white women. So, in addition to being sweet, innocent, and young, women were victims only if they were white, despite the evidence that the traffic included women of color. The term eventually embodied all the sexist, classist, and racist bigotry that was ultimately incorporated within the movement dominated by religious morality. Because of the confusion and misuse resulting from the term, the international conference of 1921 recommended that the term "white slavery" be dropped and replaced with "Traffic in Women and Children."[48] This was subsequently the language of the League of Nations' and the United Nations' studies and reports.

The 1902 Paris meeting led to the International Agreement for the Suppression of the White Slave Traffic, which was ratified by 12 nations in 1904. It was designed to commit governments to take action against "procuring of women and girls for immoral purposes abroad."[49] This agreement led to the 1910 Mann Act in the United States. This act (amended later to include traffic in males as well as females) forbids transporting a person across state lines or international boundaries (exporting or importing) for prostitution or other immoral purposes. The ambiguous term "immoral purposes" suggests the extent to which the purity movement had succeeded in becoming the lawful guardians of female virtue. The question of women's will was entirely excluded from consideration, and therefore the issue of individual liberty was lost in the language of the act. In addition, "immoral purposes" could and would eventually be defined by the courts according to prevailing male definitions of morality. Prostitute women became the scapegoats for hypocritical morality. Their victimization by prostitution was made invisible.

This series of laws formalized and legalized the ideological and practical separation, engendered by the purity crusade, between international traffic in women and local prostitution, thereby distracting attention away from the continuing enslavement of women in local prostitution.

The growing feminist movements at the turn of the century began to address prostitution and tried, unsuccessfully, to provide a political concept for analyzing male power. In reaction, antifeminist women attacked the feminists as purity crusaders and charged them with sensationalism. Teresa Billington-Grieg, who had been a member of the Pankhursts' Women's Social and Political Union but who split from that suffrage group, added fuel to this debate when she wrote "The Truth About White Slavery" in 1913. In writing the article, she gathered evidence from various police officials to prove that there is "no organized trapping." [50] Attributing the scandal in white slavery "in no small measure to the Pankhurst domination," she goes on to react to sensationalism. "Fed on such ridiculous scandal-mongering, these women have convinced themselves that a large number of men go regularly and deliberately to a safe and secret place of vice to engage in a pastime that is a life and death struggle to a trapped girl." [51] Yet that is exactly what the statistics revealing massive increases in prostitution showed. As a forerunner of contemporary proprostitution ideology, Billington-Grieg demanded a further separation of issues—that of sexual abuse of children from that of the white-slave traffic. In the former "an intemperate degenerate is passion-driven into the sudden commission of an atrocity; in the other, there is a cold-blooded, calculating deliberation which reduces the matter from bestiality to the worst possible devilishness." [52] For the female victims, this would seem like a hair-splitting distinction.

With each distinction built on the original misogynist free-force dichotomy—white slavery versus free prostitution, child prostitution versus free prostitution—the basis for validating prostitution enlarged. It was built on the racism that labeled traffic "white slavery" and on the paternalism that assumed that violation of females occurred only if they were children. The debate that had raged in Europe and America simmered down to an acceptance of prostitution. Investigating commissions accepted the formalized distinction between white-slave traffic and prostitution. The 1914 Massachusetts "Report of the Commission for the Investigation of the White Slave Traffic, so called" concluded,

Every story of this kind has been thoroughly investigated and either found to be a vague rumor, where one person has told another that some friend of the former (who invariably in turn referred the story farther back) heard that the thing happened, or, in a few instances, imaginary occurrences explained by hysteria or actual malingering. Several of the stories were easily recognized versions of incidents in certain books or plays.

But according to Ernst Bell, the most literal interpretation of white slavery was incorporated into the revised 1902 Massachusetts law in such a way that few incidents could be considered white slavery. According to the revised law, the procuring must be fraudulent and deceitful, and the woman must be unmarried and of a chaste life. If the procurer married the girl to circumvent the law, he could not be prosecuted; if the girl had made one mistake in her life, she could not be protected from being procured.[53]

Although its language was woefully inadequate, the Mann Act initially facilitated prosecution of procurers in the United States. In comparison to 1907, when only one alien was debarred from the United States for procuring, "in 1914, 254 procurers and five men living off the earnings of prostitutes were excluded, and 154 procurers and 155 persons living on the earnings of prostitutes were deported."[54]

Maude Miner collected significant material on white slavery from cases she handled in night court in New York and in her work in refuge shelters. She documented the procuring tactics and methods used to induce young women into prostitution. But despite these known methods, she asserted, "There has undoubtedly been exaggeration about the white slave traffic in some of the newspaper accounts and in the moving picture films which have also exploited vice. Yet the facts in authentic cases are too hideous to be told." [55]

The traffic in women and children persisted despite the fact that it had been socially redefined into nonexistence. At the turn of the century in California, through the rescue work of Donaldina Cameron, an enormous traffic in young Chinese girls was revealed. The girls were being purchased in China, brought to the United States, and sold in San Francisco, either in open markets or directly to individuals. Many were reported being sold into domestic slavery for $100 to $200. Brothel slaves were sold for $1,500 to $3,000. The girls were often acquired from interior provinces and exported through Hong Kong, and they believed they were coming to the United States for arranged marriages. Donaldina Cameron spent many years seeking out these girls and rescuing them from the back alleys of San Francisco's Chinatown. [56]

Marriage was the means of procuring Jewish girls in Eastern Europe at the turn of the century.

Procurers were known to go through the traditional ritual and then take their legally unmarried and largely unprotected partners off to a domestic or foreign brothel. . . . In 1892 twenty-two men were convicted in Lemberg for procuring girls from small Galician towns with promises of jobs as servants, and selling them to brothels in Constantinople, Alexandria and points east of Suez. The Austrian consul in Constantinople had rescued sixty of them from virtual imprisonment the year before. [57]

During this period, most feminists were engrossed in the battle for legal equality and the right to vote; at the time these rights were seen as fundamental to any other moral or legal changes. Some feminists addressed the issue of white slavery, but it never became a major focus of the movement, either in England or in America. Yet a few voices continued to speak out.

Christabel Pankhurst, writing for the British suffrage movement in 1913, connected the prevalence of white slavery with the denial of votes for women. Regulation had spread to India through British colonization. Pankhurst expounded on the government's responsibility for white slavery there and showed how the absence of women in Parliament prevented legislation that would provide women fair wages and thus left them vulnerable to white slavers.[58]

Emma Goldman, writing in 1917, also associated white slavery with economic exploitation, "the merciless Moloch of capitalism that fattens on underpaid labor, thus driving thousands of women and girls into prostitution."[59] And she added, "Whether our reformers admit it or not, the economic and social inferiority of women is responsible for prostitution."[60]

Lack of economic opportunity for women was in fact the source of huge profits for procurers and madams. But those profits were only possible because of customer demand—because of men buying sex or women's bodies. Radical feminist Christabel Pankhurst asserted,

White Slavery exists because thousands upon thousands of ordinary men want it to exist, and are willing to pay to keep it going. These men, in order to distract the attention of the other women who are not White Slaves, are very willing to make scapegoats of a few of the Slave Traders, but all the time they rely upon their being enough traders to maintain the supply of women slaves. By force, by trickery, or by starvation enough women will, they believe, be drawn into the Slavery of vice.[61]

Feminists like Pankhurst tried to reassert the connection between men's responsibility and the exploitation of women—the politics with which Josephine Butler had begun the movement. The political analysis of women like Pankhurst and Goldman placed the focus back on those who create and maintain the institution. According to Goldman,

Fully fifty percent of married men are patrons of brothels. It is through this virtuous element that the married women—nay, even the children— are infected with venereal diseases. Yet society has not a word of condemnation for the man, while no law is too monstrous to be set in motion against the helpless victim.[62]

And Christabel's militancy was as pronounced on this issue as it was on suffrage:

Intelligent women are revolted by men's commerce with white slaves. It makes them regard men as inferiors. So great a want of self-respect and of fastidiousness excites their scorn and disgust. The disparity between the moral standards of men and women is more and more destroying women's respect and regard for men. Men have a simple remedy for this state of things. They can alter their way of life.[63]

And by "altering their way of life" she meant sexual self-control— not repression, but responsible control.

For these feminists, as for Butler, the situation called for a fundamental behavioral change in men. If the moral values of patriarchy were to be radically altered, so would the nature of the society be. But co-optation of feminist causes successfully prevented that change.

Sporadic feminist protests continued. Through the 1920s and 1930s studies were conducted by the League of Nations and later the United Nations that affirmed a continuing traffic in women and children who were *forced* into prostitution. Regulation as a form of prostitution slavery was finally forbidden by an international treaty, the 1949 United Nations Convention for the Suppression of the Traffic in Persons and of the Exploitation of the Prostitution of Others, which called upon nations to close brothels and punish those who procure for and promote prostitution.

Even when the British feminists were the most militant, the women's rights movement that had spread throughout Europe and North America since the mid-nineteenth century had begun to wane. Its demise was complete by the end of World War I, but it left a problematic legacy in the abolitionist position on free and forced prostitution. On one hand, while campaigning for increased rights and freedom of choice for women, the movement accepted the idea that prostitution was inevitable. Apparent free choice sanctioned prostitution, and Butler would not interfere with women who had not been forced by pimps. Behind this liberalism, it was assumed that women in prostitution who were not controlled by pimps were different, unlike women who married or at least had conventional relationships. They were not like the women and girls who would have married had they not been procured and forced into prostitution. It was further reasoned that prostitutes who had no pimps and had not been procured did not need protection and support. Human rights, support, and care were reserved for those women who had been procured because, according to the distortion of patriarchal thought, they would have been married if they had not been trafficked. Therefore they were the "good women."

The distinction between forced and voluntary prostitution intensified differences in the two classes of women, a distinction that remains to be challenged by feminists and removed from universal human rights law. To do that requires taking up Butler's most basic challenge: Do men have the right at all to buy women's bodies for sex?

Industrialization of Sex

Since 1970, the most dramatic changes in prostitution have been its industrialization, normalization, and widespread global diffusion. Prostitution has overtaken populations of women, especially in newly industrializing economies. Present estimates place prostitution at 2 million in Thailand, 1 to 1.5 million in Korea, and 0.5 million in the Philippines. The industrialization of sex has produced a multibillion-dollar global market in women, at home and abroad, in highly organized trafficking and in the most diffused, informal arrangements.

Industrialization has typically referred to mass production of manufactured goods and of services for exchange on the market. I am using the term "industrialization of sex" here to refer to the production of a product—sex—that involves making or manufacturing that product from and in the human self, constructing it into that which it was not (selves are not originally sexed or prostituted) for the purpose of market exchange. Sex industrialization is a *massive* commodity production.

Industrialization of prostitution follows from (1) massive deployment of women for military prostitution during wars or foreign occupation, (2) development of tourist industries that bring in foreign exchange for economic development, and (3) export-oriented economic development that marginalizes women through exploitation of their labor, especially in export processing zones that are exempt from many of the controls that govern local industries.

The industrialization of prostitution develops in stages: first, even before many economies begin to industrialize, sex industries proliferate to service foreign military and businessmen. Rather than being a consequence (unintended or intended) of industrialization, military prostitution and sex tourism often precede or occur simultaneously with national industrial development. Prostitution and its related sex industries—international conglomerates of hotel chains, airlines, bars, sex clubs, massage parlors, brothels, and procurers—together have become a major economic force in the world today. Women (and sometimes children, both boys and girls) are the commodities through which industries sell sex.

Second, sex industries supported by the massive underground economy of pimps, procurers, and organized crime, as well as the traditional economy of multinational conglomerates operating hotels, airlines, and tourist industries, generate a significant income from selling sex through women's bodies to men. In the early phases of state industrialization sex industries thoroughly exploit women in the rural-to-urban migration process (as described in the next chapter). As economies begin to develop and women begin to gain access to the labor force, sex industries buy off some women with higher wages than the labor force will provide them, higher income than they provided through prostitution in the earlier phase of economic development. Through state and private industry manipulation of developing economies and with devaluation of female labor established in the family prior to industrialization, often prostitution is the only economic possibility for some women in poverty. However, as economic development accelerates raising the level of materialism in the society as a whole, prostitution is a more likely means for women to get the material gains of industrialization. Women turn to prostitution for material gain in the context of normalized sex industries.

However, the prostitution market is driven by customer demand for sexual service. In pre-industrial and early industrializing economies, the demand is heaviest where men are congregated in large groups, away from home and family, in the military and on business. War causes social displacement, producing populations of refugees, primarily women and children. Massive rape in war produces sex-industry commodities from whole populations of women who are raped and therefore disgraced to their families and in their communities. Raped women and girls are particularly vulnerable to networks of pimps and organized crime gangs.

In 1992 the massive raping of women in Bosnia as part of the "ethnic cleansing" by the Serbs in their genocidal war with Bosnia was reported to be carried out not only randomly in villages and on streets but in the concentration camps, some set aside for that purpose. A fact-finding team from the European Community estimated that 20,000 Muslim women had been raped since the fighting began. Other fact-finding teams from human rights organizations such as Amnesty International have confirmed the massive raping of Muslim women. However, by the time the United Nations began to document rapes in Bosnia in 1993, the dis-counting began. By late 1993 the United Nations had received 3,000 reports with 800 victims identified by name.

Because of the presence of a global women's movement, women within Bosnia appealing for help have had access to the means to bring these crimes to international attention. Therefore, the consistent discrepancy between official counts and estimated incidence is no longer cause for burying atrocities committed against women. By contrast, during the Vietnam War, the Korean War, and wars before that, massive raping of women was one of the invisible consequences of war. In 1993 the International Court of Justice took up the case of genocide in Bosnia with massive rapes being one specific concern.

While rape of women has been known as a military strategy to humiliate the (male) enemy, rape and the pornography and prostitution made from it are a kind of R & R which apparently does not exclude peacekeeping troops. Reports that rapes in concentration camps have been filmed for pornography are followed by the use of those women in those camps by soldiers for prostitution. In November 1993, United Nations Secretary General Boutros Boutros-Ghali appointed a Special Commission of Inquiry to examine charges that came out during the trial of a Serb soldier in Sarajevo who, in late 1993, was sentenced to death for murdering Muslim and Croat women at Sonjas. Sonjas, 6 miles outside of Sarajevo, has been described variously as a restaurant, a bunker, and a suspected concentration camp. Reportedly, some U.N. peacekeeping troops have been observed as frequent visitors there. According to a report of the trial in New York *Newsday*, November 1, 1993, a Bosnian Serb commander reported that some women were raped by U.N. soldiers while Serbs offered others to the soldiers for prostitution. One can only suppose that, in this hair-splitting distinction between rape and prostitution, the difference was that in some cases the Serbs took money for the sexual use of the women by the peacekeepers.

Since the Civil War in El Salvador, the number of prostitutes in its capital, San Salvador, doubled to 19,000 by 1991 under the demand of a large military.[1] Under state terrorism in El Salvador and Guatemala, political and military repression includes sexual exploitation. But because sexual abuse is part of state terrorism, it cannot be reported or even mentioned by the victim, who cannot seek medical care "because any act of resistance becomes a threat to existence" and virtually all avenues of support are closed; therefore, "what might have been merely a terrible experience with a beginning, a middle, and an end becomes an ongoing catastrophe. The devastating experience—the near annihilation of the self— exists as a detail in a much larger picture, every part of which evokes terror."[2] This includes prostitution, an often-unrecognized aspect of the multilayered torture and repression of women. "There is the practice observed in El Salvador's war zones, where young women 'voluntarily' give themselves to individual soldiers, as their private property, so as to avoid becoming the common property of the whole battalion."[3]

Prostitution (free or forced) is both a form and a consequence of sexual abuse during war and under political repression and torture, and therefore it fits into the formulation of military sexual abuse identified by Adrianne Aron and her colleagues:

Forms of sexual abuse that can be identified are best divided according to whether they occur as part of (a) the standard operating procedures (SOP) of the military while a woman is in detention (e.g., rape as a component of torture), (b) the SOP while the woman is in the community (e.g., capricious exploitation by a soldier who, because of his military connection, has license to abuse), or (c) improvised abuses generated by extreme situations.[4]

The sexual demands of military men stationed in Third World countries have produced markets that are constantly replenished with women who are bought by traveling businessmen or military men on R & R leave. Procurers work the poverty-stricken countryside of Third World nations as well as the bus and train stations of major cities, acquiring girls and young women. They maintain a constant supply to serve the massive market demand of military men and businessmen.

With massive industrialization of women for sex service in prostitution, large segments of female populations are prostituted. In some countries like the Philippines or Thailand, entire fishing villages have been turned into sites for prostitution tourism. Particularly in the Asian region, where countries like Korea and Vietnam have been devastated by war and nearby countries like the Philippines and Thailand have been strategic military locations as well as centers for R & R, prostitution has become a major industry. Today women are trafficked from these countries as brides and as prostitutes in order to relieve the economy. Men travel from Europe, the United States, Australia, Japan, and Taiwan for sex tourism, a major source of foreign exchange.

The Military Market: Korea

Sex marketing of massive populations of women during wartime preceded economic development in many parts of the Asian region. During World War II, Korea was a colony of Japan, and parts of China were occupied by Japan from 1937 to 1945. During the war, the Japanese military forced anywhere from 100,000 to 200,000 Korean women into prostitution to service their military. According to a Japanese mobilization order issued at the request of the Japanese army in April 1944 by the prefect of Yamaguchi, mobilization of labor for the war would include "100 Korean women for volunteer corps for consoling the Imperial Army."[5] One of the plaintiffs in the case that was filed in December 1991 by 3 former comfort women in Tokyo District Court reveals that this "volunteer corps" was put together by abducting the women. From witnesses' testimony, the Korean Council for the Women Drafted for Military Sexual Slavery by Japan estimate that "half of them were coercively enlisted, being kidnapped while drawing water from a well or working in a field, being captured by the police at home, or being escorted to a police station while going on their way. The other half were enlisted by means of flesh traffic methods through false job advertisements."[6]

Korean and other Southeast Asian women were deployed to Japanese "comfort stations," a version of U.S. military R & R. These stations were located in territory occupied by the Japanese military.[7] The comfort women's petition explains how procured women were deployed:

Military comfort houses existed wherever the Japanese army was located, in China, in Southeast Asia, on the South Sea Islands, in Japan, etc. When the Japanese army had to retreat with the worsening of the war situation, some military comfort women were deserted, some were forced to suffer death of honor together with the troops, and others were killed. In this way, military comfort women were treated as expendables by the Japanese army.[8]

It is estimated that 80% of the comfort women were from Korea, with others procured from China, Burma, the Philippines, and other Asian countries to service the Japanese military. Unknown thousands of Korean and Chinese women died during their sexual incarceration.

The usage of comfort stations was limited to soldiers only, and "Sekai-kan" was used by the 6th and 9th divisions, allegedly renowned for their military prowess. Soldiers had to buy coupons to enter a comfort station. They picked up a "name tag" at the "office" and received a coupon, tissues, and a condom in exchange for the money. The coupon carried the name of the woman and the room number on it. Customarily, soldiers were not allowed to pick and choose a woman. Regardless of their choice, they just had to enter the woman's room of whose number they were given. A timetable was set according to their ranks; the day time for soldiers, early evenings for low-ranking officers, and late nights for high-ranking officers. The soldiers who disregarded the rules had to face heavy imprisonment. In other words, the rules for using the army comfort stations were part of the army's rules per se. In fact, military policemen regularly patrolled the facilities. If soldiers got wild at a comfort station, they were reported to MPs.[9]

In early 1992, after years of pressure from women's groups in Korea and in Japan, Japan has finally admitted that "the Japanese government was involved in forcing the women to have sex with the troops."[10] A short time later, 4 Chinese women presented letters to the Japanese embassy in China making claims for compensation as part of a large number of Chinese women also forced into prostitution with the Korean women.[11] Documents released by the Japanese government revealed that the military high command organized the prostitution in order to discourage their troops from raping local women in the territories they occupied because they were concerned that wartime rape, an accepted military practice, might engender local resistance to the Japanese. The Korean women demanded that the Japanese government apologize to every victim and provide each one with full compensation.

The Japanese military, having procured Korean women as "comfort girls" for its own military men during World War II, then made Korean women available to American military during the U.S. occupation. Japanese journalist Yayori Matsui revealed how prostitution became part of the provisions made for the occupation forces in Japan at the end of World War II:

After its defeat in World War II, the Japanese government presented Japanese women as "comfort girls" to the United Occupation Forces. It is reported that at the cabinet meeting held on August 21, 1945, only six days after the V-J surrender, Konoe Fumimaro, then State Minister without Portfolio, made the following proposal: "We must take emergency measures to protect our women and children from sex-starved American soldiers." Three days later, the Metropolitan Police Headquarters began to gather members of the red-light trade and request, "As a stopgap measure to protect the flower-like purity of 40,000,000 respectable Japanese women, we would like you to open facilities to 'comfort' the American troops." The government proposed to contribute indirectly 50 million yen (roughly equivalent to $5 million at the present exchange rate) to help meet their expenses. . . .

A ceremony to proclaim the establishment of the "Association for the Creation of Special Recreational Facilities" (later the "Recreation and Amusement Association," nicknamed R.A.A.) was held in the square in front of the Imperial Palace on August 28 to coincide with the landing of the first contingent of American occupation troops. Soon the first R.A.A.–sponsored army brothel, Komachi Garden, was opened in the Omori district of Tokyo. On August 30, about 100 women, some of them former prostitutes and others deceived by advertisements reading "Recruiting the new Japanese woman: lodging, clothing, and food provided," had to surrender their bodies to American soldiers. R.A.A. army brothels literally sprouted up before the smoke could clear from the bombed-out rubble of Tokyo, and within three months there were twenty-five such brothels. . . . At its height, R.A.A. is said to have employed 70,000 "comfort girls." [12]

Korean prostitution for occupation forces, first Japanese and then U.S., later turned into military prostitution for U.S. forces in

Korea and then developed into sex tourism for Japanese businessmen.

Vietnam and War. In the Vietnam War, the U.S. military fought alongside and was ultimately defeated with the South Vietnamese Republican Forces. Their enemy was the Vietnamese Communist forces, who had an army in North Vietnam and one in South Vietnam. The U.S. military named their Vietnamese enemy "gooks" to objectify and ridicule them, presumably making it easier to kill them. In uniform "gooks" were Communists to American soldiers. But how did they distinguish "gooks" from the rest of the Vietnamese who were not in uniform? Or did they even bother? Were women whores, or were they "gook whores"? During wartime, particularly the Vietnam War, racism was a military strategy adopted by the sex industries to sell foreign sexed bodies to military men. Vietnamese women, racially different from their invaders, first the French colonists, then the U.S. forces, were also, like Vietnamese men, the enemy—gooks—and, in addition, they were sex, to buy or to take.

Prostitution in Vietnam was only part of a wartime sexual exploitation of Vietnamese women. Through massive raping in war men humiliate their enemy. Rape of women in traditional Asian societies often leaves them unable to return to their families or to marry. Le Ly Hayslip was a teenage Vietnamese peasant in a village in central Vietnam during the war. As soldiers moved in and out of her village daily—first the Vietcong, then the U.S.-backed southern Republican forces—she was raped by men from both sides. Especially during the Vietnam War, raped women were considered dishonored, their rape having disgraced their humiliated families, villages, and communities. Prostitution was all that was left for many women who, like Hayslip, "despaired of having a proper marriage." [13] Sex industries during war build upon the sexual violence–rape war strategy. But raped women, victims of military strategy, were only one source of prostitution as the United States increasingly poured military men into Vietnam, accelerating the prostitution market demand.

Part of the enticement for customers is that when men buy women in prostitution, it is kept secret from their wives, is forbidden by their religions, and is usually illegal. An additional excitement of military prostitution is undoubtedly the sexual reduction of women who are different racially, whose villages and families are being plundered. Sex industries build sex markets from racial bigotry. They satisfy the racist curiosities of customers pursuing the "forbidden" by providing racially different female bodies for sex-market exchange. Racial, ethnic and cultural differences are part of the sex commodification of that which is forbidden. Women of different races constitute another line the customer trespasses when buying women's bodies, heightening his excitement.

Trafficking in women fulfills the racist demands of customers by providing them with not only female bodies but bodies that are particularly "colored" and differently characterized by racial culture. When the U.S. military reduced its enemy to objects by labeling them "gooks," Vietnamese women were reduced to whores whether or not they were actually bought for sex. It is not that U.S. women were not sexually objectified and harassed in Vietnam. Military women's testimony from the Gulf War reveals they probably were. But in Vietnam their visible presence did not first suggest "whore," for they could be taken as military personnel, military wives, or even tourists. In other words, racism functions as an unsolicited protection from sexual exploitation of women of the dominant racial group (white, U.S. women) when women in the subordinated racial group are chosen by men for sexual exploitation through rape and/or prostitution. Racism in sexual exploitation sustains the separation of "good" and "bad" women. However, as the 1992 scandal of the sexual abuse of women at the U.S. Navy's Tailhook Convention revealed, when race differences do not define a particular setting, or when U.S.

women return home from duty, they resume their status as sexed bodies.

A word about national liberation movements and armies. In contrast to the U.S. and Southern Republican forces, the Vietnamese National Liberation Army was held to a strict code of ethics that prohibited rape and prostitution of local women. However, the ideal is not always the reality, and especially in male-dominated liberation movements, it is known that all armies are engaged in sexual exploitation of women. But during the Vietnam War, whereas prostitution proliferated in Saigon, under the U.S. and Republican forces in the South, it was virtually nonexistent in Hanoi, controlled by the National Liberation Forces of Ho Chi Minh in the North.

The pattern of military prostitution leading to sex tourism was repeated and severely intensified during the Vietnam War, as Thailand and the Philippines became sites of R & R for the U.S. military. Prostitution of Vietnamese, Thai, and Philippine women during and after the Vietnam War was mobilized by degrees for the American military. In Bangkok, the street Patpong became the center of the industry. In *Patpong: Bangkok's Big Little Street,* a former journalist with the Bangkok *Post* boasts that "it is doubtful if not downright impossible that Patpong Road would have its fame and fortune without that war." [14]

By 1965 procuring for military prostitution in South Vietnam had become a major problem in Southeast Asia. Laos, in its response to a 1965 U.N. slavery survey conducted by Dr. Awad, noted a sizable increase in the traffic in women and stated that "procuring is spreading from South Vietnam and Thailand to Laos." [15] First bar girls, then massage parlors for the marines at Da Nang, then "a shanty town of brothels, massage parlors and dope dealers, known as Dogpatch, soon ringed the bases."

By 1966 the 1st Cavalry Division at An Khe, in the Central Highlands, the 1st Infantry Division at Lai Khe, twenty-five miles north of Saigon, and the 4th Infantry Division of Pleiku had established official military brothels within the perimeter of their base camp. . . .

Refugees who had lost their homes and families during the war and veterans of the earlier Saigon bar trade formed the stock of the brothel. ... The American military, which kept its hands partially clean by leaving the procurement and price arrangements to Vietnamese civilians, controlled and regulated the health and security features of the trade.[16]

Eventually prostitutes were officially welcomed to U.S. bases in Vietnam as "local national guests." At Longbinh, near Saigon, it was reported that soldiers could take onto the base as a local national guest any of the 50 to 60 girls who waited outside the base. In addition to military brothels and those that ringed the bases, closed prostitution zones developed. It was reported that the Republican government in the South was taking 30% of the proceeds from prostitution in these zones.[17]

"The streets in downtown Saigon, and those near U.S. housing compounds and military bases in Cholon and scattered around the outskirts of the city, were thickly lined with bars. These bars catered almost exclusively to American males, and at any given time each bar would usually have on hand from five to twenty hostesses to make small talk with the customers and push drinks. There were similar clusters of bars in Bien Hoa, Vung Tau, Nha Trang, and Danang, and they sprang up on a smaller scale wherever significant numbers of Americans were to be found."[18] Most women in prostitution, as is the case in the Philippines and wherever military prostitution flourishes, were war widows, had been abandoned by husbands, or were rape victims. Prostitutes were women outside of the family unit. In wartime, the female condition of being a feudal vagabond was heightened by the dislocation produced by war.

At the close of the war and the time of military withdrawal from South Vietnam, many American soldiers tried to "save" prostitute women in South Vietnam from the North Vietnamese forces that would reunify the country under Vietnamese leadership in order to recycle them into prostitution elsewhere.

Young Americans made the rounds of virtually every bar and whorehouse in the capital to round up the women and sponsor them out of the country. One man claimed he made four trips in and out of Saigon, each time leaving with another "wife" and several "sisters-in-law." One prostitute who turned down the offer to leave said her would-be "husband" told her he planned to start an all-Vietnamese whorehouse in Honolulu. She said he worked for the CIA.[19]

In her biography, *When Heaven and Earth Changed Places,* Le Ly Hayslip recounts both the slave traffic and military prostitution in Vietnam, usually procured and exchanged by corrupt Vietnamese for American GIs stationed in Vietnam. Prostitution was taken for granted as an inevitable choice women made during war as if prostitution was there to be chosen. By contrast, when girls were trafficked, the trafficking was considered slavery. Hayslip's biography reveals the daily struggle against military men who assumed that she and any women who were visible were prostitutes. For the most part, Le Ly Hayslip managed to avoid prostitution, but doing so involved persistent refusals, for whenever she was on the streets she was taken for a prostitute by military men. She recounts many such occurrences that took place when she was on the streets selling merchandise to GIs to support herself and her child. And not only was she assumed to be a prostitute because she was a Vietnamese woman; even her sharp refusals in no way convinced the GIs that she could not be had for a price. And once, when she conceded because the $400 offered would support herself and her mother for a year, she considered what prostitution was as she told herself, "Just lie down and let these two American boys be men. What could they do to me that hadn't been done already."[20] Then, invoking the hair-splitting distinction between free and forced prostitution, Le Ly Hayslip described the slave traffic in Vietnam:

These girls weren't prostitutes but young women—some not even in puberty—who came into the city on buses to escape the war in the countryside. Like me, these girls were peasants, ignorant of anything but life on the farm, who had been sent by relatives to find a safer, better life in the city. When a refugee bus arrived, an older woman (accompanied by a couple of handsome young men) would ask if anyone aboard needed a job as housekeeper or nanny. Because these were jobs the girls had been told to look for, and because the handsome young men paid attention to them, the winsome young girls quickly gathered around. The woman then promised them housemaid jobs with good families for good pay, and took them to her home where they worked a few days "just to show they could do it. . . ." While the new batch of girls was thus occupied, the woman would visit her contacts and describe the new "merchandise"—sometimes complete with Polaroid pictures she took after the girls had been cleaned up. Her customers were usually corrupt officials or wealthy individuals with bizarre sexual tastes, although some of the customers exported these girls to similar clientele in other countries: to Thailand, Singapore, and even as far away as Europe and the United States.[21]

In the depravity of war, oppression creates distinctions and discernments that would otherwise be unknown. Hayslip goes on to explain that "the regular prostitutes, by comparison, had a much better life." [22] It is from these kinds of desperate distinctions that arguments of women's "choice" and "free will" in prostitution are built. Within the world of prostitution, "the cheapest whorehouses, those located near the military installations, were often no more than shacks whose owners rented a room . . . to local girls who plied their trade with resident servicemen," often in the bushes, trucks, tanks, or alleys.[23] "Many of the girls were widowed by the war or were rape victims like me who despaired of a proper marriage." [24] Next were the better hookers, better because they had a madam and whorehouse in which to prostitute. And finally, the madams whose brothels were protected by the police were on the highest rung of the prostitution ladder. Uncounted among the victims of war are the many Vietnamese women who survived by simply conceding to the enemy's prostitution demand, telling themselves, "what does it matter?" or "why not?"

With the U.S. withdrawal from Vietnam in 1972 and reunification of the North and the South in 1975, there were approximately 500,000 Vietnamese women in prostitution. The Socialist Republic of Vietnam considered prostitutes to be victims of the political, social, and economic order of the former U.S.-backed "puppet" regime in South Vietnam and found that by the end of the war, venereal disease was one of the many serious problems the new government of Vietnam had to confront in rebuilding the country. Health officials then estimated that even with an intensive campaign, it would take 6 to 8 years to bring it under control.[25] It was estimated that 54% of the prostitutes suffered from it. The women were given emergency aid, which included medical examinations and treatment. Those women who came into prostitution from rural villages were said to be returned to those villages to work and, where possible, to be reunited with their families. Women and girls who were originally from urban areas were sent to boarding schools, Schools to Rehabilitate Women's Dignity, where they were trained in a trade or profession, attended political lectures, and participated in cultural activities. The cost was borne by the revolutionary administration of each city.[26] In the late 1970s, after Vietnam had reunified its country and established a Socialist state, some Western human-rights organizations were concerned about the treatment of political prisoners, sympathizers with the fallen Republican government that had been backed by the U.S. military in the South. They, along with prostitutes, were sent to re-education centers. Although concern had been raised about whether or not the re-education centers for prostitute women were in fact the same as the centers for jailed political prisoners, in 1979 investigators from the nongovernmental organization Humanitas found that prostitute women had not been treated as political prisoners.

When I visited Vietnam in January 1991 and again in January 1993, I inquired about the success in reducing and controlling prostitution after the war. According to Professor Bui Thi Kim Quy, a sociologist and director of women's studies in Ho Chi Minh City, at the end of the war the programs were successful, for two-thirds of the women in wartime prostitution were able to return to traditional society. However, many returned to prostitution in poverty-stricken postwar Vietnam; rehabilitation programs and socialist prohibitions did not completely eliminate prostitution. Under the socialist state, pornography disappeared, pimping was controlled, and prostitution was reduced, but even in the absence of a market economy, men persisted in producing a market demand for women's bodies.

In 1986, with "Doi Moi," or renovation, the Vietnamese *perestroika,* a free market economy began to develop, and prostitution immediately began to increase. The familiar pattern repeated itself: as economic conditions improved and gave rise to increased spending, men first spent leisure money buying women's bodies. Before Doi Moi it was estimated that prostitution in the former Saigon had been reduced to 10,000 women. By 1991, on my first trip to Vietnam, my inquiries revealed that it had tripled from that low. By 1993 Professor Le Thi Quy of the Women's Research Center in Hanoi estimated from her research that there were presently 100,000 prostitutes in Vietnam, one-half of them in Ho Chi Minh City. In 1993, the 50,000 prostitutes in former Saigon constituted an increase from 30,000 2 years earlier, which constituted an increase from 10,000 in 1987. As prostitution accelerates, it quickly becomes normalized. Seventy-five percent of the women interviewed by Professor Le Thi Quy in her study of prostitution did not consider prostitution to be "beneath their dignity." [27]

By 1991 trafficking of Vietnamese women to Thailand for prostitution had begun again. Trafficking has mostly taken place via an overland route through Cambodia and has contributed to Vietnamese prostitution there. In 1993, Vietnam reported that there were 10,000 Vietnamese women in prostitution in Cambodia, many servicing the U.N. peacekeeping forces there. In the immense poverty, severe illness, and disease that impacted Vietnam in postwar years and was intensified by the U.S. embargo, prostitution was contained. But Vietnamese leadership turned to other issues to address beyond eliminating the conditions that promote prostitution.

Under socialist leadership before and during the war, feminist movements were considered traitorous. There is a strong women's organization, The Women's Union, that influences legislation on behalf of women, but it does not challenge party leadership. Sexual exploitation, then, was *suppressed* because the market was outlawed. Now, in 1990s Vietnam, with its developing market economy, there is a resurgence of prostitution as women are being marginalized in the development process. Women in the rural-to-urban migration process find few opportunities in the cities, and global sex industries are poised, waiting to buy them off. By 1993, the developing women's consciousness in Vietnam led to new policies designed to confront aggressively the upsurge of prostitution (see last chapter). With the shift to a market economy, the government has not funded these programs to protect women, but it did identify prostitution as one of its top ten priority issues for 1993.

Sex Tourism: From Military to Business Markets

Massive, industrialized prostitution was set in motion by foreign militaries in several Asian countries and perpetuated by businessmen and male tourists from Japan, Australia, Europe, and North America. Sex tourism and mail-order-bride marketing are the two major sex industries built from military prostitution. The buildup of the male market for sex tourism follows from the two forces that dominate the regions: Japan's superior economic strength and the United State's massive military deployment throughout Asia.[28] Japanese market demand for prostitution sex tourism followed the military prostitution during and after World War II; the Japanese turned first to Taiwan and then to Korea for sex tourism. The European, Australian, and American market demand for prostitution followed from the massive U.S. military prostitution in Southeast Asia during the Vietnam War, after which sex tourism industries developed particularly in Thailand and the Philippines. By the late 1970s these two different markets of sex tourism merged, particularly as Japanese men joined Americans, Europeans, and Australians in sex tourism to the Philippines and Thailand. (The other significant cause of the prostitution buildup in this region was the rural-to-urban migration of poor women who are trafficked into prostitution, or turn to it in desperation. This will be discussed in the next chapter.)

Korea. Sex tourism servicing businessmen and other male tourists escalated in Asia in the 1970s. Taiwan's tourist industry in the 1980s was primarily male. Of the Japanese tourists to Taiwan in 1984, 81.8% were male and 70% were businessmen, salesmen, and office workers. In Taipei, the capital of Taiwan, the main prostitution market is near Lungshan Temple, on Hua Hsi Street, a small crammed block, 500 square meters of market stalls, where snake blood and bile are sold to men to increase their virility. The Rainbow Project of Taiwan, which confronts the trafficking of Aboriginal Taiwanese women and girls and provides them with shelter, reported that in 1980 over 40% of the prostitutes in that area were Aboriginal women and girls trafficked from the mountain tribes.

By the early 1970s the Japanese male market demand for sex tourism expanded to South Korea and Kisaeng tourism.[29] But when Japan normalized relations with the People's Republic of China in 1972, Japanese businessmen shifted their sex tourism from Taiwan to South Korea and Kisaeng prostitution.

Presently there are an estimated 18,000 prostitutes servicing 43,000 U.S. army personnel stationed in 27 areas in Korea.[30] Small sex-industry towns with bars and clubs develop around the bases to service the military, as they have in other regions.

Prostitution of Korean women for the military and later for sex tourism took another turn in the late 1970s and 1980s when Korean crime syndicates escalated trafficking of Korean women to the United States for massage-parlor prostitution. In 1990 the U.S. Immigration and Naturalization Service was investigating several marriage brokers who paid GIs $10,000 to marry Korean women in order to traffic them to the U.S. Syndicates have relied on U.S. soldiers, some of whom are duped and others of whom are working lucrative business scams to bring Korean women into the United States as wives when they are transferred back home. As soon as they are in the U.S. the women obtain divorces and are placed in massage parlors.[31] After the mid-1980s crackdown on prostitution in Manhattan, there was a 1992 shift of Korean massage-parlor prostitution in New York City from Manhattan to Queens.

Sex tourism for Japanese as well as Western businessmen and tourists developed around Kisaeng prostitution. "Kisaeng" originally referred to independent women who were singers and dancers and who took on lovers. But the term came to refer to prostitutes and the brothel tours that take Japanese businessmen and tourists to South Korea, often supported by their companies. "Chartered tours of two nights and three days cost no more that $200—including the price of sex."

Yayori Matsui noted in 1984 that there were over 8,000 Kisaeng in prostitution in South Korea, 2,000 registered and checked for venereal disease twice a month, and that there were over 30 Kisaeng houses in Seoul alone.[32] Yayori quotes a white-collar Japanese worker whose reasoning resonates throughout the customer/market demand for prostitution: "In South Korea the spirit of rendering oneself completely to a man still exists among women, and their exhaustive service is irreversible."[33]

Kim Hae Won provides a picture of Japanese tourists going to Cheju Island in Korea for Kisaeng tourism. The selling point is the authentic, even indigenous experience, beginning with the stone statues of the protecting spirit of Cheju Island guarding the gates. Everything is sold as if it is authentic and indigenous, from food and liquor to lodging and women in traditional Korean dress. The women who arrive at 4:00 P.M. to prepare for the evening are waiting in the basement until they are called. Twenty women line up before 10 Japanese men, who take their pick of the women whom they will have for the entire night. At the dinner the Kisaeng washes the face and hands of the Japanese who chose her. Dinner is followed by traditional Korean dance and songs. The men then can take the women directly to their hotels or to nightclubs or karaoke bars. The women return to their rooms about 7:00 A.M.[34]

In 1973 the Asian Women's Association launched a campaign to halt Kisaeng tourism. On Christmas day a protest demonstration by women confronted Japanese male tourists returning from Korea with "Aren't you ashamed to go on group brothel tours?" and "Go to hell, sex animals!"[35] But when sex tourism or any part of the sex industry is exposed in one region, it moves to another. By that time sex tourism was burgeoning in Southeast Asia as procurers were looking for new markets for their merchandise and governments were seeking foreign exchange through tourist dollars. Japanese feminists in alliance with women from other countries created a movement to confront the sex tours throughout the region. After public protests and threats of exposing the customers, in 1981 "the number of Japanese men visiting the Philippines declined sharply, from 14,699 to 11,988 in March, 19.7 percent in April and 24.6 percent in May, compared to figures from the previous year."[36] A comparable reduction in flights between Tokyo and Manila also resulted from the actions. However, the effect of the action was short term, and tourism to these countries remains primarily male—Japanese and Western. Traffic in women continually moves industries to more and more lucrative markets.

Thailand. Estimating prostitution in Thailand follows the pattern in estimating the incidence of rape. As of 1993 it is estimated unofficially that there were 2 million prostitutes in Thailand, where the country's economic development is based on foreign exchange from tourism. Prostitution is the largest commodity for the 450,000 Thai men who frequent prostitutes daily and for a large proportion of the 5.4 million tourists who visit Thailand annually for sex tours. Sex tourism is the major source of economic foreign exchange for the Thai tourist industry. Police estimated 400,000 prostitutes in Thailand in 1974. They had been procured primarily for the U.S. military on leave for R & R during the Vietnam War. However, despite the continued growth of sex tourism and prostitution outlets, in 1992 the Thai Public Health Ministry counted only 76,863 prostitutes nationwide.[37]

The sex industry was one of the largest businesses in Thailand until the withdrawal of troops from Southeast Asia. In Thailand, where there was virtually no restriction on marketing of women, procurers developed ways to deal with the excessive number of prostitutes left over from the booming sex industry created for and by American GIs. Thai prostitute women, already victims of sex industries, also became victims of a drastic crash in that industry. They became pawns in traffic in women to other more lucrative or profitable areas.

The German economy and liberal prostitution laws made that country a likely focus for traffic from Thailand. Later, when the Netherlands legalized prostitution, the trafficking in women from the Philippines, Thailand, and other Southeast Asian countries expanded into that country. One report in 1977 indicated that Thai girls were purchased for $1,000 each by a ring in Frankfurt, which then was reported to rent them out for $2,200 a month.[38] Some were taken directly from Thailand to German brothels with no ruse or pretense. In 1977 a Thai welfare worker, who went to Germany to bring home one young woman abandoned on the streets there, estimated that over 1,000 Thai girls were working as prostitutes there at that time.[39]

After the U.S. troops withdrew from Vietnam in 1972, journalist Tom Weber, writing for the Chronicle Foreign Service, visited Thailand and found some of the prostitutes left in the Village of Night Girls—a prostitution area he described as full of pimps who would offer "a young virgin from a farm for $300 American dollars." Black-market operators were doing a big business in orphaned children, many fathered by GIs and left behind; they were being sold through adoption agencies. Weber asked to be taken to a typical massage parlor in Bangkok, which did not look much different from the way massage parlors look in the 1990s.

There is an expensive look about the whole operation. Inside the entrance is a large department store display window. The walls are draped in red velvet. The glare of 30 spot-lights shows off the merchandise; nearly 200 girls, all pretty and painted and wearing bright colored dresses and platform shoes. They sit on tiers of benches, looking like an all-girl choir. I asked if any of them spoke English. A few were pointed out.

After making his selection and paying the equivalent of $10, he was taken by the young woman to a small room.

After the routine of the bath she started to take off her dress. I told her to keep it on and we spent the rest of the time talking.

She grew up on a farm northeast of Chiang Mai. When she was 16, an American came to the farm and told her parents he wanted her for his wife. He paid his gift of money and took her to an army base.

She thought the marriage was forever. But after her daughter was born, the "husband" was transferred back to the States, and just before he left, he "gave" her to his buddy. Then there was another and another. Now there are no more Americans to "marry" and she lives in the Village of Night Girls.[40]

During the Vietnam War, "a highly organized U.S. R & R office in Bangkok had, in collaboration with a Thai general who ran a travel service, arranged for hotels costing no more than $5 a night." These hotels were within a short walk of a "long string of massage parlors and big bars on new Petchburi Road."[41] The GI did not have to leave that road during his R & R leave. However, in another part of town, Patpong, construction workers, journalists, and other businessmen following and profiting from the war were doing business over drinks. Patpong, a more expensive, up-scale hangout for men, did not turn into the most active center for prostitution and sex tourism until the beginning of the U.S. withdrawal from Vietnam. In 1969 the first go-go bars opened in Patpong. Then "between 1973 and 1979 virtually all the street-level shops and offices on Patpong Road were replaced with bars or restaurants."[42] As competition for sex business increased, go-go bars turned to live sex on stage and smaller bars expanded to superbars.

In a study of women in Bangkok massage parlors in 1982, the lowest-grade massage parlors were found to be frequented by wage laborers. Women and girls were presented in cages or windows:

The girls sit in the cage lit by dim artificial lights. Opposite, and outside the case, is a row of benches where the men may sit and contemplate their choice. In some places there is a one-way mirror to ensure that the girls cannot see the clients, but in the cheaper establishments the shadows have to be enough. The client picks out his girl by the number pinned on her blouse, and pays the appropriate rate at a desk to one side of the cage.[43]

In 1991, there were approximately 3,000 prostitutes in Chiang Mai, a city of a quarter-million in the north of Thailand. Again, in most of the brothels the women are presented in cages, sitting on tiers to be picked out. They wear color-coded price tags: "yellow $4; blue $8; red, $12, clear, $20."[44]

In the early 1980s there was a depression in the Thai sex industry. Concern about venereal disease and the reputation in Europe of men-only tours led to a brief government crackdown in prostitution in 1981.[45] Cynthia Enloe pointed out that "by 1986 Thailand earned more foreign currency from tourism than from any other economic activity including its traditional export leader, rice."[46] By 1990, 5.29 million foreign tourists visited Thailand. Thailand's tourists have been so disproportionately male that the tourist industry designated 1992 as the year to attract women tourists—though this effort was beat out by another male attraction, the Miss Universe pageant held in Bangkok. In 1993 it was estimated that 500,000 men bought sex every night in Thailand, according to EMPOWER, a Thai women's organization.

And Thailand continues to service military prostitution. In 1992, with the Gulf War, the U.S. Seventh Fleet docked in Subic and Pattaya, a tourist center in Thailand. The economy of Pattaya had been depressed during the Gulf War, but as the town readied itself for U.S. servicemen on R & R, one bar owner said he hoped to make up for the previous 3 months in the following 4 days.[47] That gain would largely come from prostituting of Thai women and girls.

While the massive increase in AIDS (discussed in chapter 7) in Thailand has led to an increase in the trafficking of women from Burma, Vietnam, Laos, and Cambodia since 1990, the government- and police-implicated corruption in prostitution has led to a crackdown on child and "forced" prostitution.

In early 1993, this crackdown was being enforced in southern Thailand, where the tourists are mainly men from Malaysia and Singapore visiting for prostitution. As of 1993, it has been noted that the "people involved in running prostitution have become even more powerful than they were just 2 or 3 years ago; having both the money and the necessary connections to stay in the business and flourish . . . in towns in the south brothels formed associations maybe with 50 members. Each pays a membership fee and a head fee for each prostitute to the chairman, the fee per head ranges from 250 baht to 700 baht. The money is then distributed to all concerned. . . . In the northern city of Chiang Mai women pay a daily fine to the police of 30 baht."[48] The Thai campaign, which included "saying no to bribes," came after a brothel raid in the southern province of Norathiwat's Sungi Kolot, which found hill tribe girls under 18 in prostitution and a register of bribes paid to the police.[49] This crackdown was followed by a new bill introduced to Parliament in December 1992 that, if passed, would "make customers who have sex with children or women forced to serve as prostitutes liable to prison terms and a heavy fine."[50]

However, 86% of Thai prostitution is local, not foreign, and in a recent study, only 2.1% of the prostitutes indicated they had been "forced."[51] Following the pattern of European countries,

Thailand's crackdown on forced prostitution is part of an overall normalization of prostitution that actually stabilizes the sex industry.

Several forces are at work here: (1) trafficking, forced prostitution, and child prostitution are separated from the industrialization of sex and therefore crackdowns on them will not pose any significant threat to the sex industries; and (2) while prostitution and sex industries have developed a significant economic base in Thai economy, local prostitution can be threatened by the trafficking of foreign women, who inevitably command a lower price and therefore bring down the prices of the developed sex industries, which have escalated considerably and have proven able to buy women off from the traditional labor force with which they compete for the marketing of women's bodies.

The Philippines. The U.S. military domination of the Philippines extends back to the beginning of the twentieth century but was formalized in a Military Bases Agreement at the end of World War II. The 1992 volcanic eruptions of Mount Pinatubo, which poured inches of ash over Clark Air Force Base and destroyed parts of Subic Naval Base, completed the tentative and previously resistant U.S. military withdrawal from the Philippines.

Before the volcanic eruption, Angeles City was the bar town that served the 25,550 U.S. military stationed at Clark Air Force Base. In 1990 there were 1,567 registered bars, massage parlors, and brothels, with 5,642 registered women entertainers and thousands of unregistered women. There were 5,000 military personnel stationed at Subic Bay Naval Station. But 70,000 military would crowd into Olongapo City from 550 aircraft and 90 ships that would arrive when the U.S. fleet docked there for repairs and renovation. In 1989 there were 11,600 women in prostitution who were registered as entertainers, with an estimated 6,000 bar girls, 14,000 unlicensed streetwalkers, and 500 go-go bars, massage parlors, and brothels (10% of which are owned by retired U.S. military).[52] Cynthia Enloe has documented that "of the approximately 30,000 children born each year to Filipino mothers and American fathers, some 10,000 are thought to become street children, many of them working as prostitutes servicing American pedophiles."[53] With the U.S. withdrawal from the Philippines, bar women have lost the services provided to them for their Amerasian children, including some medical care, education, and child support.

Olongapo existed only as a tourist center, one that, as Aurora DeDios explains, is "thriving in times of war and contracted economically in times of peace."[54] It was estimated that 2 million navy and marine personnel passed through Olongapo each year, spending $66 million in rest and relaxation. DeDios reported that it was virtually impossible for a Filipino woman not to be taken for a prostitute when the military naval fleets arrived in Olongapo. Just before the Gulf War, 32 warships in readiness docked in Olongapo over a 2-month period.[55] After the war, in March 1991, 6 shiploads of U.S. sailors and marines arrived from the Gulf War after 5 other battleships.[56] Seven thousand men would arrive at any one time, with 400 wives there to meet their husbands.[57]

The U.S. military withdrew from the Philippines on November 24, 1992, and the bases are now under Philippine jurisdiction. The massive sex industry is faltering, but efforts are being made to regenerate it through development of a tourist economy wherein businessmen will replace military customers. In its transformation to a nonmilitary site, "Subic Base is being heralded as the next Hong Kong," with plans to attract foreign investors by creating another export processing zone. Some prostitution centers in Olongapo have "transformed into Karaoke bars and are now catering to the Taiwanese and Japanese."[58]

As in Thailand, prostitution in the Philippines is normalized. It is treated as "entertainment," and there is no legal impediment to promoting it for the foreign exchange it produces for the country's economy. (See chapter 7 on laws.) In the 1970s the Philippines liberalized its entry requirements for foreigners to promote the tourist industry that brings in foreign exchange. Between 1976 and 1986, travel agencies increased from 300 to 491 while tour guides and promoters increased from 1,550 to 8,120. There was a similar proportional increase in health certificates issued to "entertainers" in Manila; 1,699 certificates were issued in 1980 while 7,003 were issued in 1986. The ministry of tourism reported an increase in tourism; 67% of the tourists were men from the United States, Japan, Hong Kong, Australia, and Taiwan. Of those men, 72% come to the Philippines for holidays.[59]

It is currently estimated that between 300,000 and 500,000 women are in prostitution in the Philippines.[60] With the withdrawal of the U.S. military and the development of conversion plans for Subic and Clark, the government has refused to consider the needs of women in prostitution, ignoring the Women's Education, Development, Productivity, and Research Organization report of June 1992.[61] The conversion plans call for the development of free trade zones and for tourism. The bar women have no alternative but to wait for the next wave of foreigners—businessmen and tourists. Standing in the middle of the sex-trade zone in Angeles, I discussed the conversion plans with a Philippine official and listened as he explained that Angeles was planning on developing tourism. Noticing that Angeles is not a coastal town, that there are no beaches or any other tourist attractions, I asked what the attraction would be for tourists. He told me that they plan to build a large casino. Finding it difficult to imagine tourists flying from various points in Asia, Australia, Europe, and North America merely to visit a casino, I could only reason that the casino was an implicit drawing card for continuing the prostitution, or "entertainment," industry.

By 1993, the Philippines authorities in Olongapo and Angeles had not begun to address the needs of women in the prostitution industry or to develop a plan for its "conversion." However, in a move that seems to contradict the "laissez faire" approach of the former military prostitution towns, the mayor of Manila issued an order to close down all prostitution and sex tourism outlets in

Manila in order to rid the "tourist belt" of prostitution, drug trafficking, and other illegal activities.[62] The mayor planned to turn Ermita, the prostitution zone in Manila, into a business area. Massage parlors, nightclubs, bars, and other prostitution outlets were closed down, their windows and doors boarded. The mayor offered incentives to investors to encourage the startup of new businesses. But Manila has offered nothing to the women, for whom there are no social support systems, and thus this potentially far-reaching reform has been turned into another victimization of bar women. They are not only exploited by the men who buy them but also by government prohibition of the businesses in which men buy women.

The 1992–93 reorganization of prostitution in the Philippines reveals plans to close down the sex industry in some areas, such as Manila, and redevelop it in others. The complete disregard for the welfare, future, and legitimate economic development of prostitute women establishes the base for the continued proliferation of prostitution.

In the Philippines, women have been advertised to foreigners as "Little Brown Fucking Machines." In a 1990 study by the Women's Education, Development, Productivity, and Research Organization, in the Philippines, it was found that there are 3 classes of prostitution: Generally migrants from depressed regions in the Philippines, the lowest class consists of *casa* workers, all of whom are migrants registered as food handlers; they live in brothels, are not allowed to leave, and must take any customers as they arrive. The next are bar girls, who are formally registered as employees of bars but receive no salary. They live at the bar and earn money by encouraging men to buy drinks and, from there, to buy their bodies. Then there are the streetwalkers, who are controlled by pimps. Their work is illegal because they are unregistered. Depending on their pimps, they may be more or less advantaged by working fewer hours, having to take fewer customers, and possibly receiving a better cut from the pimp than the girls in bars or *casas* receive.[63]

Alcohol and drugs help numb the effects of prostitution. In the Philippines study of prostitutes it was found that, "Given the prevalent use of alcohol and drugs in the entertainment trade, 85 percent of the respondents say that women entertainers like themselves run the risk of being alcoholics, and 73 percent, the risk of being drug addicts." [64]

Who are these women? A survey conducted in Olongapo by Virginia Miralao, Celia Carlos and Aida Fulleros Santos shows that 43% are barely out of their teens, while one-third are between 21 and 25 and 23% are over 25. In Olongapo, 89% of the *casa* women, the lowest level of prostitution, are migrants from rural areas while bar and street prostitutes are from urban areas. Most (70%) are middle children from large families of 6 or more. They remove themselves from their families to remove the burden of their support. The survey gave a description of a typical young Olongapo prostituted woman:

The third child of a large family she is left behind in an impoverished Visayan town where she finished her elementary schooling. Her father is a carpenter and her mother, a housewife. Being out-of-school and lacking in parental attention, she fell prey to a sweet-talking man who promised marriage and escape from her family problems. She plunged into marriage or a live-in relationship at 17 and soon found herself simply abandoned with a child by her vice-ridden "husband." With no financial support for herself and her child, and with minimal formal education and no vocational training, she looked for a job. But looking for a job and taking care of her child are virtually impossible to do at the same time. So, she decided to leave her child to be taken care of by her family while she looked for a job. [65]

Visiting Olongapo and Angeles and talking with bar women in both places in 1993, five months after the U.S. withdrawal from its military bases there, I heard one consistent theme that was reiterated over and over again by the women: their belief, hope, wish, that the GIs who had fathered their children would return to take them to the United States as their wives. Many women explained that in coming to Olongapo or Angeles from their rural villages, they learned that their only way out of poverty would be to marry a GI and eventually return with him to the United States. Prostitution, many believed, was an interim necessity. The GIs who had paid a "bar fine" to take the women for days or weeks treated them as girlfriends and filled them with false promises. After the United States withdrew, however, only a few of the fathers have even sent a postcard. Some have sent small amounts of money but usually with no return address, no way to trace them. But the women cling to the hope that their "boyfriends" will return and that they will eventually live in the United States. Alternatives to prostitution are so far beyond view, with no social services to help these women through the transition, that marrying an American becomes one of the only dreams of getting out of prostitution and poverty. That is the basis of another sex industry, mail-order brides.

Marketing Women: Mail-Order Brides

Marriage is the other side of prostitution. Most frequently, prostitute women are those who have been deserted or widowed, are escaping wife abuse, or are, like Lisa Mamac, seeking better opportunities than marriage in rural poverty. In poverty and prostitution, women frequently see marriage, particularly to a wealthy foreigner, as the only possibility of escape. During the Vietnam War, "marriages between Vietnamese and Westerners climbed steadily: 126 in 1965, 402 in 1968, 559 in 1971 . . . whereas marriage between Vietnamese fell from 96 percent in 1965 to only 81 percent in 1970." [66]

In the context of women's deprivation during economic development, while many traditional societies are making arranged marriage and polygamy illegal in the process of modernizing, Western, advanced capitalist countries are marketing arranged marriages for Western men with Third World women.

Siriporn Skrobanek has pointed out that in countries like Thailand, mail-order-bride trafficking in women is sustained in part by prostitute women's efforts to marry foreigners.[67] Most women do not want to remain in prostitution. In countries that offer little in the way of other alternatives, they would prefer to marry a foreigner.[68] The difference is slight. The mail-order-bride industry and trafficking arranges for women in prostitution, poor women, and women trying to find a way out of their country to marry foreign men.

Mail-order-bride selling, a practice that is a consequence of prostitution but is another form of arranged marriage, is not a new practice. For decades prior to the massive industrialization of sex, it has been a part of the trafficking in women, often referred to as "disguised traffic." However, it became a major business of the sex industry after the Vietnam War.

A number of agencies ran ads in European newspapers offering a "Super Sexy Tour" that included a vacation in Thailand and the opportunity to buy a wife. On the sex tour, the first week is spent picking out the girl one wants (after trying out several, if one likes). During the second week a final selection is made, along with "sightseeing and sweet nothings on a romantic palm-fringed beach. See a Thai style boxing match, eat a traditional Thai dinner, see traditional Thai dancing . . . by week three the tour operators will have made all the wedding arrangements . . . and be ready to hand over all the documents needed to export your new acquisition." The prices ranged from $1,500 to $3,000.[69]

Other reports indicate that some agencies were taking the men's money but not delivering the merchandise. One ad in a German paper offered 3 weeks in Thailand and the bride of one's choice for $3,000. However, the operators took the money, arranged a ceremony, and made a false promise that the "wife" would be sent later. Similarly, in Hong Kong over 100 men complained to authorities in 1975 that they had bought brides from Thailand (some paying as much as $1,000) but found that the girls disappeared soon after the marriage.[70]

The Thai sex-marriage tours are advertised in men's magazines in Europe. In 1979 Norway's foreign minister, Knyt Frydenlund, put diplomatic pressure on the Thai government to halt the tours. The Norwegian Parliament investigated the tours. The foreign minister reported that the prostitution, pandering, and slave trading was in violation of human rights and the resolutions of the 1975 International Women's Year Conference.[71] In 1987 Siriporn Skrobanek from Thailand joined with the Norwegian Women's Front as they faced the first legal suit by a sex-tourism agency against a feminist organization. The court found:

Generally one must see prostitution as a form of exploitation of women, as oppression of women. When this oppression of women takes place in the Third World and is maintained by mass tourism from Western industrialized countries, an element of racial discrimination is undoubtedly added to the sexism.[72]

One brochure from a German mail-order-bride agency advertised Filipinas:

They stand out against the greyness of everyday German routine, those beautiful creatures with black, satin hair and the charming almond-shaped eyes of the Malay. No one who falls prey to their charms need feel victimized. Ethnologists and world travellers, photographers and fashion designers agree that the Filipinas with their graceful, slim form, Chinese-influenced features, and dusky complexion, belong to the most beautiful and most desirable women in the world. Whoever enters into a marriage with such a creature gains something precious, as far as appearances go.

And in case that description is not sufficiently enticing to the German man, the brochure goes on to say, "The Filipinas are pliable and surrendering, when in love become imaginative and know how to make a man, old or young, happy in bed or at the table."

By 1993, mail-order-bride agencies had become established throughout Europe and in Australia, Japan, and the United States. Some agencies provide catalogues and others offer videotapes giving intimate descriptive details of Philippine, Thai, and, most recently, Eastern European and Russian women. In the bride traffic to Australia there have been 20,000 marriages between Filipino women and Australian men. In 1988–89 women constituted 84% of spouse arrivals from the Philippines and 83% of the arrivals from Thailand.[73]

The women are provided to men whose most sexist dream is racist: the belief that in buying an Asian bride they will have an alternative to "liberated" Western women. The industry is not only one that exploits the disadvantaged conditions of many poor women in developing countries; it also sustains men who are incapable of egalitarian relationships with women, or of relationships with independent women. If the male market for brides did not go as far as it does in sustaining the economic inequality of women, the men who buy women would be merely pathetic.

By 1984 American men were paying $6,000 for Filipino brides on the justification that "I want a wife who isn't career oriented, who participates very little in the world outside, who doesn't have high aspirations, who is useful, whose life revolves around me. . . . And yes, she had to be a virgin."[74] Between the mid-1970s and mid-1980s, worldwide mail-order-bride businesses expanded from about a dozen to over 50. Their numbers have grown beyond calculation since then.

The mail-order-bride business is a form of migration/disguised trafficking that also includes migration of women as domestic workers and as entertainers. Between 1988 and 1989 the percentage of Filipinos marrying foreign nationals increased by 94%, from 4,043 to 7,759.[75] In 1989, 7,759 women left the Philippines through mail-order arrangements, an increase of 94% over 1988.

Immigration authorities conveniently ignore the practice as long as proper documents are provided. Conveniently, the U.S. immigration service provides fiancée visas to facilitate this practice. A fiancée visa requires only that the man meet his future wife within 2 years before filing a petition. It takes a least 3 months to have a fiancée visa issued, and once it is issued, a woman can travel to the United States with her fiancé, but they must marry within 90 days of her arrival. If no marriage takes place, she must depart the United States at the end of the 90 days. In effect, this allows men to try out their new merchandise with the assurance that, if they do not like it, the immigration service will require her departure if there is no marriage. As mail-order-bride agencies hasten to remind their customers, returning a woman to her country of origin does not prevent customers from bringing over another bride on another fiancée visa. And that is exactly what many men do. On a television talk show where I was opposing mail-order-bride agencies and customers with Marie Jose Regab from the National Organization for Women, a man bragged of having brought over 4 women. When they did not work out, he simply had them deported.

Mail-order-bride selling is not only a form of trafficking in women but also a kind of prostitution that begins with men buying women for sexual as well as domestic service. Not infrequently women, if they don't work out to the customers' satisfaction, find themselves turned over to prostitution. In the Gulf region, many find themselves in harems of sorts. In 1984, a Filipino professional woman arrived in the United States as the wife of a California podiatrist only to find that he was already married and intended her to be his mistress. In 1991 another California man was being investigated for bigamy after having added a Thai wife to his household, which already included a Filipino wife he had purchased. The haremlike arrangements built from mail-order-bride buying came to light when the Thai woman contacted police, indicating that she had been sexually assaulted and held in restraint by her purchaser-husband.[76]

As soon as the Communist bloc began to disintegrate and the Soviet Union was dissolved into Russia and accompanying states, the trafficking of Eastern European and Russian women through mail-order-bride agencies began and immediately escalated. In 1993, LatinEuro Introductions had been in the market of arranging connections for North American men with Latin American women for over four and a half years when they turned to a new burgeoning market—Russian and Eastern European women.

Scanna claims that 5,000 American men are looking for Russian brides through its agency, which advertises a listing of 20,000 Russian women. American Russian Matchmaking is one U.S. agency plying the marriage market. In 1992, for a fee of $35 they were providing male customers with pictures and profiles of 12 Russian women. The women must each pay approximately one-third of their monthly salary, $80, to be profiled. Profiles include a head shot, a full-figure photo, vital statistics, and a few words about themselves.[77] The customer picks 3 women and then he is taken to Russia to meet them, on a 2-week tour that costs between $4,000 and $5,000. The agency arranges the visa for the one whom he picks. If marriage takes place within 48 hours, a conditional U.S. visa is issued that is good for 2 years—on the condition that the woman stay in the marriage. If she does not, she is deported. This effectively forces a woman who has known her purchaser "husband" for only a few days to stay in a marriage no matter what the conditions turn out to be when she arrives home with him as his purchased bride. Marie Jose Regab, International Director of the National Organization for Women, points out that recent U.S. laws have been passed to make it easier for foreign spouses, wives in the case of marriage marketing, to stay in the United States even if they cannot stay in the marriage, thus easing the conditional enslaving status of the visa. If a woman has to leave a marriage and goes to the police, court action can remove the "condition" from her visa. However, women procured through marriage agencies and placed in arranged, instant marriages also have little access to this information. "The Violence Against Women Act of 1993" pending in U.S. Congress would allow alien spouses of U.S. citizens to obtain immigration status directly for themselves.

It is even easier to traffic Russian and Eastern European women to the Netherlands, where they do not need a visa. According to police in Rotterdam, the demand for Asian brides and prostitutes is dwindling because the collapse of communism has created not only new marketable commodities in women's bodies but also a shift in market demand—men want to try and buy that which has been unavailable to them previously.[78]

When mail-order-bride selling is examined from the standpoint of the purchaser, several patterns emerge. This practice is based on the practice of arranged marriages, which considers women to be the legal property of their parents, to be disposed of so that they become the legal property of their husbands—a practice that persists in many societies in the world today and prevailed in Western societies into the nineteenth century.

Men who buy mail-order brides are purchasing human beings. The marriage or engagement simply makes the trafficking of women across international boundaries easier. Women report being terribly homesick, being afraid to go out of the house, and frequently being disappointed by the "marriage." But as one satisfied customer explained: "She is spoiling me, though, with all of the attention I get, all of my nails manicured, gives me a shower daily, body massage nightly, shines my shoes and no sooner take a garment off till she has hung it up. She is well worth the price of your catalog."[79]

Some "men's rights" movements have moved into the business in reaction to independent Western women. A newsletter from the November 1991 issue of the Liberator, a "Men's Rights Unity News Magazine," advertised "young and honest Honduran girls through mail," warning "American Women—Stay Away from Me!!!"[80] Mail-order-bride trafficking is not confined to the Asian region. We simply know more about it there because of the activism of Asian feminist groups that are exposing these practices.

Because the poverty in countries like the Philippines is so severe, the push for external migration so strong, the viable options for women so nonexistent, some Asian organizations have hesitated to challenge this form of trafficking in women, hoping that for some few women, the risk they take may improve their lives. Yet the possibility that it may work out for a few women is seriously offset by the numbers who are trafficked into sexually and physically abusing situations, and into prostitution. Ultimately the sale of human beings, whether for marriage, prostitution, or both, is a fundamental human-rights violation. When it is taken out of this context and when sexual exploitation is normalized, transferring women as property is traded as an informal "development" approach. However, it is built on two fundamental assumptions: (1) male opposition to female independence and (2) the reduction of women to saleable property.

A beginning for addressing this trafficking of women as mail-order brides was a new law enacted in the Philippines in 1990,

AN ACT TO DECLARE UNLAWFUL THE PRACTICE OF MATCHING FILIPINO WOMEN FOR MARRIAGE TO FOREIGN NATIONALS ON A MAIL-ORDER BASIS AND OTHER SIMILAR PRACTICES, INCLUDING THE ADVERTISEMENT, PUBLICATION, PRINTING OR DISTRIBUTION OF BROCHURES, FLIERS AND OTHER PROPAGANDA MATERIALS IN FURTHERANCE THEREOF AND PROVIDING PENALTY THEREFOR.

The law has been criticized by some Filipina women's groups for not being strong enough and not going far enough, and because its effective implementation would require the cooperation of the police as well as immigration monitoring, *not to mention* the implementation of similar laws in the United States, the Netherlands, and every county into which women are imported as brides. However, it is often the case that before laws are effective in controlling crime—and mail-order-bride buying and selling is a crime—they do provide the society with the moral base for condemnation of the act, as does this law, which goes on to establish,

It is the policy of the State to ensure and guarantee the enjoyment of the people of a decent standard of living. Towards this end, the State shall take measures to protect Filipino women from being exploited in utter disregard of human dignity in their pursuit of economic upliftment.[81]

Western Deployment of Sex Industries

In advanced industrialized states, sex industries are developed, packaged, and ready for new markets as they become available in the developing world. As I write, while Vietnam continues as a socialist republic, it has begun slowly to develop a market economy, and sex-tour agencies and mail-order-bride outlets have already established their base, with operators traveling to and from Vietnam, preparing to exploit this new market, which was expected to open when the U.S. embargo was lifted and the government lost control of its industrializing efforts to market forces.

The sex industries, usually run by organized crime, were the first to move in and take over the markets created by the collapse of Eastern European communist regimes. In the former Soviet Union, the Soviet mafia is reported to have chartered buses to keep hotels of visiting businessmen supplied with prostitutes through the night.[82]

Even before the toppling of communism, Poland was ready to market the sexual exploitation of women. Its first pornography was produced in 1988 and published by a press agency owned by the Central Committee of the Communist party.[83] In June 1990, Budapest got its first peep show. Censorship laws were repealed in 1989, opening the way for hard-core pornography, first imported from the West but almost immediately generated from a vast industry that developed within the country. Meanwhile, plans were under way to restrict abortion.[84] The Christian Democratic party protested pornography only to the extent that it exploits children, and one of its officials conceded that "pornography is part of democracy."[85] Feminists in Hungary have taken a stronger position, opposing pornography as offensive to women. But a 1989 poll in Hungary showed 75% in favor of legalizing prostitution.

As the Berlin wall came down, traffickers poured in from West Germany, where the sex industries operate with government sanction. Prostitution had been prohibited in East Germany except as it was available in some state-run hotels for Western visitors (often as a source of espionage).[86] Leipzig has been inundated with West German pornographers and procurers[87] setting up trailer camps for prostitution, catering particularly to businessmen pouring into the country to open other markets.

While sex industries, organized crime, and Western European procurers play on the impoverishment of Eastern European women and girls, Western media have represented the proliferation of prostitution in former Communist countries as the release from years of pent-up sexual repression said to characterize the prohibitionist system. In market terms, a rise in the standard of living causes people to start earning spendable income, and when this occurs, spending on luxury items increases disproportionately. If income goes up by X amount, expenditures on items like prostitution will increase disproportionately. Men have first access to spendable income for luxury items, and they are quick to spend it to buy women for personal gratification and power.

Sexual Exploitation Industrialized

Historically, the expansion of prostitution has been considered a consequence (unintended) of rapid industrialization. Industrialization typically provokes massive rural-to-urban migration, with an oversupply of labor pressing on the newly developing urban economy and producing fluctuations in the market. In the first phases of industrialization, as women move from the home to the marketplace, from rural to urban areas, they are marginalized from paid labor in favor of men. When some women begin to gain entry to the labor force in the first phases of industrialization, most are consigned to menial and underpaid jobs, and therefore to poverty and destitution. The industrializing labor force does nothing more than build on the pre-industrial seclusion of women—their confinement to the private sphere of marriage and the family, where their labor has no monetary value. Thus industrialization perpetuates the gender structure of poverty.

Export processing zones (EPZs) are areas in Third World countries designated for foreign business to manufacture goods and commodities for export. Usually, restrictions are limited and the host country offers deregulated incentives that permit intensive production at low cost. Companies are frequently exempt from duty on raw materials and capital goods. They receive reduced rates on electricity and housing, and reduced taxes.[88] EPZs along the Mexican/U.S. border, in parts of Latin America, and in Southeast Asia typically recruit female labor because it is the cheapest available. EPZs are phased out with advanced economic development.

Meanwhile, girls and women in the migrating process are recruited for EPZ production, and their labor in turn accelerates production and the economy. But EPZs are often exempt from minimum-wage and labor standards, so while they offer women a way out of rural poverty, they do not pay enough for them to live at a decent standard of living. Procurers work these areas.

The normalization of prostitution with the increase in standards of living has produced a massive national Thai customer demand, with an estimated 75% of Thai men having had sex with a prostitute.[89] When they are sufficiently developed, sex industries in Thailand are able to buy off women for prostitution with higher wages than they could earn in industrial wage labor sectors. In 1990, the monthly wage of a factory worker for an 8- to 12-hour day ranges from $40 to $80, while a massage-parlor prostitute working comparable hours earns $200 to $320 per month. At a lower level of unskilled employment, a domestic servant working 12 to 18 hours per day can expect to earn $12 to $20 per month, while a third-class prostitute working comparable hours will earn $40 to $80 per month.[90]

The extent to which prostitution has become a means of economic development was revealed in a 1982 study of women in prostitution in Bangkok, where it was found that most of the women interviewed considered themselves as breadwinners for their families in rural villages in northern Thailand, from where they had migrated. All of the women in the study were sending money home to their families. About 25% had told their families how they were earning the money.[91] "Eight of the girls said they had already built a house for their parents in the home village, while most of the girls aimed to do so before they quit. One girl had built two houses—one for herself and one for her parents— and was still saving to build a dressmakers' shop to which she thought she would be able to retire in two years' time. This effort of accumulation had taken ten years."[92]

Traditionally, prostitution proliferates after industrialization is set in motion by development schemes primarily aimed at advancing men. It is then assumed that as industrialization progresses and women have more access to better jobs, prostitution will decline. However, in newly industrializing economies such as that of Thailand, prostitution continues to grow, and has increased dramatically with economic development.[93] In other words, prostitution is not a consequence of industrialization. Instead, with the development of prostitution in industrializing countries today, prostitution is industrialized. Multinational sex-industry conglomerates have become autonomous economic forces.

Typically, a study of prostitution is a study of women: traditionally, the explanation for prostitution, like the customer john or trick, is found upon women's bodies. For generations if not centuries, the causes and consequences of prostitution have rested on women. However, as there would be no prostitution without market demand, there would be no industrialization of sex without commodity consumption. For many state economies in the developing world, those prostitution markets are put into motion and developed into multinational industries by foreign men— soldiers occupying bases and/or waging war, businessmen who sustain sex tourism with or after military prostitution has proliferated, male tourists pursuing sex tourism, and then, as the sex industrialization of women accelerates and the economy develops, the local men.

With military prostitution, sex tourism, and massive increases in local prostitution, the sex industries, multinational conglomerates, stand on their own, producing global markets. The international prostitution market of women's bodies for sex is perpetuated by organized crime, operated through multinational conglomerates that include tourist agencies, hotel chains, airlines, international traffickers. From all of the evidence gathered to analyze prostitution and traffic in women globally, it is evident that as industrialization accelerates, establishing an increasingly advantageous material base, prostitution ultimately is sustained by local men in developing economies.

With these major social transitions—changes in family structure and rural-to-urban female migration—under rapid industrialization, state, community, and family economies become increasingly dependent on prostitution industries both as a source of foreign exchange through sex tourism and as a means of siphoning women off from the developing labor force. States under these circumstances begin to look favorably at legitimization of prostitution. Models from Western, particularly European, countries where prostitution and sex industries have been legalized and sustained, contribute to encouraging legalization. Legalization literally locks women who are in destitute conditions into prostitution.

To speak of the "status of women" under these conditions is to discuss a condition for which there is no material base. For women to have a "status," they must appear as social facts, legal entities of the public as well as the private spheres. Prostitution makes women invisible as an economic, legal class. It is a dumping ground for women between the patriarchal family structure and the industrializing labor force. State legitimization of prostitution (to relieve its labor-force demands and to encourage foreign exchange through tourism) inevitably leads to the consideration of prostitution as a form of work in which women are discriminated against because they are marginalized and denied social security. But the social production of prostitution actually works the other way around: *Women are marginalized and reverted to prostitution* (whether they choose it or not), and that is a violation of human rights. For women as a class to have access to and a claim upon a nondiscriminatory condition, their human rights to dignity must first be assured. Prostitution pre-empts that.

5

Traffic in Women

Trafficking in women is the oldest, most traditional form of procuring for prostitution. It predates sex industrialization and is extensive in primarily rural, poor and pre-industrial societies. Traffickers are traders in human beings who either buy women from husbands, buy children from parents, fraudulently promise them well-paying jobs or lucrative marriages at the other end, or they abduct them. Traffickers take their acquisitions to market via overland routes or, through the more sophisticated crime gangs such as Yakuza in Japan, they transfer women and girls by air to their destination, usually a brothel where acquired women and children are sold as merchandise. Trafficking, as distinguished from sex industrialization, is most aggravated to and from the poorest countries, states that are primarily rural or pre-industrial.

Although trafficking in women is global, within as well as to and from each world region, it is best documented in the Asian region. The massive industrialization of sex in the Asian region, combined with the extensive work of human-rights and women's-rights advocates in exposing trafficking and developing action programs against it, has brought significant numbers of trafficking cases to light. Although widespread trafficking of women can be found in Latin America, in Africa, and to and from North America, Europe, and Australia, according to a regional seminar on criminal law and women in Latin America and the Caribbean, "The subject of prostitution has been scarcely attended to by women's groups in Latin America."[1] Consequently, most women's groups addressing prostitution have been isolated. New Latin American networking of women on prostitution and trafficking has been launched by economist Zoraida Ramirez Rodriquez of Venezuela.

Asian women's organizations distinguish between "sending" countries, from which women are trafficked, and "receiving" countries, into which women are trafficked. This distinction applies directly to trafficking in women, a virtual slave trade. Traffickers who take women from one country to another and sell them to brothels rely on internal sex markets of the receiving country whose brothels cater to local men within the country. In contrast, with sex industrialization women are prostituted within their own country to men who go abroad as customers for sex tourism and military prostitution.

To examine the market exchange of women for prostitution, I begin with trafficking between similarly situated, economically disadvantaged countries, then consider trafficking in relation to countries that have achieved moderate economic development, and finally examine trafficking in relation to the wealthiest countries.

Trafficking from Pakistan to Bangladesh

Bangladesh, on the eastern border of India, was formerly a part of Pakistan, on the western border of India. Bangladesh received its independence through a U.N. peacekeeping effort in 1971. It is among the countries on the Asian subcontinent that are the least developed. It had a 1989 per capita GNP of $180 in comparison to India—$340—or Pakistan—$370—which are both low relative to the GNPs of most developed countries: $20,910 in the United States, $23,810 in Japan. Severely ravaged by frequent floods and cyclones, Bangladesh's population of 115 million is 82% rural. Ninety percent of the country is below the poverty level and 85% of the women are illiterate.[2] Of the women employed in the labor force, 68% are domestic helpers with a mean monthly income of $339.40.[3] However, among the population of housemaids is a large number of girls who have not reached the age of majority (age 18) and who are subjected to sexual abuse.[4]

One estimate places the number of women and children in prostitution in the capital city of Dhaka at 18,000 to 20,000 while another places it at 25,000 to 30,000.[5] Prostitution in Dhaka and other large cities is hidden in brothels or is "floating," with streetwalkers whose rickshaw drivers are the middlemen between them and customers.

Despite the fact that the land mass and national boundaries of India stand between Bangladesh and Pakistan, since Bangladesh's liberation there has been a growing trafficking from Bangladesh to Pakistan. Lawyers for Human Rights estimated that there are about 200,000 Bangladeshi in slavery, bonded labor, marriage, and prostitution in Pakistan. Human rights lawyer Zia Awam estimates that 15,000 to 20,000 Bangladeshi women are in jails in Karachi, Pakistan, having been bought for marriage or left for prostitution after being taken from Bangladesh in the border areas. Between 200 and 400 young women and children are smuggled every month from Bangladesh to Pakistan and India. Depending on market demand for age, beauty, and race, these women are sold for $1,000 to $2,000 to brothels in Pakistan.[6] Sher Khan and Nanney Mian are the brothels most frequently noted in arrest reports in the early 1990s.

The networks of traffickers include Bangladeshi who procure women either by arranging fake marriages or by promising lucrative jobs in Pakistan and India. Short-term marriage is an easily employed strategy in polygamous countries. Professor Shamin from the University of Bangladesh reports a typical incident: a young, divorced woman, Jahanara, married Hossain Ali even through he was not very well known in her village. He had married another villager, Balla, 2 years before and then had disappeared from the village with her and her sister Pachi. When he returned to marry Jahanara, he explained that he had found jobs for Balla and her sister in Bombay. As a divorced woman, Jahanara was worried about her future, as were her parents, so she accepted his proposal for marriage. He convinced her to leave her child behind and go with him to Bombay. Again he returned to the village without his second wife, presumably looking for the next one.[7]

Traffickers require the assistance of border guards who either are part of the ring or are bribed with money and allowed to use the women being trafficked; Indian traffickers who conduct the women by land across India, usually from Calcutta; and guards on the border between India and Pakistan, where the women are turned over to Pakistani agents. From Bangladesh, over-the-border trafficking from Kinaipur, Khulna, Rajshahi, Jessore, and Chittagong has been reported since the 1970s. Land routes go through West Bengal, Bombay, Punjab in India, and Karachi and Hyderbad in Pakistan.[8] From India, Indian women are also trafficked into Pakistan.

It seems that Jessore and Khulna border areas are most susceptible to women trafficking to India by land routes. As it is well connected by bus and train, procurers can easily reach Calcutta where the women are usually sold. For a long time, Calcutta has been well known for prostitution and selling of women and there are well organized agents to take women to Bombay and Pakistan. Comilla is another border area where procuring young girls through marriage is most prevalent. There are men who are being employed outside the country and they in turn come back to their village home to get married. After marriage the wives accompany their husbands to his place of work and since then no trace can be found of these young women. Even the police cannot arrest husbands who are travelling with their legally married wives to other countries. They may come again and remarry. As there is religious sanction for having more than one wife and remarriage, villagers over-look the matter that these men have previously married. Parents who are poor usually agree to such marriage which in turn would bring future prospects to their daughters. Only when several incidents happen, then parents become suspicious and try to discover the truth. But then it is too late to either apprehend the procurer or rescue the women victim-ized. Most of them are sold in India and Pakistan and some to the Middle East.[9]

The Human Rights Council of Pakistan described 1992 as the worst year of human rights violations. The report of the council found that "gross violations of human rights and terrorism in-flicted on the political workers, leaders, lawyers, intellectuals, women and peaceful citizens were at a peak during the last two months of the past year."[10] In 1992 a trafficking ring held 74 people captive on a ferry on the Meghna River about 50 miles from Dhaka. Among them were 15 teenagers—girls who were being taken to Pakistan for prostitution.[11] "In June 1985, Karachi police had arrested a gang of six traffickers who . . . were involved in selling more than 500 young girls and women from Bangladesh, who were forced either into prostitution or to serve as maidser-vants. Similarly, in various police raids, about 100 Bangladeshi young women were arrested and sent to prison in Pakistan."[12]

Most cases are documented by Zia Awan, a Pakistani lawyer and a member of Lawyers for Human Rights and Legal Aid, an agency formed in January 1989 to provide legal assistance to victims deprived of their human rights and without financial sup-port. Awan meets the Bangladeshi women at the end point of the trafficking route—in jail. He has won the release of numbers of women and children who were arrested in police raids on brothels in Pakistan, and from his work emerges a picture of sexual exploi-tation, feudal power in the state, and economic desperation.

In January 1991 Zia Awan defended and achieved acquittal of 16 Bengali women from Bangladesh who had been recovered in a raid on a brothel and arrested under the Zina and Hudood ordi-nances. The traffickers were not arrested. Awan describes the jail conditions that women taken from brothels are subjected to: "It's nothing new to say that rapes are being committed. In fact the prostitution dens are the most frequented by police officials. Although rapes are not committed inside the jails, the girls are taken out to other places for such offenses. The conditions in jails are absolutely abhorrent. No concept of hygiene, no proper food, nothing. They live in a virtual hell."[13]

On April 2, 1991, an early-morning raid on a brothel of Sher Khan (against which there were already 25 cases) resulted in the arrest of a gang of 18 traffickers. In the brothel raid, 49 Bengali women and children from Bangladesh who had been procured on the pretext of being taken to lucrative jobs in Karachi were arrested for prostitution and for violating recent Islamic laws, the Zina and Hudood Ordinances.[14] Police said that the Bangali women would be repatriated to Bangladesh after they served their terms in jail. Two months later, two Indian sisters were arrested in a brothel and released on bail by Awan's human-rights organization, having been booked under the Hudood Ordinance. In August 1991, it was discovered that 15 women and 30 children were smuggled out of India to Pakistan by a woman trafficker.[15]

Trafficking of women within Pakistan follows the route of rural-to-urban migration. Prostitution practiced under the tradition of the dancing girl is the basis of trafficking into Lahore, Pakistan, where, it is reported, young girls are kidnapped. Some of these girls are runaways from the rural countryside and from purdah (veiling) to dancing, possibly to marriage or even to becoming a movie star in the city. Reportedly, there are 1,500 "dancing girls" in Lahore.[16]

When brothels are raided, the trafficked women usually are arrested for charges of being in Pakistan illegally, for violating the Zina Ordinance adopted in the late 1970s in Pakistan, which holds that sexual relations between a woman and a man not legally married is a crime punishable by whipping or imprisonment, and for violating the Hudood Ordinance of 1979, which establishes that the evidence of a woman in court is not permissible in cases that involve maximum sentences such as theft, adultery, rape, or murder.

The Zina Ordinance and the Hudood Ordinance are reversions to feudal state policies that regress women's status from person to property. Because the family and marriage are the bases of feudal power, that which lies outside of the power relations of marriage is virtually lawless and legally irrational, not subjected to objective standards of fairness and human rights. The Zina and Hudood Ordinances reflect the power of Islamic fundamentalism to enforce women's feudal place in the family, the village, and the state. In the case of prostitution, even though they are trafficked, these ordinances make women legally responsible for their victimization. Women not controlled within those feudal structures, particularly by the family, are not only vulnerable to trafficking but are also subjected to laws that punish them for being outside of that feudal, patriarchal control. Nadjma Sadeque, a Pakistani reporter and women's-rights leader, indicates that many Bengali women and girls trafficked from Bangladesh and India into Pakistan who are found in Pakistani brothels and eventually acquitted after raids do not even know what country they are from. Illiteracy and rural village patriarchal feudalism abnegate human identity for many of these women. Pakistan does not want these women when they are arrested and acquitted. And returning to their families from prostitution may well bring a death sentence for having engaged in prostitution. The result: homeless women. Stateless women.

Nepal Is Trafficked into India

Nepal is bordered on the north by the Himalayas of Tibet, China, and on the south by India. Like Bangladesh, Nepal is largely agrarian. With a 1989 population of 19.1 million and a per capita GNP of $180 compared to India's per capita GNP of $340, over 84% of the population of 15 million live in rural areas and 75%

of the women are illiterate. In the lowest category of the United Nations Human Development Index (1992), Nepal is listed at 140 out of 160 nations in the world while India is ranked 121. Nepal is Hindu in religion, and caste systems distinguish social groups. Under such severe conditions, Nepali women have lived under the extreme political repression of an autocratic monarchical regime that was peacefully taken over by a people's movement that in 1993 had restored the multiparty democratic system and was drafting a constitution.

While Nepal, moving toward democracy and industrialization, is beginning to promote economic development through mechanization and imports, trafficking in women remains a problem of enormous magnitude. Tourism has increased in Nepal, where trekking and hiking in the Himalayas have become popular. Tourism is exceeding export commodities as the "single most important foreign exchange earner in Nepal."[17] Meanwhile, women had been losing their place in economic development under the previous regime. Between 1952 and 1971, the rate of employed women decreased from 59.4 to 35.1 in the total labor force[18] while women contributed 81.4% of the household income from home production.[19] It is precisely these conditions, the displacement of women from paid labor along with the rise of tourism, that give rise to sex industries. Sex industrialization has begun; Indian men are going to Nepal for prostitution, and sexual services are being provided to European and American trekkers while en route in Nepal. The first AIDS case reported in Nepal was brought in by a tourist in 1988. While prostitution is illegal in Nepal, it is socially acceptable, and it is estimated that there are 5,000 women in prostitution in Kathmandu. While sex tourism is not yet a large-scale practice, its foundations have been laid.

The massive trafficking of women and children over the open border from Nepal to India is one of the most aggravated conditions of exploitation of women globally. In the late 1980s, official figures from Dr. I. S. Gilada, director of the Indian Health Organization, reported the following:

Bombay — 100,000 prostitutes in a population of 10 million

Calcutta — 100,000 prostitutes in a population of 10.2 million

Delhi — 20,000 prostitutes in a population of 6 million

Pune — 40,000 prostitutes in a population of 6 million

Nagpur — 13,000 prostitutes in a population of 3 million.

By 1993 it was estimated that there are 600,000 women and children in prostitution in Bombay. It is estimated that 15% of India's prostitutes are below the age of 18. Averaging 4 customers per day, they earn an average income is $15 per month. Forty percent of the country's carriers of HIV are in Bombay, with the highest proportion of HIV-positive prostitutes being Nepali.

In 1987 the Child Workers in Nepal estimated that there were 153,000 Nepali prostitutes in India. In 1993 the Nepal National Coordination Committee for the United Nations World Conference on Human Rights gave the estimate of 200,000 Nepalese women from the age of 8 to 25 in brothels in India. Most are from indigenous communities in the Nuwakot and Sindhulpalchowk districts.[20] Racism plays into the trafficking, as Nepali are lighter skinned than Indian women and therefore their sale commands a higher price.[21] An estimated 5,000 to 7,000 young girls are trafficked across Nepal and sold into brothels in India each year.[22] In Bombay alone, 60,000 Nepali women are in brothels. "Entire red light districts in Bombay and Calcutta are virtually all-Nepali, and it is said that wherever there is a brothel in India there are Nepali prostitutes."[23]

While many women are kidnapped for prostitution, a substantial number is procured from carpet factories around Kathmandu, where the labor force is 75% female, with 65% being between the ages of 10 and 14. One report in 1992 gives the story of Sanumaya Chaudhary, age 14, who was procured from a carpet factory. She was told by another girl there that there were higher-paying jobs in carpet factories in Raxaul, across the Indian border:

After three days travelling by bus and train, the girls arrived in "Rax-aul," a large city where they immediately went to the building Sanu's friend said was a carpet factory. As soon as they met the proprietor, Sanu was told to take a bath; when she had finished washing herself, her "friend" had disappeared. She was given a loose-fitting nightgown to wear and the clean dress she had brought with her was taken away.

Sanu was terrified when she realized where she was. Her story is a typical case of trafficking that goes from fraudulent job prom-ise, transfer, to arrival and seasoning. Seasoning, as I found in *Female Sexual Slavery,* "is meant to break its victim's will, reduce her ego, and separate her from her previous life. . . . Seasoning inculcates dependency and indebtedness in the victim. The meals, new clothes, and a place to stay all must be paid for."[24] "Sanu was told she could leave the brothel as soon as she could repay the sum given to her parents," although she had no way of knowing whether her parents were involved (and later investiga-tions revealed that they were not). "After about a week, Sanu grew apathetic and no longer resisted the men who were sent to her." Even Sanu's escape was as classic as the rest of her case. Because she was so young, she was forced to receive 2 to 3 customers a day compared to the average of 15 to 20 for prosti-tutes in Bombay. "By chance, one of Sanu's customers was a 20-year-old Nepali working in a Bombay electronics factory. He visited Sanu several times without sleeping with her, told her he loved her and promised to rescue and marry her." A phone call led to a raid on the brothel and Sanu was turned over to the Children's Aid Society in Bombay. Then she was threatened and harassed by police and gangs for reporting the case to the police. To complete the typical case of trafficking, Sanu married her rescuer.[25]

Procured from a factory where women's and children's labor is inadequate to their own or their families' basic needs, women are offered higher income in another region, usually across a border. Most frequently (although not in the case of Sanu), they are taken there by traffickers. When they find they are not in a factory or legitimate entertainment establishment, they are overcome with fear. Brute force and enslavement prevent them from leaving, and eventually they are seasoned into prostitution, including indebtedness to the establishment and brothel keepers for their meals, clothing, and room or bed.

Economic Disparity: First World and Third World, Husband and Wife

The social and economic relations of power that make women and children vulnerable to traffickers are (1) the economic disparity between the richest states or regions and the poorest, and (2) marriage and the family, which in pre-industrial and feudal society make women property of their husbands as well as wealthy landowners or aristocracy who own the labor of the peasants who work their land. Where there is little or no social place for women outside of feudal marriage arrangements, unmarried women are among the most vulnerable to traffickers.

1. *Global Economic Disparity.* In examining the disparity between Western and Third World countries, and considering the distinction between trafficking and sending to receiving countries, I have turned to a recently developed global measurement, the Human Development Index, so as to establish the trafficking in relation to world resources and world poverty. The United Nations *Human Development Report* of 1992 identifies the economic disparity between north and south, pointing out that between 1960 and 1989, countries with the richest 20% of the world's population increased their share of global GNP from 70.2% to 82.7% whereas the share of countries with the poorest 20% of the world's population fell from 2.3% to 1.4%.[26]

Introduced in 1991, the United Nations Human Development Index measures countries' development in relation to world resources and human needs. Human development is defined as both the formation of human capabilities (through proper health, education, etc.) and the use of human capabilities (in work, in politics, in culture, etc.). The most critical elements of the Human Development Index are the measurements of opportunity (1) to live a long and healthy life, (2) to be educated, and (3) to have access to resources needed for a decent standard of living.[27] Rather than being a purely economic measure such as the GNP, this index measures accomplishments in providing resources that sustain human development and gives positive definition to that which human rights protect, establishing what is required from society and states for people to live in human dignity and to attain equality.

At best, the index is a crude measure (which overgeneralizes and thereby underestimates) for comparing the overall effects of the uneven distribution of resources between industrialized and developing countries. The multidimensional Human Development Index measures countries' achievements of human development and rates them as having low, medium, or high development. In recognition of the fact that there is differential distribution of resources between males and females, a separate index is calculated for each sex.[28]

In considering countries with the heaviest deployment of women into prostitution, I have found that the Human Development Index's distinction between lowest and medium development directly parallels the difference I have identified between trafficking in women in feudal conditions and sex industrialization in economic development (see Table 5.1).

I am differentiating between trafficking and sex industrialization in developing countries. Unlike traffic, industrialized prostitution is located in an economic sector of the industrial economy, separated from the patriarchal, family-based society from which women are trafficked. Sex industries are sectored and capitalized, having business connections to the industrial sector such as the use of major internationally recognized credit cards to buy prostitution services and airlines, hotel chains, and tourist companies

TABLE 5.1

Selected Countries	Rating Scale (160 lowest, 1 highest)	Female Hum. Dev. (1.00 = Full Hum. Dev.)	Index (1.00 = full Hum. Dev.)	Per capita GNP US $ 1989
		Trafficking		
Low Development				
Nepal	140		.168	180
Bangladesh	135		.185	180
Pakistan	120		.305	370
Mynamar (Burma)	111	.210	.385	200
Viet Nam	102		.464	220
Indonesia	98		.491	350
		Trafficking		
Medium Development				
China	79	.396	.612	350
Sri Lanka	76		.651	430
		Sex Industrialization		
Medium Development				
Philippines	80		.600	710
Thailand	69		.685	1220
High Development				
Taiwan				
Singapore	40	.557	.848	
Korea, Rep.	34	.548	.871	4400
Hong Kong	24	.635	.913	10350
		Normalization (Receiving Countries)		
Netherlands	9	.835	.968	15,920
Australia	7	.879	.976	14,360
United States	6	.842	.976	20,910
Japan	2	.743	.981	23,810

that participate in sex tourism packaging. Sex industries flourish in the developing world alongside mainstream industrialization, profiting from accelerated economic development and marginalizing millions of women from the mainstream development process in prostitution.

Prostitution in the countries rated lowest in human development have the highest incidence of traditional trafficking in women. Women are trafficked from Bangladesh via India, from Burma via Bangladesh and India, from Sri Lanka to Pakistan, and from Burma, Vietnam, and China to Thailand (the receiving country.) Trafficking from low-development countries involves procuring, which targets the most vulnerable women, those who are migrating over national borders (usually to the adjacent country) for mere survival. Trafficking focuses particularly on indigenous and aboriginal women who are from remote tribal communities where traditional family and religious practices either devalue girl children or reduce girls to sex service, which enables and encourages parents to sell their daughters.

2. *Family Feudalism and Rural Prostitution*. The poorest poor in every country are women. Trafficking impacts most severely on women and girls in the poorest countries and regions of the world, states that are the lowest in human development.

Trafficking exploits the feudal power relations in marriage and the family. A kind of petty commerce prevails where women and girls are transferred from being the property of their husbands and the land-owning feudal aristocracy to being sexual commodities in brothels. Trafficking involves moving women from one location to another: from a family to a brothel, from a rural village to an urban center, from a less developed to a more developed country. In addition to the fraudulent schemes and brute force engaged in trafficking women, traffickers rely on the change from rural to urban, from one country to another, to keep the women from escaping or knowing how to return to their country and village of origin.

Familial ownership of women and children is *marital feudalism*,[29] a condition of feudalism that in developing countries is combined with state feudalism, wherein landowners or aristocracy control the labor and lives of peasants in the way that husbands own and control wives in feudalistic marriage. Marital feudalism persists in the absence of or after the disappearance of state feudalism, as is the case in many developing economies where industrialization has produced a distinct economic sector in urban areas but feudalism persists in rural areas and in marriage. Traffickers are most prevalent in, although not confined to, the least-developed, poorest countries in the world, where feudal relations of power define both the family and the state or the region.

Feudal power in marriage and in the state makes women and girls vulnerable to (1) disguised trafficking by fraudulent marriage and employment agencies, (2) preprostitution trafficking for domestic services, either to more economically developed regions or to wealthy households in poor countries, and (3) local prostitution resulting from the exploitation of traditional cultural or religious practices that devalue women and girls.

Rural prostitution is sometimes the fate of women outside of feudal family arrangements; under marital feudalism single women who are divorced, widowed, abandoned, or unmarried are particularly vulnerable to rural prostitution. Unmarried women are the "vagabonds" of marital feudalism, for the systems of feudalism are family based and do not socially recognize or even paternalistically protect those not confined within that system of power.

In rural areas of Bangladesh, some women not under the control of a husband are taken as prostitutes by land-owning aristocracy or tribal chiefs. Prostitution in rural Bangladesh is not accepted or tolerated, but it is understood to be necessarily imposed where "there is no viable means of livelihood for women who are single, deserted, divorced or widowed."[30] Rural prostitution, loosely structured and relatively unsystematized, involves women who may accept it as inevitable or natural or even as their responsibility to contribute to the economic welfare of the village.

In rural India, village prostitution coexists with the patriarchal family in a manner developed from earlier cultures. As a village elder of the indigenous tribe of Nats in Kuku Ka Bas, India, explained, "Our females used to entertain the princes and kings. During the early period, one girl in every family was kept in reserve to entertain princes by dancing. The other females could get married." As in Korea, where "Kisaeng" originally referred to singers and dancers, in India and many underdeveloped regions and traditional cultures based on musical entertainment, old forms of entertainment have given way to prostitution. With global sexualization of women, entertainment of men is becoming synonymous with prostitution. As feudal landowners dispossessed the Nats of their land, prostitution of wives and daughters by the feudal family head became the village's major source of income. "We try to send girls to Bombay or Calcutta to be prostitutes. There the money is more. We have a little income from agriculture, some milk, cattle and we have this prostitution," said the village elder, who was lounging with other men while the women did the work and the prostitution of the village.[31]

The Badini, the lowest caste in Nepal, have traditionally supported themselves through singing and dancing for lords and landowners. Now the girls and women bring in income primarily through prostitution. From this kind of prostitution of indigenous people, based on ancient patriarchal customs, economic development accelerates. With the advent of tourism, these customs are being packaged and sold as part of sex-tourism industrialization.

Temple dedications also give rise to commercialized prostitution. According to a report on human rights in the Himalayas:

In Western Nepal, especially in Melouli village where a holy temple is situated, parents give their young daughters, or girls that they purchase, to the goddess Bhagwati or to a family god to seek a blessing. After the child is devoted to the god, she lives with her parents, but she does not have means to support herself after she is grown up. Anyone marrying her is considered a social outcast since she is perceived as the property of the god. . . . Since the girl is never offered any job, she is forced to work as a temple prostitute.[32]

These traditional practices are banned by the government, but they continue. One study of rural temple prostitution indicated that, as in rural prostitution in Bangladesh, the women are servicing fewer customers than in urban areas, an average of 10 per month.[33]

Globally, religion provides an ideological infrastructure for marital feudalism and its concomitant prostitution. Social validation of prostitution reaches from feudalism into its sustaining ideologies, particularly religions. In India, Devadasi is a religious system of temple prostitution; "Devadasi" means offering and dedicating girls to the goddess or the god. From the dedication they are auctioned and prostituted. Devadasi "account for an average of 15 percent of the prostitution in India, and up to 80 percent of those living in the southern regions of the country."[34] It is practiced mainly among the untouchable castes.

As Gilada and Thakur point out, "Myth and traditions are often the superstructure of the will of the feudal class." While the poverty of rural families and of dedicated girls, who cannot marry, are typical explanations of prostitution, as explanations they avoid identifying the base of power, and therefore the proposed solutions are invariably inadequate. Devadasi prostitution, an ancient custom practiced among the most oppressed classes in India, is sustained by the feudal power of landowners and lords over peasants. Historically, control of the land has been secured by landowners through their connections with local priests who use religion to control the peasant class. This control includes turning peasant girls and women over to the control of their purchasers to prevent peasant revolts.[35]

Asha Ramesh and Philomena H. P. describe the ceremony of the girl, who may have been promised before birth and is dedicated before puberty:

On the appointed day, the other "Devadasis" in the Harijan colony gather in the girl's house. The girl anoints herself with oil and bathes with water drawn from the "Jogula" Bavi (Jogiti's well) if it is in the dedication centre (to which she is supposed to walk almost naked, covered scantily by neem leaves, according to tradition). She then serves food to all the other women in their begging bowls.

Decked up in new clothes, she is taken in a procession to the temple. After the priest conducts the worship of the goddess (on payments of certain fees), he gives the arati to her and blesses the "tali" or mangal sutra which he may or may not tie round her neck. All the other women then throw "akshata" (rice) at her, like any other Hindu marriage. The bridegroom's place in all the ceremonies is taken by a sword.

Once she is dedicated, the girl is barred from marrying.[36] "As the girls are dedicated to the goddess during their childhood, they are taken back home after the ritual of the dedication ceremony. A sale-auction is arranged, when the girl attains puberty. The highest bidder present at the auction gets the first chance to touch the girl and he becomes her first master. This ceremony is named the 'Touching Ceremony.' "[37] From there the woman is taken, usually to Bombay, for prostitution. "Devadasis working in Bombay brothels come to the village and lure women away promising riches."[38] The 1982 Karnataka Devadasi Act prohibits dedication of a woman as a Devadasi, but apparently the act has had little impact on the practice. In the late 1980s the Indian Health Organization, under the direction of Dr. Gilada, reported that about 1,000 girls continued to be dedicated every year.[39]

In Thailand, religious ideology and patriarchal feudalism reduce the value of women's lives to that of sexual and economic property, which in turn validates prostitution. Buddhism, according to Thanh-Dam Truong, considers female sexuality as a corrupting force. "Rather than defining sex as sin, sex is tied to the natural world, the world of suffering and ignorance. As a form of bodily craving, sex is a source of attachment to the phenomenal world, and therefore is opposed to the basic principle of non-self and detachment. The activation of sexual desire is considered to be caused by women, and sexual relations are considered incompatible with religious attainments."[40]

Prostitution is considered the result of imperfect karma. But given that karma can be improved, "Women can neutralize the consequences of their offenses through merit making"[41] and thereby with improvement of karma they can be reborn into a higher social status.

In so far as they contribute well to their families, improve their homes and communities, support their religious institution and remain grateful to their parents and respect their elders, their profession is justified. The end counts more than the means, according to the Thai pragmatism cum Buddhism. The prostitutes themselves feel atoned after their sacrifices for the good of their families. They are willing to suffer the consequences by themselves. Each evening, before "work" they normally pray to Lord Buddha and the goddess of fortune to bless them with many rich clients. In return, they would promise to offer the idols the best food and flowers.[42]

In Nepal some parents sell their children to brothels, and some "make periodic visits to Bombay to collect their daughters' earnings. This is particularly common among the poor, indigenous communities of Nuwakot and Sindhu Palchowk to the west and northwest of Kathmandu." Dr. Aruna Upreti, who is working on AIDS prevention in these areas, indicated that "in some places we found there were no young girls at all in the villages. In Nuwakot we found that the girls who came back from Bombay brought a lot of money and gold back. One father was proudly talking about the 3 *tolas* of gold and Rs. 15,000 that his daughter brought back to the village."[43]

When women escape or otherwise manage to get out of brothels and return to Nepal, many of them are welcomed back if they have brought considerable money with them from their prostitution, which also makes them marriageable. Not all return that way, however; the Asian Women's Human Rights Council (Manila) reports that "almost 22% of Nepali who were returned from the brothels of Bombay were found infected with AIDS." Furthermore, according to Laxmi Maskey, then under secretary in the Ministry of Labour and Social Welfare, "in the Nepalese context the society does not accept them if they return through the police. Realising this problem, only five years ago a women's welfare centre was established as a transit house under the Ministry of Labour and Social Welfare for such women."[44]

The practice of selling daughters into prostitution and being supported off their earnings is typically attributed to the "backwardness" or ignorance of rural and indigenous peoples. Aside from the class prejudice of such attributions, such thinking obfuscates the power relations of marital feudalism that structure the family, the village, and sometimes the state, supported and sometimes promoted by religious beliefs. It is not ignorance, backwardness, or any other negative characteristic ascribed to rural people that leads them to accept particular belief systems that support trafficking of women and girls from their villages. Rather it is the power relations of marital feudalism that governs the family and of the feudal aristocracy that controls the land that produce the conditions that lead to devaluing girls and selling daughters. It is precisely because the husbands and land-owning aristocracy gain economic advantage from trafficking that they participate in it. The social acceptance of prostitution is an extension of marital and state feudalism, which considers females as property owned by husbands and landowners, who in many traditional societies have the right of the first sex on the wedding night of their peasants. Wives and daughters are property of both landowners and husbands. That they are sold and trafficked into prostitution is an extension of the original, patriarchal ownership of women in marriage. Marital feudalism persists into developing and developed economies long after state feudalism has passed.

From Marital Feudalism to Economic Development: From Trafficked to Industrialized Sex

Trafficking and sex industrialization are not exclusive categories. The distinction I am making here between sex industrialization and trafficked prostitution is based not only on the way women are procured for prostitution but also on the social conditions of feudalism or industrialization that characterize the lives of women when they are procured and prostituted. But the distinction between feudal or preindustrial and industrial does not evenly separate women from least developed and more advanced developing countries. There is some sex industrialization in some of the least developed countries, such as India, and there is some trafficking that persists in heavily sex-industrialized countries, such as the Philippines and Thailand. Taiwan, with its dramatically expanded economic base, is an example of a country that has passed from trafficking as the main prostitution strategy to sex industrialization as an established fact. And women are trafficked from developing countries to the most developed, already-sex-industrialized countries: Japan, Germany, the Netherlands, the United States.

There are 3 patterns to trafficking between states with developing economic bases (see table 5.1, p.177):

1. Countries with medium and high human development, such as Thailand, the Philippines, Taiwan, and Korea, where prostitution is industrialized, are simultaneously "receiving" countries from traffickers bringing women in from the poorest countries in the region: Vietnam, China, Indonesia, and Burma.

2. In addition, trafficking of the poorest and most vulnerable women who are in the migrating process persists *within* developing countries that have, overall, achieved moderate human development and an accelerated economic development.

3. In yet another pattern, women and girls from industrializing or medium-level developing countries are trafficked to post-industrial or high-development countries: as domestics—which often precedes prostitution—in the Gulf, as entertainers trafficked to the United States and Europe, and through the organized crime syndicate Yakuza to Japan.

The gendering of economic development that sustains patriarchal power over women is evident in the escalation of prostitution as a location for the sexual and economic exploitation of women, while for men who begin to achieve some new economic gains from recent industrial and economic growth, prostitution is a leisure-time, recreational product. Men's expenditures on prostitution often represent money they have taken away from household economies and therefore from the development of women and children. In medium-development countries, massively deployed prostitution sustains the economic marginalization of women from the industrializing labor force—the function it continues to serve in the labor force of developed countries.

Burma, China, and Vietnam to Thailand. Thailand has a Human Development Index rating of 69 out of 160 countries and a per capita GNP of $1,220. It has a rapidly industrializing economy that shows signs of stabilizing prostitution as a patriarchal economic sector for women. In recent years women are being trafficked from the least developed countries—China, Vietnam, Laos, and Burma—to the sex markets in Thailand. At the "receiving" end, in Thailand, women are trafficked into individually run brothels and sex-industry outlets. Women are trafficked via overland routes from China, especially Yunnan Province, through Burma, and from Burma into Thailand. A new road from Thailand through Burma to southern China is expected to accelerate the trafficking.

Burma, now Mynamar, has been controlled by a ruthless military dictatorship for 30 years and has endured 45 years of civil war. As of 1993, the country was still riddled with human-rights abuses. As a result of the long-term civil war in Burma, there are an estimated 70,000 refugees in camps along the Thai-Burma border and 100,000 Burmese working in Thailand. Often when they are deported by Thailand, they are dumped in these camps. In January 1992,

The "deportees" were dumped two hours' walk from a refugee camp, where they arrived after dark. Some of the women were from Nepal, Laos, Shan State and many other places that were impossible for them to reach. Many had absolutely no funds. They were met by many agents offering to take them to Bangkok for work. Even some of the men deported along with the women tried to sell them to the agents in order to get enough money to make their own way to Bangkok.[45]

Burmese women in the migrating process, women fleeing from the military regime there, are vulnerable to traffickers who supply women and girls to brothels in Thailand. Terre des Femmes estimates that 40,000 Burmese women and children, mostly from minority tribe groups, were working in the Thai sex industry in 1992.[46] In 1991, Antislavery International reported to the United Nations that 1,500 Burmese women and girls were forced to work in prostitution in Ranong, a fishing port turned tourist center on the west coast of Thailand opposite the southern tip of Burma.[47] Most Burmese women trafficked to Thailand are taken to Ranong. In June 1992, a police raid on a brothel in Ranong found 33 Burmese women[48] who had been held as prisoners and severely beaten. Of 43 prostitutes from Ranong interviewed in June 1991,

All spoke the official (central Burma) dialect. They came from all over Burma, with one third of the women from Rangoon. They ranged in age from 18 to 37 years of age, with 72.1 percent of the women in their late teens and early twenties. Nearly half of the women (44.2 percent) had no formal education, while 18.6 percent had completed Primary School. About half of the women (48.8 percent) had spent between 6 to 8 months in Ranong at the time of their arrest. None had worked as prostitutes before coming to Thailand. All came from poor families in Burma. 26 percent of the women had not worked outside their own (usually their parents') homes. About a third of the women had previously earned a living selling food or goods in their own or their parents' stalls. Others were domestic helpers or farmers.[49]

Of these 43 Burmese women in prostitution in Ranong, "30 percent of the women were lured into prostitution by people they trusted—7.0 percent were sold by their husband or boyfriend and 23.3 percent by a friend. 65.1 percent were sold by a stranger who in most cased lured the women with promises of high wages as waitresses, maids and food vendors."[50] All of the women were poor, and none had been in prostitution before. In another set of interviews of 10 Burmese girls and women in prostitution in Ranong, in June 1992, it was found that 4 had been enticed by people whom they knew and trusted to cross the border into Thailand for more lucrative work.

Burma has experienced a dramatic increase in AIDS, with 1,076 people testing positive for HIV in 1991. According to an April 1992 report from Project Maje on the AIDS epidemic in Burma,[51] "the traditionally high status of women in Burma, and the lack of flashy nightclubs, discos or massage parlors, has led some foreign visitors to believe that prostitution is nonexistent there. But there are numerous brothels, and street prostitution is more and more common." As opium, a major product of Burma, is refined to heroin, AIDS has also spread through drug use in a country with almost no medical resources.

The report goes on to describe the trafficking, which is conducted in collusion with police and the military:

Gangs bring young victims across to Thai border towns like Chiang Rai, Mae Sai, Kanchanaburi, and Ranong, where they are sold into forced prostitution from USD $100 to USD $560. The slave-prostitutes include ethnic Burmese from the south (some are immigration detainees bought out of Thai jails by brothel owners), and northern ethnic groups like Shans and hill tribespeople. Imprisoned in the dark brothel rooms, speaking no Thai, the prostitutes from Burma have little chance for escape. They are in demand because Thai customers perceive them as "AIDS free," coming from a relatively closed country.[52]

But if the Burmese ethnic minorities trafficked into prostitution in Thailand arrive AIDS free, they do not remain so for very long. Women and children, girls and boys are tortured and turned out to the lowest-level, cheapest prostitution in Thailand. When the HIV testing of prostitutes reveals that they carry the AIDS virus, they are most frequently deported. Many want to return home to die.

In 1992 a scandal broke out over one "deportation" and over some women's attempts to re-enter Burma:

Crime Suppression Division Deputy Commander Bancha Jarujareet told the newspaper that officers last June rescued 25 Burmese women from a brothel in the southern city of Ranong. He said all tested positive for the virus that causes AIDS. Police deported the women to Burma, where Bancha said he has now learned they were injected with cyanide to prevent them from spreading the disease. The official said he was unaware who gave the women the cyanide or whether they had died. . . . Nitiya Thippayanuruksakul, director of Emergency Home, a Bangkok shelter for abused women, said Thai police at the northern border crossing of Mae Sae told her a group of 20 Burmese prostitutes deported last year from the home were murdered by troops of Burma's military regime. "The police told us the girls were injected with something and buried. All 20 of them killed," she told United Press International.[53]

By mid-1993, this report was considered unconfirmed by some U.N. agencies. However, other reports indicate that other Burmese prostitute women and girls deported from Thailand with AIDS have also been murdered, their bodies found at sea.[54]

As the market goes, Chinese women and girls are more valuable to the Thai sex industry than Burmese women. Traffickers earn 5 to 10 times as much for selling a Chinese woman to a brothel.[55] After reaching its heights in the 1930s and 1940s, trafficking in China had been virtually suppressed by the Communist Revolution and halted by 1949. But since 1979 and the development of a free-market economy, trafficking has escalated dramatically in China. However, increased trafficking is not only a function of market changes. Feudal marriage practices, although made illegal by a new marriage law in 1950, have persisted in 80%-rural China. The Marriage Law of 1950 outlawed arranged marriages, polygamy, concubinage, and the practice of paying a price in money or gifts for a wife. By 1990, however, China had recognized that bride buying and the trafficking surrounding it were major problems. Reportedly, 30,000 women and 1,000 children have been sold in recent years, according to an official Beijing radio broadcast.[56] There is an enormous market within China for wives, and traditional (feudal) weddings can cost 10 times a rural peasant's annual income. Men can buy wives for one-fourth to one-half that price. Well-organized nationwide networks of traffickers have developed. A traffic in women from Vietnam, with its higher female population because of war, has begun to China's marriage market. In an effort to control them, China has officially authorized matchmaking services that are licensed and controlled, and thereby is beginning to abandon its attempts to modernize marriage and to establish legal equality in it.

Women are sold as wives, as domestic labor to wealthy families on the coast in China, and as prostitutes in other countries. "The abduction of women is rampant in impoverished villages in Sichuan, Yunnan and other provinces," according to the Chinese paper *Outlook Weekly*.[57] Given that feudal family structure in China has required wives to live with the families of their husbands and has often meant separation from their families of origin, buying trafficked women for marriage is not inconsistent with customary practices. The disappearance of women trafficked into prostitution is merely the next step. Gangs trafficking women into Thailand operate primarily from the Yunnan Province of China, bordered by Burma and Laos, only a short distance from the Thai border. It has been estimated that in 1991 gangs trafficked 5,000 Chinese women to Thailand. From Thailand some are taken on to Malaysia and Singapore.[58]

High-Development Receiving Countries: Domestic Workers to the Gulf. Women in the process of migrating from rural poverty to industrializing cities do not seek prostitution as a way to support themselves. However, many women in the migrating process do seek jobs as domestic servants, either for wealthy families in their own country or abroad. Agencies abound in many Third World countries for placing women and girls in domestic service abroad. Frequently, they are trafficked. The conditions of women domestics are often as exploitative as prostitution, or lead to it.

In the 1970s men from Arab states began to recruit labor from the subcontinent of Asia and from Southeast Asia. Of all Philippine domestic workers abroad 17% are in the Middle East. In addition, 200,000 women from Bangladesh are working in the Gulf states, as are 1.5 million Indians. In 1987 Saudi Arabia had

36% of the Filipino market in domestic laborers, or 9,090. But the largest number of Filipina domestic workers was in Hong Kong, where their numbers increased from 10,000 in 1980 to 89,801 in 1991.[59] By 1992, 48% of the total Filipina domestic workers abroad were in Hong Kong, according to the Asia Migrant Center in the Philippines.[60] A report compiled by the Philippine Embassy in Singapore found that over a 7-month period, from January to July 1990, the following complaints were lodged:

Physical assault, 80 cases; maltreatment, 144; molestation, 20; torture and harassment, 5; accused of stealing, 12; suicide, 6; murder case, 2; non-payment of salary, 66; difficult working conditions, 67; illegal employment, 99; want to go home, 128; employer wants to send worker home against her will, 54; seeking for transfer, 109; waiting for visa, 4; claiming ticket, 2; passport, 2; and prostitution, 1.[61]

Of the women who migrated from the Philippines as export labor in 1989, 300 were expelled from Cyprus when their temporary visas expired. Afraid and unable to return to the Philippines, the women went to Lebanon where there were about 4,000 women working as domestics and entertainers. The women expelled from Cyprus waited for new working papers. There they found jobs in bars and clubs. It was reported that their passports were confiscated by their new employers. "The news stories also state that the Filipino women were rented out for $6 a night to some 30 bars in Beirut."[62] After news of this situation was released, the labor attaché of the Philippines conducted a rescue mission and brought 190 women with 6 children back to the Philippines after finding them in deplorable conditions in Beirut. Aurora DeDios reported the following story of one of the women, as told in a hearing after her return to the Philippines.

Ana relates that her manager was someone she met on a public ride who told her the salary she would get abroad as an entertainer was $350. However, in Cyprus, she was not even given a salary for four months. After 5½ months, her impresario brought her to Lebanon on a guaranteed $350 salary. In actuality she received only $20 a month.

Kuwait is the destination of a large proportion of domestic workers from Asia who emigrate for labor. Indian, Bangladeshi, Pakastani, Filipina, Thai, and Sri Lankan women are all purchased for domestic labor in Kuwait. In 1989 Kuwait rated among the countries that rank the highest in human development, with a per capita GNP of $16,150 and with 860,000 immigrant workers before the Iraq-Kuwait War. In 1991 there were 350,000 domestic servants from Sri Lanka in Kuwait, an estimated 20% of whom had been trafficked.

Because wages for immigrant workers in the Gulf region are determined by the income level of the immigrant's country, a Thai will likely earn 4 to 5 times what a Bangladeshi earns.[63] The exploitation of domestic laborers in Kuwait is so severe that in 1988 the Philippine government banned agencies recruiting domestics for that country.[64] In 1993, 221 women domestic workers in Kuwait took refuge in the Philippine embassy, filing charges that they had been beaten, raped, or denied pay by their employers, who were holding their passports.[65] It was reported that the Kuwaiti government required $1,463 to fly each one home, although the actual airfare to the Philippines was only $592.

Receiving Countries: Immigrants Drive Down the Prices. Having already discussed the sex tourism and commercialization of prostitution in the Philippines and Thailand in the previous chapter, I now turn to trafficking of Thai and Filipino women to Japan.

Japan is a major receiving country of Asian migrant women with over 150,000 in 1993. Over half of these women were Filipinas and the rest were Thai (40%). In 1991, 65.20% (57,038) of Filipina "entertainers" had been trafficked to Japan.[66]

A significant amount of the trafficking in Japan is controlled by one of the major crime syndicates in the world, the Yakuza, which reportedly had 86,553 members in 1989.[67] This crime gang's activities range from prostitution trafficking to drug trafficking and extortion. Having the menacing reputation of the Mafia and

La Cosa Nostra in the United States, the Yakuza, like these gangs, has become more involved in corporate control. According to police estimates, the Yakuza draws over $10 billion per year and may take in as much as $30 billion.

Many of the Filipina and Thai women trafficked into Japan are brought in and sold by the Yakuza. Agents bring the women to Japan, and "on arrival at the Airport, women are handed to brokers, some of whom are Thais, others are Yakuza . . . at the price of Y1.5 to 7 million." Thinking they are going to Japan to be entertainers, they find themselves prostitutes. Some escape. "The number of such Thai women who reach the embassy amounts to as many as 300 to 350 every month." [68]

"Receiving" countries are viewed by migrating women as "lands of opportunity," and sex industrialists as well as those in the market for domestic laborers consider women from "sending" countries, which are lower in economic development, a primary source of cheap labor. In the sex-industrialized states of the West, prostitute women often consider immigrant women in prostitution a threat to their incomes, as cheap new labor on the market drives prices down. In early 1991 Bangkok police formed a crime-suspension division that was quoted as having rescued 534 "sex slaves" from traffickers in 6 months. One of the causes of the increase in trafficking was attributed to "inflation" among the prostitutes, "who will not work for as little as $1.50 a trick." [69]

With immigrant prostitution—women trafficked from the poorest to the world's wealthiest countries—the market and the trafficking are always in flux. The *maisons d'abattage* I saw in Paris in 1978 had disappeared by 1990:

Small prostitution hotels in one part of the North African *quartier* of Paris are known as *maisons d'abattage*. I was warned to stay out of this section of the 18th *arrondissement* of Paris because it is dangerous for women, at any time of day or night. But I did walk through the area. I needed to see the *maisons d'abattage*. It was early evening when another woman and I emerged from the Barbes-Rochecauart Metro station. We were jostled and pushed as we made our way through the crowded shopping section. Once we were on the quiet side streets no other women were to be seen. As we walked through the neighborhood streets of this North African section of Paris, we were suddenly struck by the sight of a crowd of about 300 men in a narrow street ahead. We stopped and gazed, assuming there must have been an automobile accident or a fight. The frantic, jostling crowd of men spanned the full width and half the length of the small street. As we approached the rue de la Charbonniere, just above the crowd of pushing and shoving men we saw a small "Hotel" sign.

We continued down the street and around the corner. We stopped again, stunned to see a small neighborhood police station with a smiling policeman standing in the doorway, while about 20 yards away from him, next door but in the same building, was another "Hotel" sign and another group of men, about 100 North Africans pushing, body-to-body against the gates of the hotel. It was only 6:00 P.M. on Saturday of Easter weekend. The crowds of men were to grow larger as the evening progressed. Although closed prostitution houses are illegal in France, these hotels are not only tolerated but obviously supported by the police.

In each of these *maisons d'abattage* (literal translation: houses of slaughter), six or seven girls each serve 80 to 120 customers a night. On holidays their quota might go up to 150. After each man pays his 30 francs (approximately $6.00) at the door, he is given a towel and ushered into a room. A buzzer sounds after six minutes, and he must leave immediately as another man comes in. The girl never even gets out of bed.

The girls are told that they will get a certain percentage of the money if they meet their quota. From their earnings is deducted the cost of room and meals; after these deductions—with the hotel doing the bookkeeping—the girls always find they are indebted to the house.

In 1990, when I returned to that area in Paris to see the *maisons d'abattage,* I found that the buildings had been converted into apartment complexes. The lowest form of prostitution represented in the *maisons d'abattage* had not only moved, as it frequently does, but it had also changed, and since the 1970s it has become concentrated in one of Paris's most famous parks, the Bois de Boulogne.

In 1992 it was estimated that 85% of the prostitutes in the bois were illegal immigrants. In Paris as a whole there are 6,000 to

7,000 prostitutes, one half of whom are immigrants.[70] In recent years immigrant prostitution in France has been increasingly trafficked from South America, particularly Brazil, Ecuador, Peru, and Colombia, often through agencies that are connected to the milieu or networks of pimps who control prostitution in the bois. Likewise, in Germany it is estimated that 70% of the prostitutes are foreign.

Paris police informally estimate that there are 2,000 women in prostitution just in the few blocks of and surrounding rue St. Denis. These women are known as the "bonne gagneuse." Taking 15 to 20 customers per day at the rate of 200 francs each (about $35 U.S. dollars), they make twice as much as the prostitutes in the Bois de Boulogne who do their work in the bushes and make 100 francs ($17) for each "hand job." Police estimate that 80 to 90% of the prostitutes in Paris are controlled by pimps.

In January 1992, the French government took measures to close the Bois de Boulogne to traffic which effectively cuts off the primary route for customer access in the park, but it also closes a main artery of commuter traffic between Paris and its suburbs. The measures to close the bois, if implemented, may eventually restore the park to Parisians for their leisure just as the hotels, the *maisons d'abattage,* in the 18th *arrondissement* were restored and turned into apartment complexes. The women disappear; most of them reappear elsewhere.

Local prostitution in Paris and in major cities throughout the world is interconnected with the traffic in women. Once women have been trafficked, they are then absorbed into the local prostitution scene as another "colorful" addition. In New York City the movement of prostitution from Manhattan to Queens has involved the shift of immigrant Korean massage parlor business but includes South American women immigrants as well. Reports from 1992 police raids have revealed networks that traffic South American women into Queens.[71] Most illegal immigrants are likely to be put to work for less than Koreans, who had at one time been at the bottom of the market.

The Prostitution Sector: From Trafficking to Sex Industrialization

Trafficking in women relies on the feudal privatization of women in the family, where wife and children are property of the husband. Family feudalism keeps women economically outside of local or developing economies, a marginalization enforced by traditional marriage. Where trafficking is heaviest, most of women's income-generating labor is located either in informal-sector employment or in illegal and unregulated income-generating market transactions, neither of which are recorded in national income accounts. "In India, 89 percent of women workers belong to the informal sector and live and work in sub-human conditions or starvation and squalor. These women workers are most visible as hawkers and vendors; they are mostly providers of urban services, home-based petty manufacturers and traders among others."[72] In urban Bangladesh, the majority of low-income females in slums work as domestic maids.[73] The informal sector is where women go to earn survival income, as vendors, as domestics—it is where women are marginalized from the standard labor force. It is the base for prostitution in that it establishes women's economic marginalization, impoverishment, and vulnerability.

With the development of an urban economy, some women continue to be victims of traffickers, but other women migrating to cities simply find no other economic means of existence than prostitution. They are not trafficked in the traditional sense, nor are they forced through brute coercion. They are simply vulnerable to the only means of economic existence available to them because they are women, and because they are women they are homeless, and poor. Sex industrialization builds its economic base off that human need. Sex industries rely on the industrial sector *not* providing the means for women in the process of migrating to meet their material needs.

With the industrialization of sex, eventually neither traditional customs nor overt coercion is necessary to prostitute large populations of women. The massive industrialization of prostitution relies on a normalization of that commerce in the economic sector. If a developing country has been targeted for military prostitution or sex tourism, or if the economy is relying on foreign exchange and on immigration of its labor force, trafficking in women eventually gives way to a sex-industrial economic sector.

Prostitution may well be among the highest costs women pay for their country's development.

6

Pimping: The Oldest Profession

Across nation-states pimping, "living off the earnings of a prostitute," is illegal. But proprostitution movements in the West now propose to decriminalize pimping so that pimps can be treated as lovers or husbands, not enslavers of prostitute women. But it is a fact of prostitution that once a woman "tricks" for a man, she is never again not his "whore." He thinks of her as such, whether or not he is otherwise known to her as husband, lover, brother, or father.

In all the world regions, estimates from organizations addressing the exploitation of women in prostitution, including some prostitution groups, show that 80% to 95% of all prostitution is pimp controlled. While 53% of the women interviewed by Evelina Giobbe in a study of prostitution were brought to it by a pimp, 90% of the women had pimps while in prostitution.[1] To analyze pimping in prostitution from a feminist perspective, it is necessary to determine whether or not women in prostitution are in situations they can leave. As I found, pimping is a condition of female sexual slavery.

Female sexual slavery is present in ALL situations where women and girls cannot change the immediate conditions of their existence; where regardless of how they got into those conditions they cannot get out; and where they are subject to sexual violence and exploitation.

Some women who willingly try out prostitution do not realize until later that they cannot leave. When they try to leave they learn that they must escape their pimps. In attempting to escape, women face physical brutality and torture. One 16-year-old who was procured in Minneapolis described the "going-away present" her pimp gave her when she tried to leave:

Well, first he put his foot in my face which broke my nose and knocked me out and I got out the door—we lived on the third floor of this building and I couldn't get out the door in time before he caught me and there was just punches in the face and he had long fingernails which scarred up my body pretty much and kicking because I kept falling on the floor from being hit in the head. . . . I finally got out the door and was running out the middle of the street and he was trying to drag me into the place again when the police came.[2]

Female sexual slavery includes not only women in prostitution who are controlled by pimps but wives in marriages who are controlled by husbands and daughters who are incestuously assaulted by fathers. My definition of female sexual slavery breaks away from traditional distinctions between "forced" and "free" prostitution and between wives and whores. When women and/or girls are held *over time, for sexual use,* they are in conditions of slavery. Specifically, female sexual slavery is not an illusive condition; the word "slavery" is not merely rhetorical. Slavery is an objective social condition that requires escape in order for the victim to get out of it. Slavery is one aspect of the violation of women and children in prostitution, in marriage, and in families.

However, prostitution that is not pimp controlled is not slavery. It is another form of sexual exploitation. Sexual exploitation and female sexual slavery are each different aspects or dimensions of the sexual relations of power in the patriarchal oppression of women.

The Pimp-Whore Relationship

According to Melinda, a former San Francisco prostitute,

Once a woman starts hoing [whoring] for a man, there's no way out—unless she runs. Once I started, my man wasn't going to let it stop. He wasn't a flashy pimp. He was a lazy good-for-nothing who leeched off of women!

The first time I came home without enough money and he put his foot in my ass—that's when I realized I was his ho and he was my pimp and that's the way it was going to be. Then the beatings were regular. He'd hit me up side my head with a 2 by 4 or a dog chain. When I was pregnant he'd kick me in the stomach. He put me in a tub and tried to drown me once. . . .

Pimps have two ways of holding on to women. One is verbal abuse, psychological beatings where they make you feel like you are worthless, like you're trash. The other is fear. Beatings are the other way he'll keep her because by having so much fear in her heart she is afraid to leave him. Yet by that time I was so much in love with him it really didn't matter as long as he was there. When he put his arms around me nothing could hurt me. When he told me he loved me I believed everything would work out all right. I'd been alone for so long and he'd told me I'd be with him for the rest of my life.

Melinda recounted some of the "escape" valves she devised to relieve the pressure temporarily. She considered long evening dinners and drinks with her girlfriend before they would start working the streets together to be an "escape," a time when she was away from it all. Prison was also temporary escape. "I got busted left and right. I knew if I'd get convicted that would be one way I could get away from my man for maybe four months. I could get away to regroup my mind to deal with another year." But these escapes were temporary as long as she was emotionally dependent on him.

A prostitute woman may be able to divert her pimp's attention away from her by bringing another woman to him. If she can convince a woman on the streets to "choose" her pimp and if he accepts the woman, she may get some relief from his attention and she may even get an opportunity to leave. But when a woman tries to escape from the life, whether or not there are other women around, she will invariably be hunted down. If she goes to relatives or friends, her pimp knows to look for her there. Once he locates her, he will "sweet talk" her (until he gets her alone) by telling her how much he has missed her, how he had lost his mind the last time he had beat her and could never do that again, and how miserable and lonely life is without her. This line of sweet talk, just like procuring strategies, is the same across cultures.

In San Francisco in 1977, Joey was convicted and sentenced for pimping and pandering. Jessica began dating Joey in January 1975, when she was 19. Soon after she fell in love with him, he began to talk to her about the easy money to be made in prostitution. According to Jessica, he told her that "within a month or two I could get him a car and I could get myself a car and we would travel around the world." He was persistent and convinced her to try prostitution if she really loved him. He instructed her on how to approach customers and set prices. He got her false identification with a new name "so that you can have a life under your real name that won't be soiled."

She did not succeed. When she came home 3 nights in a row without any money, he began to slap her around. For a year and a half the beatings increased. She eventually realized that despite her love for him, her dreams were not going to come true. She decided to leave him, and that was when she realized the extent of her enslavement.

He hunted her down and burst into her aunt's house, breaking down the door. His physical and verbal abuse terrorized her. He left without her but returned 3 days later.

He told me to bring my baby. So I got the baby and stuff. And we got to the freeway going towards Oakland. . . . I went with him because there was no other way out. The back yard was all fenced up and I knew— the door was already pushed open, it couldn't close—I knew if I didn't walk out, he would come and get me. We got on the freeway. He asked me about an incident that happened when I first left him and he accused me of lying to him and he hit me in my nose. It started really bleeding bad. Then he said "I'm going to pull off, take the next exit off and beat your ass until you can't move." And I kept asking him, "What about Michael?" Because Michael [her baby] was right in the back. He was looking at me with the blood on me. He just said, "You're going to get it now." We got off the freeway and he started beating me real bad . . . hitting me with his fists and trying to turn my neck. I lost track of how many times he hit me. I just know he hit me so many times that after a while I was so weak, and then he said "I'm not going to hurt myself hitting you." And so he went to the truck and got the base of a jack and he hit me on the head.

He took her home with him. His other prostitute, her stable sister, seeing the severity of her condition, helped her get out and call the police a few days later. When she got away, the police took her to the hospital, where she found that her skull was fractured.[3]

Do all pimps treat their prostitutes in these ways? The Council for Prostitution Alternatives found that of 55 women in their program in 1990–91, 63% "were horribly beaten by pimps an average of 58 times per year."[4] Many women do not know the full range of a pimp's wrath until they try to leave. Considering pimps' control and violence, it is not surprising that in 1980 Mimi Silbert reported that 41% of the prostitutes she studied found no advantages to being with a pimp and only 4% indicated that they loved their pimp.[5]

Rules of the Pimp

Regardless of their race, and regardless of whether they operate on the street, from a house, or in higher levels of organized gangs, all pimps have a clear rundown on the pimping rules. They see themselves as players running a game. After he retired from the life, notorious pimp Iceberg Slim called this knowledge "whorology." The first rule is, "The best pimps keep a steel lid on their emotions and I was one of the iciest . . . any good pimp is his own best company. His inner life is so rich with cunning and scheming to out-think his whores."[6] This knowledge is learned and passed on from one pimp to the next on the streets and in prisons.

A favored pimp philosophy likens the game to movies: the pimp is the producer and director and he runs everything according to his own will. Iceberg Slim explained the best philosophy he ever heard while in prison: "I picture the human mind as a movie screen. . . . Son, there is no reason except a stupid one for anybody to project on that screen anything that will worry him or dull that vital edge. After all, we were the absolute bosses of the whole theatre and show in our minds. We even write the script."[7]

The movie-set analogy appears in a contract confiscated from a pimp in a Washington, D.C., raid in 1977. The terms of the contract read,

You are reading this because you have passed one of the requirements to become a member of the illustrious family of ———. This life is just like a large scale movie production with me as the producer and you as the star. The world is your audience for the entire universe is your stage. It is also like a large scale business; you are the stockholders. In this business there is a president, director, and a teacher and a treasurer. All of these offices are held by me. In this business, there is no room for confusion. Anyone or anything opposing my will must be and will be destroyed.

Pimps exploit girls' boredom that results from traditional female socialization, which leaves many young girls looking for excitement and glamour in their lives. One pimp wrote about the exploitable vulnerability of many teenage girls:

Here we have a group of "have-nots," plain women who have, as a result of their plainness, lived plain unexciting lives, perpetuating their drab, plain existence, their drab morality on a potentially beautiful girl child. . . . Mothers, teachers, school nurses, aunts, grandmothers, etc. in collusion to put a beautiful girl child in her place. . . .

Most potentially beautiful women arrive at the age of seventeen or eighteen for all intents and purposes a shell . . . like an unfinished house which is potentially a mansion; while the structure may be there, it needs to be finished on the outside . . . a woman who is potentially beautiful must also be finished, inside and out.[8]

Pimps look for and target young girls or women who appear to be naive, lonely, and bitter and rebellious. Such women are often runaways from sexual abuse in their homes or from violent marriages. On the street, they are likely to be broke and without job skills.

The following pimp procuring scenario is typical: Suddenly he appears, he is friendly, he offers to buy her a meal and, later, he gives her a place to spend the night. She hears compliments for the first time in ages, as well as promises that he will buy her new clothes and have her hair done. This romantic-movie scenario is played out. But it may be days, weeks, or even months before she figures out what has happened to her.

In 1989, from the Göteborg Prostitution Group in Sweden, Lena's story reveals how a pimp creates the conditions by which a woman ends up prostituting herself. Lena was incredibly attracted to Thomas, who offered her a job in a pizza parlor. After they had been seeing each other for some weeks he let it be known that "he'd had a girl who was a street hustler and that it wasn't half as bad as it sounded." Thomas knew Lena wanted to make lots of money. Her first reaction was, "I didn't see how anybody could or how they dared." But Thomas kept bringing up the subject of hustling. As it became a familiar topic, she finally said that she "was going to give it a try." He prodded her by saying that she would never do it. "Then I started thinking more and more about it." And finally she decided to go to the streets. She did not get any customers the first time but "I promised him I'd be brave enough to go down there again." "I was kind of shocked that I dared to do it," she added, but Thomas reassured her.

Thomas's romantic spell over Lena and his seductive coaxing were broken the first time Lena encountered the Prostitution Group. Even though Lena initially rejected their representation of Thomas as a pimp, after she talked with the women from the Prostitution Group, "Thomas and I started fighting more and more." That was the beginning of the end of prostitution for her.

Usually the pimp's approach fulfills all the star-studded romantic images that popular magazines, television, and movies have promoted. When Officer Mary Christenson went undercover for the San Francisco Police Department to arrest pimps for pandering, some of the opening lines she heard were, "You are going to be my star lady," or "I'm going to make you my foxy lady" or "my sportin' lady," or, as one pimp put it, "you are going to be my hope-to-die woman . . . 'cause that's how long we going to be together." [9]

After his initial come-on, a pimp follows the strategy that most likely will win her over. If the girl he is procuring appears to be rebellious and daring, he can come right out with his proposal, offering her a challenge. Mary, who looked street wise, apparently seemed easily available to one pimp:

PIMP: I'm a businessman. We could be partners. You've got nice cord pants on, but you look like you should be wearing satin. I can take you to the hairdresser and buy you some nice clothes.
MARY: What is my role in this?
PIMP: Well, you'll be my woman. I'll turn you out on the street. Give you some schooling. If you are my partner you'll have your pockets filled with money and you'll fill my pockets too.

Lots of money, new cars, travel, the best clothes, flash, and glamour are the promises. Another pimp started off by explaining that he would take care of business, be her protector, stay with her forever, and that tricking would only be necessary until he got a big settlement from an insurance company on an accident. This, according to vice officers, is a frequent procuring line used by street pimps, who often represent themselves as about to come into some big money. Ultimately the appeal is to glamour:

PIMP: I'm going to be sure that you have your clothes, everything else
you're suppose to have.
MARY: Like what?
PIMP: Anything that you want, anything. No limit to what you'll have,
things of that nature. . . . Do you understand me? Seeing my lady
getting it together and saying you understand me. . . . You're supposed to have the best. I like to see my lady with the best on. I like
every mother-fucking body around to look at my lady.

For many girls it is attention and apparent affection that wins
them over. In 1977, a young woman testifying to a crime committee in New York State reported being picked up at a bus stop in
Minneapolis and eventually put in prostitution in New York City.
She stated,

At the time I did it because I really liked him and it was more or less
having someone, you know, and he said, you know, to prove to him that
I really love him I had to do this because we needed the money. It was
things he said, but I did it because I liked him. He made you feel like you
were somebody important.[10]

When a pimp hits on a woman or teenager who is resistant,
"prudish," or scared, he usually does not introduce prostitution
immediately. He'll just be a nice guy who buys her a meal and
offers her a place to stay. Then he makes his play for her as a
lover. When a sexual relationship between them is established and
he is sure she loves him, his next move is to set her up to prostitute
herself as a condition of her love for him, with lines like, "If you
love me, you'll do anything for me." To prove her love she must
have sex for money with someone she does not know. If she
resists or refuses, he will likely pout, create a scene, and insist that
she does not truly love him. To restore his affection, she finally
agrees to do what he asks, telling herself that "one time won't
hurt," or "what does it matter." This rationale, used by women
faced with unwanted sex from husbands, fathers, lovers, and
rapists alike, is an entry into prostitution too. When she concedes
to it, he has her hooked. When she turns one trick, he starts

pimping her. He gives her nightly quotas, takes the money she earns, and begins to treat her as the slut he intends to make her think she is. He tells her, "You are nothing but a goddamn whore," and makes her believe that only out of the goodness of his heart will he have anything to do with such a despicable creature. She knows that is what society thinks of her. She knows she is a criminal. And most likely, she has nowhere else to turn.

Seasoning

The Council for Prostitution Alternatives in Portland, Oregon, reported that almost half of the 234 women who sought help from them in 1990 reported being raped by pimps on an average of 16 times per year.[11] Likewise, 49% of the women had been kidnapped by pimps. Rape, kidnapping, and other forms of physical abuse and torture are often systematically practiced as forms of control over women in prostitution.

Typical of what continues in the 1990s is the story of Blood Stewart, who in 1976 picked up 14-year-old Jennifer in the vicinity of Penn Station in New York City. She had run away from her parents' Long Island home and was confused, bewildered, and alone in the big city. Blood befriended her until he got her to his room. There he beat, raped, and tortured her for 3 days. Journalist Mark Schorr unraveled the details of this case: Blood Stewart presented himself as Ralph Moss and listened to her sad story.

She decided to trust him, so she told him her real name and age. Then she showed him the letter she was sending her father. "I know you tried stuff with her (Jennifer's girlfriend) . . . and she told me where you touched her." Still, the note was apologetic: "Daddy I'm really sorry. I feel like dying for what I've done to you." Ralph Moss offered to help. He would act as a go-between, speak to Jennifer's father man to man, and straighten out the problem. Jennifer could sleep over in his hotel room that night, and the next day they'd return to Long Island to work things out.[12]

When she entered the hotel with Stewart, the young girl had no idea what was ahead of her.

To demonstrate his absolute power and reduce Jennifer's defenses, Blood stripped her naked, then raped her, police say. They maintain that he terrorized her with his big "007" gravity-blade knife and told her, "If you don't do what I tell you, I'll use this on you."[13]

He then informed her that she was going to work the streets for him. After 3 days of abuse he sent her out to work in front of the New York Hilton. She hurried inside and hid in the women's restroom in the lobby. When she finally got the courage to come out, she spotted a security guard and ran to him asking for help. In a back office she poured out her story; the police were called and ultimately Stewart was arrested. What Jennifer experienced after being procured was a seasoning that was meant to break her will and distort her perceptions so that she would not know where to turn or how to get away. Jennifer escaped before she was broken.

Seasoning is meant to break its victim's will, reduce her ego, and separate her from her previous life. All procuring strategies include some form of seasoning. Often the extent or form of it is determined by the resistance of the woman or girl; sometimes it is a measure of the sadism of her procurer. Seasoning inculcates dependency and indebtedness in the victim. The meals, new clothes, and a place to stay all must be paid for. What appears at first to be freely given is later tallied up to be paid back, whether it is an act of affection, a meal, or some seemingly mutual sex. The pimp intends for affection and lovemaking to hook a woman, to make her emotionally and psychologically dependent, while she, on the other hand, is likely to be thinking in terms of a mutually developing relationship.

At the same time that *Female Sexual Slavery* was originally published, in 1979, Linda Marciano revealed her story as Linda Lovelace in *Ordeal*.[14] Linda's story was prototypical of that of all victims of pimps' love strategies. She was seduced by a man whom she did not know was a pimp. She began to live with him. He ran a bar with after-hours nude sex shows and prostitution. When she discovered the nature of his operation, she then tried to leave him, but the next day she found herself delivered to 5 businessmen in a hotel room:

"You're going to fuck all five of them."

"Chuck, don't talk crazy."

"Oh, you're gonna fucking do it all right," Chuck said. "Believe me, you're gonna do it. I've *promised* these men. I've given my word. You tell me you don't want to run my business. I give you every chance in the world and you tell me no. Okay. You don't want to run it, then you can be part of it."

"No, Chuck." He smiled at that. "I mean it, Chuck, I'm not doing anything with anyone."

"You got no fucking choice," he said. "I already got their money. And that's something I want you to remember. The first thing you do is get their money. I've taken care of that for you this time, but in the future you'll have to be responsible for that. Now strip off you clothes."

"I'm not taking off my clothes."

I tried to sound strong but that wasn't the way I was feeling. I suddenly realized that Chuck was crazy, really insane, that he actually expected me to take off my clothes and go out there to have sex with five strangers. When he took his hand out of his trouser pocket, he was holding his pistol and pointing it at me. It was the first time anyone ever pointed a gun at me but it wouldn't be the last time.

"I'm going to shoot you right now," he said. "Unless you get out there and do what I'm telling you." [15]

When Chuck Traynor turned Linda over to pornographers, she became the symbol of the sexual revolution for sexual liberals— Linda Lovelace. Many times, Linda desperately but unsuccessfully planned her escape. Eventually she did escape and finally in 1980 told her own story.

Procurers who employ the strategies of befriending or love and romance use both tactics together. They may begin by befriending a forlorn runaway and then calculate a romantic connection. The strategy of befriending and love is designed to fit the vulnerabilities of its potential victim. A procurer's goal is to find naive, needy teenage girls or young women, con them into dependency, season them to fear and submission, and turn them out into prostitution.

In breaking down their victims, some procurers rely only on the dependency that results from taking their acquisition so far away from home that she cannot return without money for transportation. The language barrier that a victim of international traffic faces will make it difficult for her to fend for herself in a new country. Harsher methods may involve beating, raping, sodomizing, drugging, and starving a woman before turning her out on the streets or over to a brothel. Seasoning does not always precede prostitution. It is as effective in forcing some women to remain in prostitution as it is in putting others into it.

A critical early step in seasoning a girl is changing her identity. She is given a new name and any necessary papers, such as a false driver's license, social security card, and birth certificate, so that the police will not be able to trace her real identity or determine her true age. But a new identity has an even more important function than providing cover from the police. It separates the woman from her past and focuses her totally on the moment in time when she belongs to this man. According to anthropologists Christina and Richard Milner, "A pimp wants his woman's mind more than her body. It is love, loyalty, and obedience he requires as well as a capacity for self-discipline." [16]

In their field research on pimps, the Milners found out that "turning out a square broad means that you must literally change her mind." [17] (And it appears that Richard Milner did not question the ethical limits of research. He reports that when he was posing as a pimp for purposes of his research, he was required to recommend a particular pimp to a new girl the pimp was trying to procure. Even though Milner probably knew from his research what the girl's fate would be, he provided the recommendation anyway.) Steve, a pimp, discussed with the Milners why a new prostitute's mind must be changed:

She must cut all family ties, because, you see, she can't be with her family and ho [whore] too. You can't cope with bringing disgrace upon your mother or father, your sister, or whoever it is. You have to get away from them. There's nothing I could do with you over there because they're telling you one thing and I'm telling you something else.[18]

Brock, another pimp, put it to the Milners this way:

You create a different environment. It's a brainwashing process; the whole thing is creativity. When you turn a chick out, you take away every set of values and morality she had previously and create a different environment. You give her different friends.[19]

Seasoning, among other things, creates perfect obedience in the newly procured woman. The pimp must have complete authority. One pimp who tried to procure undercover officer Mary Christenson promised her that when she went to work for him, "I am not going to beat on you. . . . I don't want no tricks to beat you up." She responded, "You won't beat me?" "I ain't that stupid," he replied, "long as you obey, understand me, and act like a lady, then I don't think we should ever have any misunderstanding, okay? Just do like I say, 'cause I'm not going to tell you to do nothing wrong." Another pimp described how he would protect her out on the street: "The only thing is, you can't make me mad at you. I don't want you hiding out any of the money you make. You give it all to me and I take care of you."

The romanticized role of pimp as protector stands in sharp contrast to the actual methods and behavior of procurers. Convincing his women and society at large that he is the prostitute's protector is just another one of the pimp's con games. Pimps do not protect prostitutes from violent customers. Often they are hanging out down the street in the local pimp bar when their woman faces a sadistic trick in a room by herself. Sometimes pimps, particularly those who run houses or massage parlors, will set their women up with a violent trick to teach her a lesson if she isn't working hard enough.

Nor do pimps automatically respond when their prostitutes get arrested. Depending on his mood and circumstances, a pimp may choose to leave his woman in jail, ignoring her call to be bailed out, or he may get her out immediately if he wants her back on the street working. All the promises made in the first meeting—glamour, travel, money, affection, protection, even child care if she is on her own with a small child—turn out to be means of enslavement. A certain glamour is necessary for the pimp's display of his new acquisition to other pimps and for her work in hooking customers. But as for travel, she soon finds out that she finances it with her work and that when she and her pimp go to to another city, state, or country, she will continue to work long hours to meet her daily quotas.

Prostitution is not the economic alternative for women that many have believed it to be. The money a woman makes is usually not her own. The pimp takes most or all of it. He tells her where to work, how many hours a day, and what quota she must make before coming home. If he is angry at her or just wants to instill some obedience, he will threaten to "pimp her hard," that is, raise her hours and quota. Often a pimp will make arrangements for his woman to leave the money she makes in a convenient place when she comes in at night; he will pick it up the next day. This technicality is meant to protect him from prosecution: since he doesn't take money directly from her, he can't be charged, he hopes, with living off the earnings of a prostitute.

Even the child care he promises to provide for the young mother is part of his strategy. Almost always when a prostitute with a child is taken in by a pimp, she will ultimately find her child used as a weapon against her. By offering to take care of the child, to take the child to the babysitter or to school, to pro-vide for his or her well-being while the mother works, a pimp gains physical control of the child. If a woman wants to leave her pimp, she may find her child held as hostage, forcing her back to work.

When the pimp controls his woman's body and soul, then she is set up to bring other women to him. One pimp told Mary

Christenson, "You get them for like, you know, sisters, you know, understand what I'm saying. Just get 'em to come and help you and the more, you understand, more that you get, the more sisters that you can get, honey, the better it is for you. They'll help you and by you being my main lady, you see, you don't have that to worry about, see, 'cause they ain't going to never be able to take your place, you understand me? You bring 'em home, I'll do the rest." And the cycle of loving her, seasoning her, and pimping her starts all over again.

Police Brutality

The last resort for escape is to go to the police. But this is hardly an option for women who know they are legally and morally condemned by those from whom they would seek help. Indeed, police brutality of prostitutes is periodically reported by women working the streets.

One night in March 1977 when Mary was working the streets to get enough money to pay her rent, she was solicited by an undercover police officer. When he identified himself as the police, she didn't believe him. A rapist had been working the area and the prostitutes were quite anxious about who his next victim would be. She thought he was a trick who was going to take her someplace and beat her. Mary resisted arrest. When she tried to get out of the car, she was severely beaten. A nearby taxi driver noticing a man beating a woman, rushed to intervene, whereupon a backup police officer arrived and beat the taxi driver. Mary was taken to a police department's holding tank, a room in a downtown hotel where each night police held prostitutes as they were arrested until there were enough to call for a paddy wagon to pick them up and take them to the police station.

Another prostitute was already in the holding tank when the officers arrived with Mary. She witnessed and later testified to the beating that Mary received in the hotel's lower chambers.

According to Mary and the witness, Mary was beaten to unconsciousness. The officers claimed that in the room at the hotel holding tank, Mary had tried to kick them and her injuries had occurred when they had tried to restrain her and had all fallen to the floor. I first met Mary when she left the hospital a few days later. Her face was swollen and puffy, and both of her eyes were blackened; a bone behind her eye had been fractured, and part of her cheekbone was crushed. She was still dazed and bruised from the beating. She had had surgery while in jail. As we talked she kept saying, "Why did they beat me so badly? Why did they have to mess up my face?"

The only thing unusual about this case is that it went to court. At the time, Margo St. James, head of COYOTE, had been organizing to expose the police brutality of prostitute women, and in this case she personally befriended the victim, bringing her clean clothes in jail and giving her support. As a result of agitation raised by her organization and some women's groups, the police officers who beat Mary were suspended and formally charged with assault. In court the defense's winning strategy was the fabrication of a prostitute conspiracy theory; the defense alleged that Mary and the other prostitute, along with COYOTE, the prostitute organization, were out to dishonor and discredit the police department. In addition, like so many victims who try to help their case by making the story more believable, Mary testified that she had been hit by a police officer at the hotel holding tank when it had already been established in court that she had been unconscious when the officer hit her. An acquittal of the officer followed.

I talked to Mary again after the trial and tried to encourage her to continue with her plans to get her high school equivalency diploma and enter a vocational training program. But she was bitter—not at the police, but because, as she saw it, she had been suckered into trying to get justice through the courts. As a victim of incest from her stepfather and, later, of battery from her boyfriend, Mary had come to accept beatings as inevitable, but she just couldn't understand why it had been so bad this time. She was ridiculed by her friends on the street and felt, as they did, that she would have been better off if she had just accepted the beating and let it go at that.

Escape

Some pimps will allow a woman to buy back her freedom for an arbitrary amount of money that she must raise and pay him. In some cases women have been able to walk out of the life after paying the required fine. But most often the "fine" is just like the sweet talk; it is part of the game the pimp has been running, another fraudulent means of holding on with no intention of letting go. Some women manage to elude their pimps and escape into another town or state, taking on a new identity and the enormous task of putting their lives back together. Others, overwhelmed emotionally as well as physically, escape through suicide.

In 1976 Cynthia testified before a San Francisco grand jury about the times when she had tried to leave her pimp. The first time she left him, she was looking for an apartment when he began following her down the street. "I went into a restaurant. I was running around the tables screaming. I told the man to call the police. The man told me to get out of the restaurant." The pimp took her home and beat her so badly she couldn't leave the house.

Some time later, when she was beaten again by her pimp, she attempted another escape. She recuperated from the beating in a motel room until he tracked her down there. The motel manager gave him the key to her room; he went in and again beat her, complaining that she was avoiding him and not working. Again she managed to escape from him and ran to the motel office for help. Later, the rest of the story came out when the motel manager testified before the grand jury:

DISTRICT ATTORNEY: She ran around your motel screaming for someone to call the police, right?

MANAGER: Yes.

DISTRICT ATTORNEY: You grabbed her, pinned her arms back, and told
the guests in the motel not to bother calling the police.

MANAGER: I tried to get her out of the office.

DISTRICT ATTORNEY: She was saying that A. was trying to kill her? Did
it ever occur to you that he was trying to kill her?

MANGER: No, it didn't occur to me.

While the manager was holding her, the pimp came in, grabbed
her, and took her away. Again she got away from him and finally
went to the police. He was arrested and pleaded guilty to one
count of pimping. When he was sentenced 1 to 10 years, he
complained to the judge that the court was picking on him; he
claimed that on the streets it was known that pimps who pleaded
guilty never had to go prison.

A prostitute is known to be "out of pocket" with her pimp
when he punishes her for talking back to him, disobeying him, or
contradicting him. When the word goes out that she is "out of
pocket," she is fair game for other pimps, who may have a free
hand with her without triggering a war. When I rode on patrol
with San Francisco police officers on the Prostitution Detail in the
summer of 1978, we stopped to talk to a prostitute who had been
kidnapped by 2 pimps from Oakland 3 nights earlier. She had
been picked up off the street, taken to Oakland, raped, and
robbed. As she was telling us about this, she lifted her wig slightly
to show us that they had shaved her head before dumping her
back on the streets of San Francisco. This is a common occurrence
in the high-crime prostitution section of the city. While we were
talking with her, another prostitute joined us and reported that a
similar thing had happened to her a few months earlier. The
kidnapping had somewhat dimmed in her memory, and she was
presently more concerned with the slashes on her arm and back.
She took off her jacket to show us her slashed arm and lifted the
back of her shirt to display her back, which had been criss-crossed

with razor slashes by a trick a few nights earlier. She didn't consider reporting it the police. She appeared to accept the violence as inevitable.

Conclusion

Eleanor Miller,[20] based on the work of Bernard and Cohen,[21] differentiates among men who control women in prostitution. She distinguishes between a "man" and a pimp according to the number of prostitutes they have: a "man" has only one prostitute while a pimp may have many. The "man" is said to provide protection and to watch over "his woman" while the pimp considers himself more like a manager.[22] In her study of prostitution Miller extends this distinction into a continuum: "At one end is the pimp, a flamboyant male who manages a 'stable' (group of prostitutes) in a fairly bureaucratic way. At the other extreme is the 'man,' who is the husband/lover of the woman and really does work with her."[23]

Miller also notes that unless a man has reduced the relationship to a mere business transaction devoid of personal connection and intimacy, the prostitute is unlikely to refer to him as her pimp. As long as there is a relationship, he is "my man."[24] Pimps who develop a stable of several women usually maintain some form of private relationship with each one, and the addition of new women is treated as in polygamous marriage, each new woman being referred to as a "wife-in-law."

Most of prostitution is pimp controlled, and most women are in emotionally entangled relationships with pimps. As Hoigard and Finstad have shown, the tendency is for women to deny that they are controlled by pimps.[25] "Denying you have a pimp thus becomes a way of expressing that your own experience does not coincide with the stereotypical pimp-prostitute relationship."[26]

This is not significantly different from women's experience of abuse in marriage. As long as women remain in the abusive relationship, they tend to deny that their husbands abuse them. However, the difference, which at times may be slight, between prostitution and marriage is that the former is only sexual exploitation while marriage or a marital-like relationship may or may not be sexually exploitative. But all prostitution is sexual exploitation, and so every relationship that sustains it is abusive: with a customer, with a pimp or "my man," or with a boyfriend or husband. While degrees of abuse and ranges of affection may vary in these relationships, they all promote, aid, and encourage the sexual exploitation of women through prostitution.

The parallel to marriage is important here because as the sexuality of prostitution has been transformed into the prostitution of sexuality, sexual exploitation has increasingly become the normative condition of private relationships. Miller is correct to assume that there is a continuum between a pimp and "a man," but to the extent that he—pimp or "man"—is involved in a relationship with a prostitute woman, the real question regarding his role is whether she is subjected to sexual exploitation *from him* and/or *because of him*.

The proprostitution lobby objects to laws against pimping on the grounds that such laws deny women in prostitution a boyfriend, a lover, a real relationship, a genuine connection to another. This objection ignores the exploitation of women by pimps—the violence and abuse characteristic of pimps and the fact that pimps earn their livings off the sexual exploitation of women as commodities. It ignores the issue that faces all women in sexual relationships today—the question of whether or not their relationships are based on sexual exploitation or intimacy and love. A lover, husband, or boyfriend who promotes the sexual exploitation and commodification of a woman is a pimp, and together, pimping and procuring are among the most ruthless practices of male power and sexual dominance. These practices go far beyond the merchandising of women's bodies for the market that demands them; they crystallize misogyny in acts of male hatred of femaleness as rendered into a commodity for whom the marketer and the purchaser have contempt. Procuring today involves "convincing" a woman to be a prostitute through cunning, fraud, and/or physical force, taking her against her will or knowledge and putting her into prostitution. Procuring involves tactics for acquiring women and turning them into prostitution; pimping keeps them there. That some women, by their definition, choose to prostitute and choose to be with pimps as lovers or husbands is no more a defense of pimping than is a woman's choice to remain in a marriage with a man who abuses her a defense of that marriage.

7

The State: Patriarchal Laws and Prostitution

Laws on prostitution vary significantly from one country to another but generally fall into 3 categories: prohibition, which makes all prostitution illegal; regulation, which legalizes and regulates prostitution; and abolition, which decriminalizes prostitution. In all three systems and their variations, pimping—living off the earnings of a prostitute—is illegal.

Regardless of which legal approach to prostitution a given state adopts, a form of prostitution—visible street solicitation, which is usually the lowest category in the prostitution hierarchy—singles out women for social and legal condemnation and punishment. Street prostitution is illegal or unacceptable in most countries. Because it is visible, it is the source of the most frequent arrests, fines, and imprisonment of prostitute women. Women in street prostitution are among the poorest, the most vulnerable and victimized women. In terms of sexual politics, street prostitutes serve two functions: they are easily identified commodities for the customers and the market exchange, and they are scapegoats who take the blame for prostitution to satisfy the criminal justice system and the public's hypocritical morality. The term "street solicitation" most often refers to women picking up men for prostitution, not to men buying women for sex.

Arrest, harassment, and fining of women for visible street prostitution generally takes place while police largely ignore prostitution in brothels, hotels, and clubs. Consistently across societies, women in street prostitution are hassled and fined, but never to the point of being totally removed from the streets, where they are always available for male customer demand. Visible prostitution both makes market commodity available to men and threatens the social distance male customers require of prostitution in order to keep their lives as tricks and johns separate from their roles as husbands, lovers, fathers. Police harassment of women on the streets assures customers that those fine lines they draw between their wives and their whores will be upheld by the police for the customers' unrestricted access to women. It is also meant to, but never really does, satisfy parents who worry about the effect on their children of visible prostitution and pornography in their neighborhoods.

Although many if not most street prostitute women are controlled by pimps, their visibility on the streets suggests they are neither within the confines of marriage nor enclosed in brothels. Considered women outside of patriarchal control, street prostitutes are treated as if they are "vagabonds" who are neither in the grips of feudalism nor industrialized by the sex market. Punishment of visible street prostitute women for "soliciting" replaces the social, patriarchal control of women either in the family or by the sex industries.

There is no legal approach to prostitution that isn't abusive and doesn't exploit women. Each patriarchal state system in its own way locks women into prostitution. In prohibitionist systems, where prostitute women are criminals, they can hardly expect justice to turn in their favor or protection to be granted to them. Where prostitution is legally accepted and regulated, the exploitation of prostitutes by pimps and customers is forgotten. Where prostitution is tolerated, as in France, prostitutes are still hassled on the streets. All legal approaches to prostitution are masculinist systems that yield to the male market demand and concede to the misogynist myth that prostitution is a necessary and inevitable sexual service required by men. States' laws promote men buying women for sex and support social hatred of women for doing it.

Prostitution laws have developed to sustain the sex market by supplying customer demand while appearing to control venereal disease. The question that the law has not addressed in any legal system is, Do men have the right to buy women's bodies to use them for sex?

1. *Prohibition*

In the prohibition system of prostitution law, all prostitution is illegal, and both prostitutes and customers are criminals. Pimping is criminalized because it promotes prostitution and because pimps earn income from prostitution. There are two different prohibitionist systems: socialist/communist and capitalist.

1. *Socialist Suppression.* In socialist/communist states, prohibition aims at eliminating prostitution because it is inconsistent with the ideals and values of the state. Prostitution is rejected as a capitalist market transaction and as a form of exploitation. While prostitution is illegal for the prostitute woman as well as the customer, usually in the socialist/communist system there is some recognition that prostitute women are victims. At the same time, as in all patriarchal states, men in socialist/communist states have it both ways by closing prostitution outlets, while maintaining some supply of women for government officials, diplomats, and foreign businessmen to buy for sex, condemning pornography while it is secretly available.

Today, China and Vietnam are among the few prohibitionist

countries under socialism. Until the 1949 Maoist revolution, China was a major center in Asia for international trafficking in women. Under the socialist government there, and in the Socialist Republic of Vietnam, prostitution was declared illegal with a view to eliminating it. Pimps and procurers were severely punished. Especially in Vietnam, women were considered victims of prostitution and were "rehabilitated." Under Mao, China claimed to have completely eliminated prostitution; and Vietnam, since the conclusion of the war there, reduced the number of women in prostitution by two-thirds. Sexual exploitation of women in pornography virtually disappeared from the mainstream of society.

China's and Vietnam's successes in controlling prostitution presume totalitarian state control, exclusion of a market economy and tourism, poverty that is more or less uniform throughout the country, village collectives, communes, or cadres that oversee and regulate correct standards of behavior, and collectivization of production that does not provide individual men with significant access to or control of spendable income. When men do not have the income to buy sex and there is no market economy, the conditions for prostitution have been suppressed.

In the gender structure of poverty, men receive the first economic advantages in rapid economic development. Therefore, men of every class are the first to gain spendable income. Local prostitution markets are built on the sexual inequality of economic development. The influx of foreign businesses, businessmen, and tourists produce new market demands for prostitution, and they bring in foreign exchange through prostitution. Mail-order-bride agencies that originate in Europe and the United States develop large businesses as women turn either to prostitution within their countries or to marriage abroad as the only evident means of improving their economic condition. But because socialist/communist states only suppressed prostitution, they never confronted the underlying gender inequality, sexual exploitation, and misogyny from which prostitution is built. In the U.S.S.R., now Russia, there was a massive proliferation of prostitution as soon as the socialist state was dissolved and Russia opened fully to a market economy. Prostitution and pornography industries poured into the newly opened countries from the West. Not only did prostitution proliferate but also, immediately, signs of the normalization that accompanies sex industries began to appear. The change from communist to capitalist state, signaling both a rapid development of the market and an intense valorization of materialism, threatens to leave young women behind. In a 1990 survey of young women who were asked to identify their professional aspirations, prostitution was rated seventh out of the top ten. Building upon the communist state's devaluation of women, capitalist exploitation of women leads directly to expansion of prostitution which, in turn, increasingly is being considered an "alternative" by young women.

Officially prostitution is prohibited in the former socialist countries. But in a "free" market, prohibition prostitution law is a function of capitalism. Police are more likely to take bribes than make arrests, and they implicitly understand that they are not to interfere with market demand. In 1990 throughout the Soviet Union, 5,849 women were arrested for prostitution. In the shift from communist suppression to capitalist permissive repression, arresting women for prostitution is meant to be a public rejection of prostitution that does not interfere with market supply. Customers are not arrested.

2. *Capitalist Prohibition.* Capitalist states with prohibitionist systems, consider prostitution immoral and treat it as illicit sex. In the prohibitionist system in capitalist economies, prostitute, pimp, and customer are all criminalized, but the overwhelming preponderance of arrests are of prostitute women. In the United States, there were 43,224 prostitution-related arrests in 1990, up from a total of 36,093 in 1977, an increase of 4.2% from 1989, according to the Uniform Crime Reports. Arrests for prostitution by race were approximately as follows: 65% white, 32.6% Black, 1.8% Asian and Native American. In 1989, New York State

TABLE 7.1
Offense—Pimping

	1989		1990		1991	
	m	f	m	f	m	f
Profits from prostitution	36	34	57	36	78	53
Running a brothel (madams)	86	69	84	60	70	61
Pimping with coercion and pimping a person under age 16	12	0	11	1	8	0
Controlling premises used for prostitution	9	5	14	2	7	6

Cross-tabulation of Prostitute Arrests, 1989–91, Division of Criminal Justice Services, New York State. Also see New York State Uniform Crime Report, 1989.

reported arresting 11,951 adult women, as compared with 1,317 adult males, for being engaged in prostitution. Yet only 690 customers (632 males) were arrested and only 293 persons were arrested for promoting prostitution (pimping).

Analyzing 1991 arrest patterns for pimping in all of New York State reveals a gender effect that differentiates between arrests for procuring and arrests for managing brothels or prostitution businesses. Eight men and no women were arrested for the kind of pimping that involves actually putting women into prostitution and not merely living off their earnings. In contrast, table 7.1 shows an increase in the arrest of women on pimping charges for running brothels or prostitution businesses. This is attributed to an increase in prostitution outlets such as escort services run by "madams." Coercive pimping is not only the category with the least arrests but is also an almost all-male category, with arrests of 12 males in 1989 declining to 8 in 1991. These data reveal not only that there are infrequent arrests of men on pimping charges but also that the arrest pattern is gendered, focusing on women who run their own "escort" services.

These figures are consistent with earlier arrest patterns. From January 1974 through the first three-quarters of 1977, there was a total of 36 indictments for pimping that involved promotion of prostitution in New York City (97 in the entire state), and 6 convictions (18 in the entire state). Four pimps were convicted of pimping in New York City in 1977. However, a Minneapolis policeman has estimated that 300 or 400 women were taken from Minneapolis to New York City by pimps every year. He had specific knowledge of at least 200 pimps operating between Minneapolis and New York City.[1] Comparing juvenile female and male prostitution has revealed that 63% of girls compared with 5% of boys have been arrested for prostitution.[2]

Statistics from arrest records in San Francisco and New York City are representative of nationwide practices. In San Francisco in 1977, "2,938 persons were arrested for prostitution and 325 persons were arrested as customers of prostitutes. Although it has been estimated that there are ten times as many customers as prostitutes in San Francisco, 419 persons served time in jail in 1977 for prostitution; not *one* customer of a prostitute served time in jail."[3]

One inevitable result of the prohibitionist system that defines prostitutes as criminals is the reluctance of prostitutes to turn in their pimps to the police. To do so is to identify themselves as prostitutes and therefore criminals. The legal bind of prostitute women reinforces their emotional and psychological dependency, which is often enforced with physical abuse. The criminal justice system, by treating women as criminals, closes them out of the legal system. Usually they are separated from their families and former friends, as the world of prostitution requires. Closed out of society, prostitute women, until the last few years, have been excluded from services that have been made available to victims of wife abuse and rape. Until recently, it has not been possible to secure the support that would provide the shelter, access to health services, counseling, and training needed to separate from prostitution and establish a new life.

Adult prostitute women—"criminals" according to the law, "sexual servants" or workers engaged in "sex between consenting adults" according to sexual liberals—have been social, legal throwaways, turned over to sex commodification with no other recourse. Children in prostitution are a different matter. In the United States in the 1970s, new legislation and funding became available to protect children from the sex industries: the Protection of Children Against Sexual Exploitation Act was passed in 1977; the Runaway Youth Act, in 1974; and the Child Abuse Prevention and Treatment Act, in 1974. Criminologist Rosemary Gido, working with Project SAFE and Trudee Able-Peterson, the Director of Victim Services Agency Streetwork Project in New York City, was able to take advantage of that funding for child victims of prostitution and pornography to create programs to help girls get out of prostitution. This work in turn has implications for adult women because customers are buying females at younger and younger ages, expecting 12-, 13-, and 14-year-olds to act like women. Although there has been no comparable government support for adult women over the age of 18—an indication of the government's refusal to confront prostitution as sexual exploitation of women—these projects have laid the groundwork for protections for adult women in prostitution.

In the United States, WHISPER and the Council for Prostitution Alternatives are among the projects that, from a feminist perspective, have led the way in developing services for adult prostitute women, enabling them to leave prostitution. In addition, Margaret Baldwin was the architect and driving force behind a recent 1991 Florida law[4] that enables a prostitute woman to claim both compensatory and punitive damages against "the person who coerced that person into prostitution" or coerced her to stay in prostitution. Here "coercion" "means any practice of domination, restraint, or inducement for the purpose of or with the reasonably foreseeable effect of causing another person to engage in or remain in prostitution or to relinquish earnings derived from prostitution." This act is broad in its implications, for its definition of "coercion" includes "promise of marriage" and "exploitation of victimization by sexual abuse."

2. *Regulation*

Under regulation, prostitution is legalized and enforced through systems of state-regulated brothels. Originally developed as an approach that would insure easy military access to prostitution, regulation claimed to (1) control the negative side effects of prostitution for men, its customers, through regular (weekly) venereal-disease checkups that promised to control the spread of the disease, (2) reduce rape by making prostitute women available for purchase, (3) reduce pimping and organized crime by making brothels available legally, and (4) locate prostitution away from people who are bothered by it in their neighborhoods.

However, these claims are merely idealized patriarchal rationalizations that trade off prostitute women for rape victims and other victims. Where sex industries flourish and are legitimized by the state, 80 to 90% of the women are controlled by pimps. Regulation does not reduce rape and it *enforces* prostitution, especially in brothels or eros centers in many countries, including South Korea, Germany, Beirut in Lebanon, Tunisia, Holland, and Nevada in the United States.

Germany has boasted that its system is the model for regulation of prostitution. Prostitution in Germany cannot be banned in cities with populations over 20,000; each city may regulate the practice itself. Pimping and procuring are illegal, and prostitutes, who must be at least 18, are required to have regular venereal-disease checkups and to carry health cards. Income from prostitution is taxed, but prostitutes are not eligible for unemployment or social security.[5] In most cities, prostitutes are restricted to a certain section of the city and are allowed to work on the streets, that is, to be visible, only between 8:00 P.M. and 6:00 A.M.

In 1976, police in Hamburg estimated that half of the women in prostitution were registered. In that year 3,000 prostitutes were registered in West Berlin and 800 in Munich.[6] It is estimated that 80% to 95% of the German prostitutes have pimps,[7] and organized crime proliferates, especially in trafficking women from Asian countries. In the late 1970s, according to Die Arch, a prostitute refuge center in Hamburg, women could not get into most of the city's eros centers without a pimp. Because of regulation, eros centers—large prostitution buildings—are in designated sex zones of the cities. In a 1991 interview, Domenica Nienhoff, a leader of a movement for women in prostitution, tells us that rather than eliminating men's control over women, legalization has left 70% of the women in Germany with pimps.

Domenica, described as the "top role model for the successful, self-conscious prostitute," is warning women against prostitution. She ran the house of prostitution with the "biggest success quota," that is, "the house with the most women who got out." Even though in her own prostitution Domenica is a "dominatrix," she knows that "I only do what the men want. They pay me for it. That means I play out their wishes. The men are actually the true masters of the situation." [8] Contrary to the belief that women are in control and hold the power in prostitution encounters, Janus and Bess, in their *Sexual Profile of Men in Power,* found that the client is always the powerful one. A higher-class customer, a businessman or politician, who sees all life as an exercise of power, demands painful ritual acts from prostitutes with the "knowledge that as he is directing, casting, and paying for the whole thing, he is completely controlling the situation. In this perverse logic, it is just when all is hopeless and he is seemingly shorn of all power that he is most in command." [9]

By contrast, while men take control, women in prostitution frequently are not sexual in their own lives. Sex often is excluded from their private lives. Domenica explained to Alice Schwarzer, editor of *Emma,* the German feminist magazine, that privately she has no sexual life. Sex has come to mean dehumanization. She prefers in private to be regarded as a human being.

Germany has legalized, sanctioned, and normalized prostitution, but women have not gained civil rights. However, once prostitution has been regulated, socially it becomes normalized—

accepted as a legitimate trade or work for women—and once prostitution has become socially legitimized through legal sanction, then women are able to win some social service protections. A 1991 case in Berlin recognized that a woman's work as a prostitute is a legitimate occupational activity and that therefore she is to be awarded financial assistance for retraining.[10] In other words, only when sexual exploitation is regulated and thereby guaranteed to the consumer market can women claim compensation for getting out of it.

State regulation has not eliminated pimps. Rather, it offers them legal cover. It has facilitated trafficking of Asian women, particularly from Thailand to Germany and the Netherlands. The trafficking syndicate appears to have been taken over in part by some procurers connected with the thriving sex industry in Germany. According to a report in *Der Spiegel* in December 1977, the largest ring of procurers ever found in Germany was broken up when 11 men and 1 woman from Argentina and Uruguay were arrested for procuring women from those countries and bringing them to Frankfurt, where they were put into prostitution on the street as well as in eros centers. Authorities became suspicious when they observed that a large number of prostitutes in the Frankfurt area were not from Germany but were instead from South American countries. After the arrest of 50 prostitutes in a large raid, information on the gang came to light. According to the report, so many women were procured that if a woman escaped or ran away from the gang, they never bothered to go after her because they were able to replace her immediately. The prostitutes who were brought in from Argentina and Uruguay worked for three months on tourist visas and then were taken to Italy, where they were married to unemployed or retired Italian men who were paid $1,000 for the marriage. Italian marriage made the women members of the European Common Market and therefore able to return to Germany to continue their work.

It was with the boom of the German eros centers in the mid-1960s that Austrian pimps started to move into the German scene, according to Wolfgang Hollreigal, a Viennese reporter who spent considerable time studying prostitution in Austria. These large, state-sanctioned prostitution hotels, where women (through their pimps) lease rooms or apartments, created a new boom in business. The competition that Austrian pimps offered to the German pimps created rivalry between gangs. Gang rivalry and, later, a decline in profits, caused Austrian pimps to return to Vienna, where prostitution is governed by laws similar to those of Germany. According to Hollreigal, there was one well-organized gang that dominated prostitution in Vienna. It had about 75 members and controlled 600 prostitutes, in addition to being involved in other criminal activities. Certain "assistants" in the gang travel the Prater (the Reeperbahn of Vienna) every night to collect their money from the women working for them there. The women are paying the gang for protection from the gang.

In 1976, two Austrians who were part of a ring of procurers were arrested, and six others from West Germany were the objects of a nationwide manhunt. The case broke out after a girl escaped from an eros center in Essen and reported to authorities that procurers had taken her there from Villach, Austria, and forced her into prostitution. Further investigation revealed that many young girls were missing from the Villach area, and several Villach girls were located in Essen.

When I inquired into the case 2 years later, authorities explained that the other Austrian women found in Essen were prostitutes with expired passports who, when they were picked up by the police, claimed that they too had been forced. Assuming they were lying, authorities dismissed the issue of force completely, even though police know that many women, when picked up, are terrified of giving evidence against pimps and procurers. Prostitutes' unwillingness to testify is often an easy excuse for not investigating cases that police would rather not handle anyway.

The U.S. version of eros centers is found in Nevada, which boasts of allowing regulated prostitution throughout the state except in Reno and Las Vegas. One prostitute described Joe Conforte's Mustang Ranch in Nevada as "just like a prison." The security is tight there; the iron gates and guard tower that supposedly keep troublemakers out actually keep women in. Located in a deserted area outside of Reno, Mustang Ranch looks and feels like a 1940s-style prison. In the short time I was there with a colleague in 1978, we observed the central room, which has a large bar and is decorated in red with several huge sofas. About 50 girls work there at any one time. There were about 20 working the afternoon we arrived—15 white women, 3 Black women, and 2 Asian women, with a few male prostitutes around. The place was almost silent, for the girls are not allowed to talk to each other, nor are they permitted to read. They just sit around until the buzzer sounds, announcing a new customer-john-trick. Then they line up at the front door. Dressed in body stockings or bikinis, they stand mute until the trick chooses one from the lineup. Five tricks came in during the 15 minutes we managed to stay on our visit, which was cut short by the management.

In 1978, according to the woman we interviewed (who no longer works at Mustang), a woman at Mustang had to work a minimum of 3 weeks before she could leave. In order to remain at Mustang, she had to earn $1,000 a week in the summer and $500 a week in the winter. A work day was 14 to 16 hours, with 3 weeks on and one off. The women weren't allowed out unless they could hustle a customer who wanted to take them into Reno. Occasionally, they received permission to leave for 2 hours of shopping.

The cut was 50–50 with the house. However, extra charges left the women with more like 40% of the take, for they paid 10% of their take for room and board (but not more than $10 daily), plus $1 a day to the night maid, $1 to the cashier, $1 for each pair of panties washed, and $2 for each house gown washed. And then there are the weekly venereal-disease checkups—$20 for the exam and $2 for each prescription written, plus the cost of having the prescription filled. According to the ex-employee we interviewed, almost any kind of drug is dispensed.

It has been the practice of pimps in Oakland, San Francisco, and Los Angeles, when they are arrested, to send their women to Mustang to work until they get out. Some people say that prostitutes get in through pimps. Despite the prison-like setting and the long working hours, many girls prefer the Mustang arrangements to the streets. Prostitution at Mustang is legal, and if it chooses, Mustang can provide minimal protection from customer violence. It claims that condoms are required, as are weekly VD/HIV checks. Local authorities don't interfere with Mustang's own private security system. Mustang seems to exist outside the law, and it is impossible to know the nature and extent of violence there. By 1990 Joe Conforte's profits from Mustang were $2 million.[11]

3. Proprostitution Neo-Regulation

New neo-regulationist laws and government policies assert prostitution as a woman's right. In 1990 the government of the Netherlands reported its position on prostitution to the United Nations:

It follows from the right of self-determination, which is enjoyed by an independent adult man or woman on whom no unlawful influence has been brought to bear, that he or she is at liberty to decide to act as a prostitute and allow another person to profit from his or her earnings.[12]

The Netherlands differentiated between Dutch women (and Western women generally), whom they considered to be "at liberty to decide to act as a prostitute," and Third World women, "who come to Europe apparently of their own free will to work as prostitutes, but are generally actuated by economic motives and are not genuinely acting voluntarily."[13]

The Dutch approaches to legitimizing prostitution are lodged in contradictions: they recognize self-determination in a condition that is destructive to the self; they reduce self-determination to an individual choice when, as framed by international human rights, self-determination has meant the rights of peoples; and they recognize that Third World immigrants going to developed countries such as the Netherlands are fleeing poverty but they do not recognize poverty as a factor for most Dutch or other Western women in prostitution. The law has been developed in response to a highly vocal but small proprostitution lobby. It ignores the silence of homeless women, women in poverty, abandoned women and single mothers, who would leave prostitution if they had economic alternatives.

European proprostitution groups promote prostitution but are against trafficking in women. Making the distinction between "free" and "forced" prostitution, their economic interests are apparent: Third World and Eastern European immigrant women in the Netherlands, Germany, and other regulationist countries lower the prostitution market value of local Dutch and German women. German prostitute women are complaining that there are too many drug addicts, women from Asia, and "cheaper" women from Eastern Europe who "spoil the market."[14] The price of immigrant prostitution is so low that local women's prices go down, reducing the pimps' and brothels' cuts. Thus the self-determination rhetoric of neo-regulation actually fronts for the sex industry's need to control prices by controlling immigration. The result: a movement against "trafficking in women" that promotes local prostitution on the basis of an erroneous distinction between "free" and "forced" prostitution to protect market prices. However, many prostitutes and prostitution organizations throughout the Netherlands along with international human rights and feminist organizations have protested the new laws, claiming that prostitutes are being made functionaries of the state. The result by 1994 is reconsideration by the upper house of the Dutch parliament of this approach.

The normalization of prostitution in European regulationist countries has actually promoted trafficking in women to the Netherlands. Neo-regulation relaxes the policing of prostitution, making it easier for traffickers to move in and out of the country. Trafficking from the Philippines, Latin America, and Eastern Europe has expanded in the Netherlands as it did a few decades earlier when Germany legalized prostitution. Now with the government promotion of tourism in Thailand, prostitution tourism brings in foreign exchange, and regulation of "hospitality workers" encourages trafficking of women and girls from China, Vietnam, and Burma.

In a recent study of window prostitution in Utrecht, Willem Pompe found that organized crime families control much of prostitution in the Netherlands. Prostitution as a "nuisance factor" in local neighborhoods led to the development of an out-of-sight-out-of-mind area for streetwalkers and a chain of 40 houseboat brothels on the river Vecht. In the houseboats, as in the storefront brothels in Amsterdam, women are paid $20 a customer but rent their cubicles for $8 to $40 per 8-hour day. These cubicles are 9-by-9-foot windowed stalls in which the prostitute women sit under red lights, simply pulling a curtain across the window when they have a customer.

Pompe reports that over half of the 150 prostitutes are immigrants from South America and the Caribbean. Many of them are illegal aliens, many are under 18, many work for pimps. In his research Pompe noted that police, trying to maintain good relations with the brothels, follow a policy that "is one of inhibition rather than aggressive supervision and control." Further, the largest of the brothel operators, who owns 60% of the houseboats and runs drugs, "leads a clearly criminal organization which, in the United States, would be described as a 'family.' "[15] In other words, regulation strengthens the control and role of organized crime in prostitution. The Netherlands estimates business from the sex industry at $830 million per year.[16]

4. Abolitionism

The abolitionist movement against state regulation of prostitution led by Josephine Butler in the nineteenth century fought for "the abolition of the regulation of prostitution, not as its name might lead one to believe, of prostitution itself."[17] In response to regulation, abolition, or toleration, decriminalizes prostitution for both prostitute and customer. Abolitionist legal approaches prohibit pimping, procuring, and trafficking and criminalize third-party involvement in brothels and prostitution hotels.

Abolition formed the foundation for the 1949 United Nations Convention for the Suppression of the Traffic in Persons and the Exploitation of the Prostitution of Others, which stated that "prostitution and the accompanying evil in the traffic in persons for the purpose of prostitution are incompatible with the dignity and worth of the human person and endanger the welfare of the individual, the family, and the community." The U.N. Convention legislated against pimping, brothels, and trafficking.

The perspective of abolitionist organizations, particularly the International Abolitionist Federation, is that laws prohibiting or regulating prostitution should be abolished while laws against pimping and procuring should be strengthened. Abolitionists press for the vigorous prosecution of pimps because they force women into prostitution or prevent them from escaping it. According to the abolitionist position, any condition of prostitution that is coerced and forced is a violation of human rights. Abolitionists reject state intervention for the purpose of regulating prostitution because they consider that the main advantage of legalization is to the male customer and not the prostitute. Instead, the abolitionists hold that it is not the function of the state to become a regulating factor and therefore a legitimization of prostitution itself. When the state regulates or "legalizes" prostitution, it is in a position to conveniently ignore the traffic in women because it sanctions prostitution as a legitimate form of work, as an accepted social institution, and therefore does not concern itself with whether or not women are trafficked or coerced. Thus it is essential to the abolitionist position that government laws not be formulated in such a way as to sanction prostitution.

France is one of the countries that signed the 1949 U.N. convention. When in 1991 a minister of the French government proposed a plan for state regulation of prostitution, Denise Pouillon-Falco of the Union Contre Le Traffic des Etres Humains led a successful drive to suppress the plan on the basis of its conflict with French law and the 1949 Convention. In 1980 international attention was focused on Grenoble, France, when 4 young women who were severely tortured by pimps and customers faced their captors in the open courtroom. Their courage, a vigorous district attorney, and an angry judge broke the gang of 17 pimps, gave maximum sentences to those who had not escaped to Italy, and required that extensive civil damages be paid to the women. The courts collected the fines that were never picked up by the women, who feared for their lives and left the country. In 1978, according to the French Ministry of Interior, *proxénètisme* (pimping and procuring) was the third-largest business in France, with a $7 billion annual profit.[18] However, *proxénètisme* is more vigorously prosecuted in France; 1,451 cases were handled in one year.[19]

Proprietors of prostitution hotels, or *hôtels de passe,* are *proxénètes.* To avoid being charged with running a closed brothel, they often rent out rooms to travelers or immigrants. The remainder of the rooms are rented on a daily or weekly basis to women in prostitution. They are required to take between 10 and 20 customers *(passes)* daily just to meet room rent. Most proprietors will not rent to a woman without a pimp because they know that the pimp will ensure that the women meet their quotas.[20]

There have been charges that police protection and kickbacks have hampered enforcement of laws against *proxénètisme* in France. Vigorous enforcement is restricted by the use of many of those in the *milieu* as established police informers, a practice that creates a brotherhood of hotel proprietors, pimps, and police. The law, based on habitual behavior, defines a pimp as *anyone* who gives assistance to a prostitute, takes money from her, or lives with her.

Although there are no laws forbidding the act of prostitution, each country espousing toleration carries other laws on its books that are used to control and/or harass women in street prostitution. In France, for example, laws against loitering and soliciting are used against prostitutes, who receive stiff fines when cited for these offenses.

In 1975 prostitutes took over a church in Lyon and began a strike that spread to every major city in France. The strike was sparked by a sudden increase in fines (averaging $45 each in 1975) of prostitutes in Lyon. Many women in prostitution on the street received several fines each night and alleged that the police were pocketing the money. The French prostitutes condemned proposals to adopt the German system of prostitution and set up eros centers in France. "We will never become the civil servants of sex," said Ulla, an organizer. The prostitutes denounced the system that would make them functionaries of the state, which then would become the biggest pimp of all. While some of the women involved in the strike did not have pimps, it was learned later that one of the main organizers worked for a big-time pimp who encouraged the strike in order to protest the way his income was being affected by the fines.

The abolitionist position does not concern itself with prostitution as long as women are not forced. In 1979, in *Female Sexual Slavery,* I took an abolitionist position regarding *individual* women in prostitution, recommending policy that would recognize that as long a woman can freely leave prostitution at any time she chooses, neither individuals nor the state should interfere with her personally. In 1983 I argued that it is possible to "accept the abolitionist position for individuals but feminism requires that in exposing patriarchal power we must separate the individual from the institution which controls her, and that we examine the institution of prostitution as a product of male domination, of sexual violence and enslavement."[21] However, individuals cannot be separated from the institutions. More importantly, this position perpetuates the false distinction between "free" and "forced" prostitution, which assumes that prostitution itself is not damaging to women and therefore is not a form of sexual exploitation.

By the mid 1980s I had reformulated my position on prostitution law, having recognized that decriminalization is necessary and appropriate only for prostitute women, not customers. At a 1986 meeting of UNESCO convened by Wassyla Tamzali to consider the causes and effects of prostitution, I proposed the criminalization of customers in a statement we prepared together that was adopted by the group. It recommended that state laws consider the

need to depenalize the prostitute (in the States where she is still penalized) and, on the contrary to penalize the client, without forgetting to apply the laws which repress procuring in all forms and its accomplices.[22]

Law: Irrationally Validating Violation

In the West, contemporary prostitution, an extension of industrial or commercial economic sectors, is legally "controlled" by systems of prohibition, regulation, and abolition. These legal systems and criminal-justice approaches to prostitution, when considered in relation to Third World prostitution, form part of Western patriarchal hegemony in that they overlie customary law and social practices in many Third World countries in such a way as to aggravate conditions of prostitution. Sometimes imposed by colonialism, often to replace customary law that regulated practices that were rural in character and sometimes religious in origin, prohibition, regulation, and abolition are often combined in the legal strategies of Third World states, where massive deployment of prostitution in the poorest and developing regions also provides an economic base for the state.

India. India, one of the poorest, most overpopulated countries, with the largest AIDS epidemic worldwide, is officially an abolitionist state. If there is one clear proof of the failure of abolition or toleration, it is the case of India, which signed the 1949 Convention and on that basis adopted the Suppression of Immoral Traffic Act in 1956, updated in 1986 with the Prevention of Immoral Traffic in Persons Act. Sociologist Jean D'Cunha has studied patterns of arrest under these laws and has exposed bribery practices. She has pointed out that focusing on traffic and forced prostitution has done nothing to reduce or control prostitution. Rather, trafficking and prostitution have flourished.

Jean D'Cunha's research reveals that between 1981 and 1985 there were a total of 471 raids on brothels and prostitution hotels in all of India (by 1993 it has been estimated that there were 600,000 women and children in prostitution in Bombay alone). D'Cunha estimates that at this rate, "each brothel would be raided once in 600 years." In the raids there, 469 brothel keepers were arrested, all were released on bail, and only 2 were convicted. During that period 304 procurers were arrested. Women in prostitution are arrested, as they are in all countries, regardless of the law, for street prostitution and soliciting. D'Cunha found that while women arrested for prostitution were given fines or an average of 7 days in prison, a brothel keeper convicted in 1982 was sentenced to a fine or one day in prison.[23] Police bribes keep the system of prostitution in operation:

It has been observed that police officials from the Vigilance Cell of the Crime Branch, Bombay, collect around Rs 30–50 per month as a bribe per brothel, depending on the earnings of the brothel-keeper. Brothel-keepers pay the police around Rs 500 if the latter receive information that a new minor has been forced into prostitution.[24]

The Philippines and Thailand. In the Philippines and Thailand, all three forms of law are brought together. Technically, prostitution is illegal in both countries. In the Philippines, state law defines a "prostitute" specifically as a woman. Feminist groups and women's organizations in the Philippines have called for repeal of that penal code.[25] However, while female prostitution is illegal, prostitution is promoted under another category, that of "entertainer," which is legalized and regulated for the sex industries that bring in significant foreign exchange through sex tourism. Women register as "entertainers," the euphemism for prostitute, paying 200 pesos to the mayor's office for a permit and submitting to regular health checkups for venereal disease (although the men are not required to have health checkups). At the same time, and contradictorily, the Philippines ratified the abolitionist law, the 1949 Convention for the Suppression of the Traffic in Persons and the Exploitation of the Prostitution of Others. In other words, as far as the United Nations is concerned, the Philippines is an abolitionist country; as far as the government is concerned, it is prohibitionist; and as far as the tourist economy is concerned, it is regulationist. And to the state, the brothel, the pimp, and the customers, the women are commodities.

In Thailand, the Prostitution Prohibition Act of 1960 prohibited prostitution. However, in 1966, when Thailand became an important location of R & R for military fighting in Vietnam, two laws were passed. The first legitimized entertainment as an industry and the second protected "personal services" as a form of business. These laws had the effect of regulating business for entertainment and for providing personal services. By 1972 the new Investments Promotion Act "gave foreign companies free movement of capital" for the purpose of increasing "the inflow of foreign investment to fill the gap caused by the decline in aid, and to diversify the structure of exports by concentrating on the production of manufactured goods and services through joint ventures."[26] These laws have supported the growth of the tourist industry, which overwhelmingly serves men. By 1986, after a steady decline of female tourists from 34% in 1977 to 27% in 1986, 73% of the tourists were male.[27] The enormous sex industry spawned by this male tourism as a result of foreign investment policy has made Thailand both a country from which women are trafficked (sending country) and a country to which women are trafficked for prostitution (receiving country). Consequently, new laws based on the abolitionist approach and designed to punish trafficking were being introduced into the Parliament in 1992. However, the bill introduced into Parliament goes further than the 1949 Convention by proposing to crack down on customers who "patronise a brothel which provides sex with boys and girls or women who have been forced to serve as prostitutes." The law likewise cracks down on brothel owners and procurers of women and children smuggled into the country. While outlawing trafficking, such an approach perpetuates the distinction between "free" and "forced" prostitution, legitimizing sex-industrialized prostitution and imposing penalties for those who "maltreat prostitutes," as if prostitution itself is not "maltreatment."[28]

AIDS

Prostitution may be the only high-risk AIDS context in which high-risk sex is promoted, despite the costs in human lives. Creating the illusion of controlling venereal disease in order to promote the prostitution market was the original basis of regulated prostitution. Since the 1980s, neo-regulationist promotion of prostitution has focused on controlling the spread of AIDS. In the last decade, the normalization of prostitution coincides with the advent and acceleration of this new, deadly, sexually transmitted disease. The receptivity of the sexual-liberal public in the West to the promotion of prostitution, the tendency for some countries to treat prostitution as a form of work like any other, correlates with the escalation of AIDS and women becoming the highest-risk group. But prostitution alone and its normalization does not account for the increase in AIDS among women. Men's promiscuous sexual behavior with multiple partners in polygamous societies and in sexually liberal societies, as well as in prostitution, establish the epidemiological base for the spread of HIV/AIDS.

Amazingly, the response to prostitution and AIDS has not been containment but condoms. Certainly if there is no other choice for women, no other protection, no means out of prostitution, condoms, like clean needles for drug abusers, is a stop-gap measure—one that may save a few lives but cannot effectively address the problem.

At the individual level, customers offer to pay more to women on the streets for sex without condoms. Brothels in Thailand have reportedly advertised AIDS-free prostitutes, certified by HIV tests. But because they do not require tests of the customers, HIV can be contracted in any encounter after a woman has tested negative for HIV. Regulating prostitution through weekly or biweekly tests and exams of prostitute women, who may see 4 to 10 to 20 to 100 customers every day, any of whom may carry and transmit the disease, does not control the spread of VD, STD, or HIV.

Women have a higher likelihood of contracting AIDS from men than men from women. Furthermore, men who buy sex in prostitution are members of the very population that engages in the promiscuous sexual behavior that is likely to transmit it widely throughout the female population. Wherever men get HIV infected, they carry the virus to prostitutes and to wives and other women. In other words, it is men's promiscuity that is responsible for the spread of AIDS to populations of women made available for male promiscuity.

HIV infection is sexually transmitted and 75% of the reported 8 to 10 million HIV cases worldwide have been heterosexually transmitted. By April of 1991, 345,000 AIDS cases were reported to the World Health Organization, but WHO estimates an actual 1.5 million AIDS cases worldwide. By the year 2000 it is estimated that there will be 30 million to 40 million women, men, and children who test positive for HIV, 12 million to 18 million of whom will be AIDS infected. However, almost as quickly as the World Health Organization issues its AIDS estimates and projections, the acceleration of this venereal disease causes new upward estimates and projections.[29] Current estimates show that by 1991, there were 700,000 reported HIV infections in Brazil, with 8.3% of the population of Uganda being HIV infected and 1 million estimated HIV infections in the United States.[30]

The preponderance of HIV/AIDS transmission occurs through heterosexual contact in the context of multiple sexual partners. This fact makes polygamous societies and prostitution populations especially high-risk groups. In the era of AIDS, NORC, (National Opinion Research Council), has reported from its survey sample in 1988 that more than 40% of single men under 25 reported 3 or more sexual partners.[31] In a survey of heterosexual, educated, white, single adults conducted by Masters and Johnson in 1986, it was found that 72% of women and 63% of men "had become more cautious about sex as a result of worries about AIDS." However, in this same study, 47% of the women did not insist that their partners use condoms although they were more careful in selecting sexual partners.[32]

Not surprisingly, then, in 1991 the United Nations reported that women were increasingly the high-risk group and projected that in that year there would be 200,000 women who would become ill with AIDS—more than the total AIDS population in the preceding decade.[33] In the United States, AIDS has become the leading cause of death of women between 25 and 34 years of age,[34] making women the highest-risk group. AIDS cases involving women increased in 1990 by 37% while the cases of gay men with AIDS increased 19%.[35]

Most of AIDS in India is spread by heterosexual prostitution, and it was estimated by WHO that by the end of 1992, 35% of women in prostitution in Bombay would be HIV positive, up from 3% in 1988.[36] Between 1990 and 1991, there was a 100% increase in estimated HIV infections in Thailand, with 50,000 in 1990 to 100,000 in 1991. In 1992, estimates showed that between 200,000 and 400,000 Thais carried the HIV virus. In Thailand there was a reported 234% increase of women with AIDS.[37] WHO estimates that from 125,000 to 150,000 Thais will die from AIDS by 1997.

The Population and Community Development Association of Thailand estimates that 5.3 million Thais will be infected with AIDS by the year 2000.[38] A government minister estimates that by the year 2000, 2 million to 4 million Thais will be infected with the HIV virus. "According to a survey of military conscripts in the north of Thailand, 73% of them lost their virginity with a prostitute and 97% regularly visit prostitutes."[39] There is not a sufficient quantity of AIDS-free women and children for the tourist sex market. The National AIDS Committee of Thailand launched AIDS-education campaigns and has tried to control the spread of AIDS, but the escalating sex industries seem to move faster than the program. AIDS appears to follow the sex-industry hierarchy: for low-paid brothel prostitutes, the national median infection rate in June 1991 was 15.2%; in some areas it was as high as 63%. For high-paid prostitutes operating in nightclubs, the median is 4.8%, but as high as 29%.[40] Furthermore, in 1990 the U.S. Centers for Disease Control reported a 67% increase in AIDS in teenage girls, twice the increase for teenage boys. The increase among teenage females is attributed to intravenous drug use, either by the girls themselves or by their partners. In the United States in 1993, 49% (N = 19,878) of female AIDS cases was from intravenous drug use while 37% (N = 14,997) was from heterosexual contact, of whom 3,773 female AIDS cases came from heterosexual sex with someone who did not identify his HIV infection at the time.[41] A six-city study by the Centers for Disease Control, reported by Masters and Johnson, showed that in Las Vegas 26% of prostitutes tested were infected with the AIDS virus while 74 out of 157 prostitutes (47%) were infected in San Francisco. Higher rates were found in other cities: Miami, 58%, Los Angeles, 70%, Newark, 86%.[42]

Most of AIDS prevention in prostitution has focused on condoms. As women throughout the world know, the condom is one of the least effective means of preventing pregnancy because condoms do not completely contain sperm. "They provide only a flimsy barrier, and they are subject to manufacturing or packaging defects that may cause them to leak." A 1987 test showed that 1 out of 5 condoms leaked.[43] Other research shows that if used properly condoms are an effective barrier. But whether or not they leak, they are still not an effective barrier, either in protecting women from pregnancy or in protecting them from AIDS. Guidelines for HIV counseling from the Department of Health for New York State (1990) point out that "no barrier method, including condoms, can guarantee 100 percent protection as product failure and incorrect use may occur."[44] The patriarchal sexual relations of power account for most of the failure rate as men impose their sex-without-condoms demand on women, and as sex is treated as an uncontrollable, especially male urge that should not be disrupted by stopping to use a condom.

Condoms have not been entirely ineffective in controlling AIDS. WHO reported that in testing in Zaire, they found that one-third of the prostitutes in Kinsashai tested positive for HIV. Two years later, after a condom campaign, new infections declined from 18% to 3%. However, WHO statistics are not reliable. For example, in a Bangkok "teahouse," 80% of the prostitutes tested HIV positive although doctors had certified them to be free of AIDS.

Thailand's National AIDS Committee launched a new campaign for 100% condom use in prostitution. Failure to use condoms carries punishment measures, and the brothel will be closed down if a brothel employee requests medical care for AIDS.[45] For each female life infected with AIDS from prostitution in a brothel, the punishment is that the brothel will be shut down for one day. Multimillion-dollar U.S. projects are being implemented worldwide to promote the use of condoms in prostitution as a protection from AIDS, and Thailand reported that condom use rose from 14% to 71.5% by mid-1991.

However, condom use to control AIDS will only be partially effective. Even with the risks there are other factors that make condoms a high-risk strategy for controlling AIDS in prostitution. The fact of multiple sex partners, the refusal of many customers to use condoms especially when they are drunk, and the offer of some customers to pay higher prices if they do not have to use condoms place prostitute women's lives, and all the other sexual partners, of the customer at constant risk. But this appears to be a risk that the World Health Organization is prepared to accept, for their response to prostitution and AIDS continues to be focused primarily on condom distribution. And that means that women will continue to contract it and die in increasing numbers. The educational programs designed to control the spread of AIDS have different messages for different populations. Single-partner sexual relations are encouraged along with condom protection for nonprostitute women in white, Western countries who are learning that it takes *only one act of unprotected sex* to become HIV positive. By contrast multiple sex partners are not discouraged for prostitutes. Instead, HIV testing on a monthly or, under the "best" of circumstances, weekly basis is considered sufficient protection for them. AIDSTECH, a U.S. Agency for International Development (AID) project, has mounted an educational campaign to promote condom use in prostitution. One poster from the City Health Department in Olongapo in the Philippines shows a happy Filipina walking away with a trick saying, "AIDS doesn't bother me. I know a safe trick (referring to condoms in her hand) and I always carry it with me." The AID-funded program organizes educational seminars in prostitution bars before customers come in, showing women how to put condoms on customers. In the Third World, these approaches amount to willfully risking female lives in order to sustain the sex industry and to provide supply for male customer demand.

What is clear about the response to AIDS in prostitution is that in the Third World and among women of color in prostitution in Western countries, the inadequate protection of condoms—which is known to risk thousands of lives even though it reduces the risk factor—is considered superior to changing masculine, misogynist sexual practices and habits.

At no time in patriarchal history has the outbreak of venereal diseases massively transported to and from prostitutes by customers been a cause for helping women get out of prostitution. Prostitution itself, that is, the prostitution of sexuality, is not considered harmful because the women in prostitution are considered to be an expendable population to be thrown away when no longer useful to the sex industries. AIDS prevention, which should be oriented toward getting women out of prostitution, is reduced to massive marketing of condoms to keep the sex industry and condom manufacturers going.

This is the most deadly of all the sexual double standards. While heterosexuals and homosexuals are being advised that condom use is a necessary *but insufficient condition* for safe sex, prostitution projects promote condoms to promote prostitution. By contrast, drug abuse projects, wherein clean needles are distributed to addicts to save their lives, does not involve promotion of drugs. Furthermore, a disinformation campaign has been launched: a proprostitution-lobby newsletter, *AIDS Action,* issued by the Appropriate Health Resources and Technologies Action group in England and distributed worldwide through the Department of Public Information Office of the United Nations, carries this false representation in its September 1991 issue:

The belief that sex work should not exist at all is one of the biggest obstacles to successful AIDS prevention among sex workers. Health messages aimed at clients which say: "Do not have sex with a prostitute," and those aimed at sex workers which attempt to find alternative employment have generally proved ineffective.[46]

Wrong.

First, most women in prostitution would leave if they could. Second, there is an alternative, a successful program that is a model for addressing prostitution by eliminating it. It has been tried and tested in Malmo, Sweden. This is not the only model. Others will be discussed in the last chapter. The Malmo project was begun in September 1977 in Sweden, in a region with a very high incidence of prostitution: 1 prostitute per 146 sexually mature men; 1 prostitute for every 63 women between the ages of 17 and 35. The project presumed that if it offered alternatives, the women would leave prostitution. It was designed to address all of the needs of women—economic aid, assistance in finding housing, help in finding jobs, medical assistance and counseling, support and protection for separating from pimps. Support was given to women whether or not they stayed in prostitution. But probably the most effective strategy that was utilized by the Malmo project, in addition to providing a wide array of services, was a mass media campaign designed to highlight the women who broke away from prostitution and to publicize the networks developed for and by women to support them in getting out. In other words, the media were used not to normalize prostitution but to legitimize women in getting out of it. By the fall of 1981, 72.5% (N = 111) of women had quit prostitution and of those who didn't, many were drug dependent.[47] There were only 60 prostitutes in Malmo by that time. The project was closed down in 1983.

Successful campaigns to reduce and even eliminate prostitution and to help women get out of it are based on several factors: the understanding that prostitution harms women, the intention to interfere with market supply for male customer demand, and the determination to provide women with emotional, psychological, health-services, *and* economic alternatives. Resocialization of both public attitudes and women in prostitution is possible, but it must supplant the proprostitution legitimization of the sex industry's reduction of women to whores.

The approach of the Malmo project was to eliminate prostitution. It included a legal approach that was supported by extensive social support for women and a massive anti-prostitution educational campaign. The Malmo project signals the direction for states to take in order to become disengaged from their legal role in promoting prostitution and the sexual exploitation of women.

8

Patricia Hearst: Prototype of Female Sexual Slavery

1994 Postscripted Prelude

There is a captivation with the disappeared woman or child—the suspenseful waiting—each piece of news generating more curiosity, more attention to accounts, holding an increasingly larger public with fascination. There is a sense in which the disappeared woman is unattached, loosened from patriarchal grips, outside of her family of origin, her marriage, disconnected from husband or lover. There is an unknown as to what the new configuration of the disconnected, unattached woman's new life will be. Woman is assumed to be wild and roving when she is not controlled by patriarchal power.

During the time Patricia Hearst eluded the FBI these assumptions formed the backdrop to the public's construction of their image of her and blighted the knowledge that rather than being released from patriarchal power, she had been kidnapped into another version of it.

250

I have included in this work a revised chapter from *Female Sexual Slavery* on Patricia Hearst because her experiences crystallized the way women experience female sexual slavery in prostitution. Her kidnapping is emblematic of the nature of women's victimization in that she became the woman no one wanted to, or dared to, understand. In the mid-1970s I followed her story through the kidnapping, the Hibernia Bank robbery, and the shootout at the sporting goods store, while the American public was riveted on each account. I was compelled by her plight, but even more so by the American public's refusal to understand her. Their increasing confusion stood in contrast to the one and only consistent voice of support for her, that of her mother. While I had no sympathy with the politics of the Hearst empire or with many of the public policies promoted by Mrs. Hearst, I saw that her loyalty to her daughter was unwavering as she repeatedly told an increasingly unbelieving press that Patricia was an innocent victim who was "looking down the barrel of a gun." She was one of the few who had not forgotten that Patricia had been kidnapped. Two years later, when Patricia's testimony in court corroborated her mother's belief in her daughter's victimization, the jurors, representing the American public's refusal to know Patricia Hearst's case as female victimization, concluded that she was lying.

While I followed this case, I was doing research for my book *Female Sexual Slavery*, interviewing women in prostitution, riding with vice police in the prostitution areas, interviewing district attorneys, and following pimps' cases in court, and I began to see clearly that Patricia Hearst's experience was representative. More, it was what sociologists call an "ideal type," meaning that in Patricia Hearst's story were all of the elements of women's victimization. Taken to an extreme, with intensified drama due to her family's wealth and notoriety, her case produced clarity by revealing to us more about women's victimization than we had known before.

Yet as her tragedy unraveled, Patricia's plight was not always clear to me. While I could criticize the failure of public opinion as misogynist, I was left with confusions, lapses in my explanations. That became personally painful because to the extent that I could not understand what happened to Patricia Hearst, who was a typification of female victimization, I would fail to understand the range and depth of those multitudes of invisible victims to whom my work was committed.

This started to affect my life and even disturb my sleep. I began to think of the loneliness of women's victimization—how the world closes women out, as it had Patricia, and how our experiences cease to be treated as human while unreal expectations of bravery and inhuman endurance—"if only she had," "why didn't she"—reminded me of what I had heard too many times (once being too many) when I had been raped years earlier. I thought frequently about her mother's comments and wondered if Patricia, wherever she was eluding the FBI, had heard them on television. If she did hear them, I wondered, would she know that one other human being saw her as she was—"looking down the barrel of a gun"? Would it matter that someone saw her in her own reality, a world that the rest of society refused to know?

I worried that my attempts to make sense of the misogyny surrounding the Hearst case were "getting under my skin." I could not afford to lose my perspective because, after all, as a rigorous sociologist I believe that research provides access to long-obscured women's realities. At that time I was studying under Herbert Blumer, the renowned sociologist and leader of the school of symbolic interactionism. One day, as I listened to him deliver an important lecture in which he portrayed the interpretive experience that is the cornerstone of sociological study of interaction, all the conflicting details of Patricia Hearst's story fell into place for me. Sociological interpretation had brought me to the place where feminism had already taken me, and I finally put the two together in such a way as to forge my "method": in interpretation one can only derive the *meaning* of a situation for another by *interpreting* that meaning *from the point of view* of the person going through the experience. Patricia's point of view and her knowledge of her situation was what she would take into consideration in making interpretations of her and others' actions. Her interpretations had been distorted by the police, the media, and the public's objectified interpretation of her. Normal human interaction involves repetitive acts of interpretation of the meaning of the other. Authentic interaction is interpretation that involves seeking the closest possible approximation of the meaning of the other. This core of the interpretive act is the foundation of human social action. When the other's actual situation and response is framed in terms of ideology, the meaning attributed to the other will be distorted, and the other becomes objectified.

By feminism as a method I refer to the act of restoring the objective situation by explicating everything in the situation from immediate objective conditions to institutional arrangements, gender and class conditions and patriarchal relations of power. Elaborating the situation provides the context for interpreting action. But ultimately, when women are refused subjective interaction, when women's victimization is construed ideologically as consent, a step further is required. I realized that meant that I must put myself in Patricia Hearst's situation, take on the objective conditions of her situation, and interpret the meaning she must have conveyed. At the time she was on the FBI's ten most wanted list, and later she was a prisoner in a federal prison, so the only way I could know the meaning she gave to her experiences was to put myself in her situation and ask, What would I have done in that situation?

I resisted this next step of really putting myself in her place, really knowing. I was already too far into my study of female sexual slavery to turn back. In my worry that this research was "getting under my skin," I had already begun that process. With this question: "What meaning did she give to her situation from her point of view?" I could begin to interpret her meaning because the question required that I take on her point of view, that is, put myself in her situation and then try to see it as she saw it.

So I began to reconstruct her situation from details I gathered and impressions I had developed. And finally I dared to ask myself, from what I hoped was the best approximation of Patricia Hearst's point of view, What would I do if brought before Cinque, known to me as a rapist and murderer, having been kept in a closet and tortured by him for 57 days? What would I do when he offered me my freedom or the opportunity to join the SLA? Immediately the confusions I had experienced gave way to full clarity. I knew then that only a complete fool would believe this to be a genuine offer. A survivor would make the choice to stay alive, in this case a choice to stay with the SLA, a choice that survivors know is no choice at all. *It is merely the next thing you do.*

My personal crisis with this study and with Patricia Hearst's victimization was resolved. But Hearst's ordeal continued. I wrote an article based on my research and interpretation of the Patricia Hearst case and published it in the feminist journal *Chrysalis.* And one day after her trial, Patricia Hearst's parole officer gave her the article. When she went back to prison, she asked to have me visit.

When I arrived at the Federal Correctional Institution in Pleasanton, California, Patricia was at a large table, surrounded by her sisters, being pre-interviewed by David Frost. I wasted no time. I went directly to her and we introduced ourselves to each other. She pulled up a chair for me next to her and within a few minutes David Frost left. Patricia turned to me to say, "I'm so glad to meet you at last. I have a question for you. Your article about me was the most accurate, fullest description of what I actually went through. How did you know?" I shrugged and said, "Oh, I was just trying to understand," unable to explain to her my satisfaction that my interpretations were finally vindicated. As I began questioning her for the interview I was there to conduct, I quickly realized that she was still fighting for her freedom.

. . .

Patricia Hearst was kidnapped, beaten, tortured, raped, and then imprisoned for the crimes that resulted from her victimization. Her case was prototypical of female slavery. When I talked to her in prison in July 1978, I asked her if she saw it that way, too. Her voice was emphatic: "What happened to me happened because I was a young female college student, an easy target. Women are always the easiest targets! It was unique only in the sense that what happened to me happens to many women but for me it was taken to the extreme. I feel that I can identify with many forms of oppression—I have been kidnapped, beaten, raped. I have been a prisoner in both county jails and federal prisons."

Patricia was kidnapped by self-styled leftist terrorists, not by a pimp. She was turned out as a revolutionary bandit, not as a prostitute. The rhetoric of her captors was different from that of pimps, but the seasoning that broke Patricia was as calculated as that of the best-trained slave procurers. The social attitudes and legal actions that coalesced around Patricia directly parallel those toward other women in slavery. In the public's mind she became the cause of her own victimization. In the eyes of the law she was a common criminal—not for hooking, loitering, or disturbing the peace, but for bank robbery.

On February 4, 1974, a member of an organization calling itself the Symbionese Liberation Army (SLA) kidnapped 19-year-old Patricia Hearst, an heiress of the Hearst publishing and corporate empire, from the Berkeley apartment where she lived with her fiancé, Steve Weed. Three days later, from a secret hideaway, the SLA announced that Patricia was a prisoner of war, and shortly after that escaped convict Donald DeFreeze (who called himself Cinque) set forth a ransom demand for a $6-million-food-giveaway program for the poor.

It was only a few days after her kidnapping that theories began to develop in radical circles that Patricia Hearst planned her own kidnapping. According to prevailing conjecture, she was a rich kid out for fun, rebelling against the social restrictions of upper-class life. At the time, no one knew much about people in the SLA except that they had taken responsibility for the murder of Oakland schools' black superintendent, Marcus Foster, and that they claimed to have revolutionary combat units around the country. While there was not an immediate round of applause from left radicals for the SLA, there was an instant hatred for Patricia Hearst—a rich kid who was "getting what she deserved." The lines were drawn as the right-wing and conservative public expressed pity for the poor young girl and sympathy for her abused father.

Details of Patricia's background, her childhood, school days, and affair with Weed fed the daily press. The portrayal of Patty as a docile and easily led but rebellious teenager seemed to support both leftist theories and right-wing pity. Public opinion shortly after the kidnapping was still malleable, able to shift according to new theories or available gossip—and there was some genuine worry and concern for her well-being.

But the events of April 3 and 15, 1974, changed everything. On April 3, a tape recording was released by the SLA in which Patricia announced her decision to join the SLA, and on April 15 she was photographed with others in a robbery of the Hibernia Bank in San Francisco. Her kidnappers had made her a symbol of corporate abuses and oppression by the rich. The public up to then had been tentative about what symbolic value to attach to these events. But Patricia's rhetoric and visible acts of apparent defiance immediately caused attitudes to shift and resolidify. The left's smug arrogance (they knew she was a rich kid out for thrills) merged into the right's condemnation as they saw their cherished values being trampled by one of America's former finest. Public opinion tended toward a sense of inevitability, with comments ranging from "what can you expect from the rich" to "there is no way to control these teenagers today." These judgments catapulted into an inevitable hatred of Patricia; she became everybody's symbol. She was envied, condemned, pitied, or ridiculed for being a spoiled brat or loving daughter, a kidnap victim or a revolutionary, a brainwashed neurotic or a common criminal, a rich kid out for adventure or a helpless victim. She became a symbol, no longer a human being either to the SLA or to the public.

As events passed from the bank robbery to a silent year and a half underground, then to her arrest, imprisonment, and trial, people began to complain bitterly about Patricia's taking up so much space in the news. It was a weird twist of logic. She had no control over the press that was exploiting her newsworthiness. The public had been captivated by her and then hated her for occupying its attention. As a symbol she ceased to be a woman; she could be disposed of whenever she was no longer of use. She had once told a CBS news reporter how frightening it was to be with the SLA, never knowing whether the "people you're with (are) going to kill you because you out-lived your usefulness to them." Later, after the trials, after she had been released on bail and then returned to prison, the public was bored and resentful.

Patricia was enslaved as much by the public's use of her as a symbol as by the SLA's need for a publicity trip to carry off its reactionary version of revolution. I discussed this with her and found that she had analyzed it herself: "I think people's own fears about themselves were exposed. People saw in me weaknesses in themselves that they were afraid of—like fears that they could be broken down. It's hard for people to face that. They couldn't stomp that out for themselves. It was cathartic for them to stomp me out."

And stomped out she was. After almost two years underground with William and Emily Harris, the only remnants of the SLA after a Los Angeles shootout, Patricia was arrested with them in San Francisco on September 18, 1976. Usually, when a kidnap victim is forced to commit crimes while with her captors, there is no prosecution for those crimes. Nevertheless, not only was Patricia charged for the Hibernia Bank robbery, but her case was mysteriously moved ahead on the crowded court calendar. The government was taken with a fever to bring this victim to justice, to make a lesson of her long before her remaining captors would face trial for her kidnapping.

Patricia was able to explain her participation in the Hibernia Bank robbery only in terms of her enslavement and abuse by the SLA. At her trial she testified that after she was abducted from her apartment, her life was constantly threatened while she was held, bound and blindfolded, first in one hot, stuffy closet and then in another for 57 days. (The jurors were taken to see the closets.) For 2 weeks she was allowed to go to the bathroom only at her captors' will, and later she would be allowed to go when she knocked on the door. After she had spent 2 weeks in the closet, her hands were tied in front of her; she was grateful that they no longer had to be tied behind her. Her menstrual period stopped. She was fed periodically, but initially she couldn't eat. When she did eat, she was often forced to sit blindfolded outside the closet in the humiliation of knowing that her captors were watching and ridiculing her while she was trying to eat. She was given a bath weekly by her captors, who wore ski masks while her blindfold was off, and the very removal of the blindfold caused her extreme pain and distortion of vision when the light hit her eyes. From inside the closet either she would hear music continuously playing outside the door or she would hear her captors' guns: "I could hear a lot of clicking and noises; and, it sounded like clips going in and out of guns and sometimes . . . they'd make noises like they were shooting and I could tell that they were standing right in front of the closet and doing it at me."[1] During her 57-day confinement, the SLA moved from Daly City to a Golden Gate apartment. Patricia was stuffed into a garbage can for the move.

She was told that she had to pay for the capitalist sins of her parents. In pain and humiliation, she was dependent on her captors for air, for food, for the opportunity to urinate, for her life. This dependency was reinforced when she was ordered to make the first taped message telling her family, "Mom, Dad, I'm okay," and asking her father to cooperate with her captors. A tape recorder had been brought to her in the closet, and she was given instructions on how to make the first message. Later the SLA women berated her for not doing well enough and reported her to Cinque, who meted out her punishment with sexual abuse.

At one point she was approached in the closet by Angela Atwood. "She said I was going to sleep with William Wolfe," Patricia recalled. Later, according to Patricia, Wolfe entered the closet and raped her. She was raped again by Cinque about a week later. During her trial, Patricia testified to her hatred for William Wolfe. In response, Emily Harris called a news conference and denied that Wolfe could have stirred such negative feelings in Patricia, declaring him to be one of the sweetest, most gentle men she had ever known. But Mizmoon, an SLA member who died in the Los Angeles shootout, recorded in her poetry a feeling closer to that of Patricia's:

> Willy . . . I hate him
> I want to scream
> next time he touches me
> Get your God Damned Hand off
>   My Body!
> (but his hands never were)
> damned . . . he's bein' only
> friendly . . . I'm not being
> paid to have him maul me
> Get your damned mind off my body![2]

After 57 days Patricia was allowed to leave the closet, and 2 days later, she reports, Nancy Ling Perry cut her long hair down to an inch all over her head. Humiliation. Prior to leaving the closet, she was allowed out occasionally for some exercise and political discussion. During these discussions she realized that the SLA knew more about her father's wealth than she did. She was endlessly interrogated with questions she could not answer and demands for information she did not have. This tactic kept her in the untenable position of trying to meet her captors' impossible expectations while her sense of futility and helplessness increased, engendering in her guilt for the wealth and practices of the Hearst empire.

The pivotal point concerning her willingness to join the SLA came on April 3, 1974. In a tape-recorded communiqué from the SLA, Patricia's voice pronounced:

I have been given a choice of, one, being released in a safe area, or two, joining the forces of the Symbionese Liberation Army and fighting for my freedom and the freedom of all oppressed people. I have chosen to stay and fight.

Did she mean what she said? Did it matter whether she meant it or not? In open court on February 9, 1976, she described the situation in which that decision had been made. She recalled how her captors, as an April fool's joke, had notified her parents that she would be released on April 1. She testified:

Well, a few weeks before, DeFreeze told me that the war council had decided or was thinking about killing me or me staying with them, and that I better start thinking about that as a possibility. Then he came in later and said that I could go home or stay with them. I didn't believe them.[3]

Patricia had to make a decision at that moment, a decision that followed 57 days of abuse and torture while she was confined in a closet. "I didn't believe them." Her decision was not whether to join the SLA and play at revolution or go home to Mom and Dad. Her decision, based on as reasonable an evaluation of her circumstances as she could make in her situation, was *whether or not to stay alive*. She made the decision of a survivor; the world saw it as an act of defiance—the kind of frivolity that only the rich can afford.

What would make her word so suspect? It was remembered, of course, that she had evaded an embarrassed FBI for nearly two years, but it was quickly forgotten that her life as a fugitive was spawned by a vengeful kidnapping. But her kidnapping was of negligible consideration in her trial. Her report of it was the only thing that all parties—defense, prosecution, judge, and jury—

accepted. Why? Steven Weed had many times publicly described the kidnapping of his then-fiancée, Patricia. Male corroboration was enough. Weed was not even required to testify at the trial. For the rest of it—her life as a kidnap victim, as a fugitive—we have only *her* word, *her* testimony. That was not enough.

On Lying

Did Patricia Hearst tell the whole truth and nothing but the truth, so help her God? Given her conviction, the jurors apparently believed that she lied in court in order to save her life. It was believed that the attorneys gave her a story that would fit their strategy. Whether before the U.S. courts or the SLA war council, Patricia's life was dependent on her word. And in her trial, her word—which ultimately was her only defense—counted for very little. At times it worked against her; it never seemed to work on her behalf.

Who would believe her?

Not the prosecution that overzealously pursued justice against a kidnap victim placed in a bank robbery.

Not a judge who, after Patricia's conviction, had the option of choosing the lenient route of sentencing her under the Youthful Offenders Act, which would probably have given her immediate probation. He instead chose the harshest possible sentencing, giving her a full 7 years in federal prison, noting that *her* conduct could not be condoned, that a lesson must be made of *her* to serve as a deterrent to others.

Not her lawyers. The defense strategy used by F. Lee Bailey was, in my opinion, a clear statement to Patricia and to the world that he lacked confidence in his client's veracity. Would he have portrayed her as a mindless, brainwashed victim if he hadn't believed she was guilty as charged? I think that by representing her as hopelessly empty-headed, he not only catered to the stereo-typed public image of her but also tried to remove her agency from the very action she chose on her own behalf, the only key to her survival. He legitimized *his* picture of her by the use of experts. (Patricia told me that she saw about 12 different psychiatrists during the period between her arrest and the trial.) As a defendant, she was simply a witness in her defense while one psychiatrist after another presented his or her expertise, attempting to uphold or break down the credibility of her word through that expertise. According to this strategy, she did not have to be believed. Judge and jury were asked to believe not Patricia's words, but the experts' analysis of *her motivations for those words and actions*.

In analyzing Patricia's experience of the SLA, the media, the FBI, and the courts from an interactionist approach, it becomes clear that Patricia ceased to be considered a human being by these parties. There was no interactive involvement with her experientially that was based on her, who she was. She was the "other," a thing, a symbol. And it was in this context that she had to represent herself as interactive, as truly human, a real woman. When the judge dismissed the relevance of the experts' testimony on Patricia's state of mind, all that was left for the jury was her word. They did not believe her. In fact, one juror I interviewed had developed considerable respect for Patricia's captors: "It is difficult for me to conceive that all seven of those people were crazy, all mad dogs. . . . These people appeared to treat her in some reasonable fashion." Neither did the jurors believe she was raped. Another man on the jury stated he was not sure: "It could have gone one way or another," and "it was only her word," he said. Another juror, discussing Patricia's confinement in the closet, asserted, "We [the jury] didn't think she had been in the closet that long. . . . In deliberations we felt she had been in the closet *only two weeks*" (emphasis mine). Clearly most people never think about what it might be like to be locked in a closet—for 2 weeks or 57 days. But that kind of statement represents a refusal of empathy, a distanced, noninteractive, not-human assessment.

If any one of the jurors had put themselves in Patricia's place and tried to understand what she faced and how she faced it in order to survive, especially when they had the responsibility of judging her, they would have transcended her symbolic representation to find a human being.

Each of the jurors I interviewed described Patricia as listless, empty, and pale during the trial. In awaiting her answers to her attorneys' questions about the brutality she experienced from the SLA, the jury expected to hear emotional outbursts. But as one juror said of her testimony on being raped, "She described it so calmly and didn't have any emotion in her voice." This led another juror to assert that she had simply been programmed by her attorneys. "She fit exactly what she was portrayed to be—a selfless, helpless, defenseless creature." This rationale made it possible to reason that Patricia was lying through her body as well as through her words. Her clothes, her tone of voice, her complexion, her sad eyes all meant—to the jury and the vigilant public that followed this trial—something other than what they were.

The only voice in this proceeding that credited Patricia's word—a voice that was not officially heard in the deliberations—was that of Mary Neiman, an alternate juror who would have held out for acquittal even if it meant a hung jury. But she never made it into deliberations. Agreeing that Patricia was listless in the courtroom, Mary saw this condition as a result of her experiences and an indication of her truthfulness. Talking to Mary made it clear that her point of reference was a personal, *interpretive* involvement. She tried to think of how any of her daughters would have responded in similar circumstances. "If she were lying, she would have tried to make herself look better," Mary said. While dramatic testimony would have impressed other jurors, Mary was convinced by Patricia's simple, unadorned statements. For example, when asked why she wrote on the wall of one apartment in Spanish and signed her name "Tania," she only said that everybody else did it and they expected her to do it, so she did. Surviving couldn't be as simple as that, the other jurors decided. They needed to see violent force from the SLA determining Patricia's every action, held over her every move.

Shortly after her trial, Patricia's lung collapsed, and after surgery her doctors reported that she was in a very debilitated condition. A legitimate medical authority made her pale, listless state real, legitimate, even believable. The doctor was believable. But it was too late. She had already been convicted of robbery.

Patricia had gone through all of the phases of dehumanization from distancing to disembodiment. But after she was arrested she could/did stop dissembling, acting as if disembodiment was her real self.

Patricia Speaks about Surviving

"I think people wanted to see something dramatic from me. They wanted to see me break down. I did everything I could to hold myself together. It would have been so humiliating to break down after all I had been through." It was not stubbornness but pride, a personal claim to her own self, that prevented Patricia from giving the jury and the public the performance they were expecting.

Four months passed between her arrest in San Francisco and the Hibernia Bank trial. She had been broken by the SLA and then kept in their constant companionship for 2 years. It was hardly surprising that she had not been able to compensate for the effects of those 2 years in 4 months. She accounted for her demeanor in the courtroom: "I was still very sick. I had lost a lot of weight. I had malnutrition and had just had pneumonia and the flu. I had not recovered psychologically from what had happened to me and I was very tired. During the trial, I was kept in the holding tank where all the drunks were at the county jail. I never got any sleep with all the yelling and carrying on in cells around me."

Two years after her trial, when Patricia had returned to prison after having been out on bail for 18 months, she was able to reflect on why this had happened. In our discussions I was taken by the relativity of her statements, the way she evaluated her present conditions in terms of her previous enslavement. Being back in prison (having exhausted all appeals in her case) was not such a big deal after all she had been through. At the time of our meeting she was faced with the likelihood of 6 more years behind bars. But her response was, "Prison isn't the worst place to be. They try to threaten you with discipline slips here. I never get any, but if I let that little piece of paper have any meaning for me, I would never make it. I can't think of it as anything more than a piece of paper. After all, what can they do to hurt me? Nothing! They can't put a gun to my head and threaten to shoot me."

When victimization is ongoing, unrelenting, and becomes an enforced way of life, injustice, abuse, and deprivation become relative to their circumstances. With the SLA Patricia was continuously threatened with murder. When the FBI was in mad pursuit of the SLA and the shootout occurred in Los Angeles, Patricia watched the shootout on TV with horror as other SLA members were fired upon and eventually the house was burned down. During it all she heard police and newscasters repeatedly state that they believed she was in the house that the police were shooting at and burning down. When I asked her what she thought was the single most important thing that she could attribute her survival to, she simply, almost off-handedly, responded, "Luck. I was just lucky so many times to not be someplace when I would have been killed, like being in the house in Los Angeles when it was burned down. Every time something awful happened that could have killed me, I missed it."

Surely, there was more to her survival than luck. Patricia began to open up:

I guess you have to have an ability to do something to stay alive. Some people just give up and don't make it. Staying alive means that you don't give up. You want to stay alive so much that you do anything you have to—it's a selfish state in the sense that you are only able to focus on yourself and how to get through it alive. That is the point in surviving when you feel you have made it at the loss of your self-respect. Self-respect is most important to surviving. You have to be able to look at yourself in the mirror in the morning. When I realized the things I had to do just to stay alive, I started feeling confused and guilty about it, wondering, "How could I let myself do this or that?" My psychiatrist helped me a great deal with that guilt.

It was the shift from living in a crisis-dominated, moment-to-moment effort to survive, to being in jail, faced with a different challenge to survival, that first allowed her introspection on her behavior in a crisis state.

Patricia described how, during her time with the SLA, she had to turn inward and draw from her own reserves in order to survive. She depended only on herself: "No one else can get you through something like this. People are so used to TV programs where, when someone is in danger, there is always someone there in minutes to rescue them. My youngest sister had an awfully hard time facing that I wouldn't just automatically be rescued. When you are held captive, people somehow expect you to spit in your captor's face and get killed."

The Missing Years: Was She Patty or Tania?

The stages in constructing a woman into a prostitute fit Patricia's report of her circumstances. First, facing the immediate terror of being kidnapped and physically abused, like the rape victim, she tries to make sense out of what's happening, to figure it out, to get away. She makes every reasonable interpretation of her captors' behavior that she can make from the information she has available to her. Used to interacting with and interpreting the world around her, she finds that her interpretations no longer work. The act has distanced her from her life as she knew it before the kidnapping. One of the psychiatrists, Dr. West, found that for Patricia,

Her usual coping techniques, mobility, independence, autonomy, use of allies, winning the esteem of others by performing well, self-assertion and so on—these were all useless. Her external points of reference for maintenance of her identity had disappeared. All sources of self-esteem were cut off. At times, the entire situation began to seem unreal to her and, at other times, it was she who seemed unreal or it was another person who was having these unthinkable experiences.[4]

The second stage, disengagement, is how the woman handles the situation as a result of her captors' forced redefinition of her world. Unlike rape victims, who will eventually get away from their attackers, however shattered they may be from the rape, a woman enslaved cannot physically leave. She must find another way out. It is a common human response when one is faced with tragedy to react conditionally with "this *couldn't* be happening to me." But when tragedy becomes unending, when abuse is the total environment, the conditional is transformed into the permanent and becomes dissociation: "This *isn't* happening to me." Then the woman becomes disembodied to take on the role assigned to her. As SLA heroine or Bailey's client, "She fit exactly what she was portrayed to be." But others' constructions of her were taken to be her, therefore she was dissembling.

In Patricia's case, as in most slavery, all of the phases of breaking down a woman's identity for prostitution, from distancing to disengagement to dissembling, eventually became collapsed into one, repeated in different scenarios. Whether it is enacted by the SLA, an international ring of procurers, or individual pimps, the seasoning of women enforces dependency on their captors, and in that dependency they construct new identities. Dr. West testified in Patricia's case that after she was released from the closet,

She was persuaded to take on a certain role and she complied with everything they told her to do. . . . And if she took her part with the group, she just tried to blend in with others and behave in a fashion that she understood was to be accepted. For her, it was be accepted or be killed. Now after they finally went through the sort of little ceremony where she was taken out of the closet after about eight weeks and allowed to take off her blindfold and sit down and eat with the others for the first time as a member, sort of, sometime soon after that, she was given her name by Cinque. . . . Then after she . . . had assumed the role of Tania, she began to try to be like they wanted her to be—if she was going to be Tania, that meant writing *venceremos* [we will win] on the wall with a can of paint or something, if that's what was expected of her.[5]

Temporality

The experience of rape is different from that of slavery or long-term abuse in one significant respect: time. Female sexual slavery invokes the same stages as the prostitution of sexuality, which may extend over days, weeks, months, and even years. In this context Patricia's experience sheds light on the experiences of women forced into prostitution. Simply, when one foresees the probability of escape in 10 minutes or 10 hours, one will behave differently than if, in addition to all the torture and violence, one foresees no probability of escape. In the latter state, the world becomes closed; vision narrows only to present experience. The victim's world is only what is contained in the immediate moment. And, finally, distinctions blur between one's identity and the identity one has learned, been forced into, or taken refuge in as a captive. What makes this slavery is the loss of one's self, which Gabel describes in terms of false consciousness: *"Identification with the enemy is the worst form of depersonalization; it is the loss of freedom to be oneself."*[6]

When there is a possibility of getting out of a situation, a woman will do what is necessary to survive, whether that be going passive or physically fighting back. The strategy chosen depends on the context of the situation, the degree of force used against her, the extent to which she is not immobilized by terror, the training in attitude and physical self-defense she has had. But when there is no possibility of getting out, survival inevitably necessitates redefining oneself to fit the new circumstances.

For women in long-term captivity and subjected to sexual terrorism, fear is different from, and cannot be compared to, that of male prisoners of war. Overwhelming fear increases the sense of terror. Dr. West found this phenomenon to be critical in the violence Patricia experienced: "I would say it was more violent than any military captive, because these, after all, were soldiers and had been trained and gone through various kinds of hardening experiences before they were captured." [7]

Patricia's case provides a clear understanding of the stages of becoming a prostitute, of the way identity and will are reconstructed when time is frozen and the way distancing, disengagement, dissociation, and disembodiment occur.

During Patricia's captivity, her social world consisted only of people who hated her. With them she lived in the moment only, never knowing and not having control over what the future would be. Her world consisted only of the SLA, their actions, and their rhetoric. It was an unreal world in that she was cut off from life as a process, a progression. What we normally take for granted as life evolving through interaction and involvement was denied by this group, which lived only in the context of their rhetoric, not by experience—only by "correct" positions on issues, not through interaction and relationships around issues. Patricia could not take into account a total environment, for she was removed from it and did not know the world beyond the SLA's representation of it to her and her experience in the confines of their various hideouts.

Positive change or growth is impossible in a situation in which time is rigidified into the present only; where interaction is denied, interpretation becomes meaningless. Change normally evolves out of interaction in relationship with people and one's environment; it is a progression, a movement over time. When time is halted, progression ceases and the world is narrowed, making interaction almost meaningless. This is the situation of the very young child who has not learned interaction but is totally self-centered, living in the present moment. Gabel describes this state as the "loss of the dialectic of the possible and impossible." [8] When "the possible" is truly denied, the future is cut off. Life is only in the immediate moment. One does not think about whether or not to go to a movie, take a certain job, plan a course of study, have a child, or become a revolutionary for lack of anything better to do.

In addition to the torture and imprisonment in closets that inevitably caused her to take on a new identity, the politics and rhetoric of the SLA formed the not-real world in which she was held. Life for the SLA was an abstraction, a denial of the process of existence. By making their rhetoric into their style of behavior and by assuming a political superiority to the real world, they separated themselves from the real world. It was in the world of the SLA that Patricia Hearst took on the identity of Tania.

When I first met Patricia two years after her arrest and trial, she was looking well. She had gained weight and recovered her psychological as well as physical strength. But her focus on the present, the immediate situation, was startling to me. She spent considerable time talking about what happened that day, but when I asked questions that involved thinking about the past or the future, her answers initially were brief, one word. For example:

Q: What was the most significant factor in your survival since you were kidnapped?
A: Luck.
Q: What do you want more than anything else in the world?
A: Serenity.

As rapport grew between us and as Patricia started to take time to reflect on these questions, she would, on her own initiative, come back to these questions with fuller responses, giving substantive, insightful meaning to her initial one-word answer. She was, I think, two years after her trial, still filling out that time frame that during the SLA days had been narrowed to the moment. She had a profound understanding of her experiences, of how she was treated and how she has been judged, but in those years she sometimes had to make an effort to break through the time frame of the present moment in order to reflect on the past.

In an attempt to avoid living her life in reaction to her immediate past, she became philosophical.

I try not to be bitter. All that does is eat away at *me*. It isn't a good way to get back; it doesn't accomplish anything. I mostly try to laugh at the people who threaten me.

I could look at the last five years as wasted. But it could have been worse. I try to pick the good out of it all. I think there is a lot to be salvaged. I've learned a lot about my strengths and weaknesses. In getting my whole ego and personality destroyed and then building it back up again, I've had an opportunity to get stronger than I was before.

Being in jail does not facilitate rebuilding an ego or redefining one's identity. One prison succeeded another for Patricia. She had passed from the hands of the SLA to those of the U.S. government, and, she had become its prisoner. After being arrested, Patricia spent 14 months in solitary confinement "for her own protection," and later she was held with other prisoners who hated her either for being rich or for being a snitch. "I feel like I'm becoming a professional prisoner. I'm here. I have to deal with it. The people who run this prison keep telling me this is such a nice place. Like I'm lucky to be here. I feel like saying to them, 'You're no better than the SLA.' I mean, I'm their prisoner. I'm not here because I'm their friend."

As soon as she was released on bail from the U.S. prisons, she became a prisoner in her own home. This time her captors were her lawyers. The first security company that was hired told her she could not leave the house at all, a restriction that was imposed by her lawyers.

They were really overreacting to the possibility of someone else doing something to me.

Bailey told me never to go out because reporters would be waiting for me. It took me several weeks to figure out that it was all right to go out. Bailey also didn't want me to go to nightclubs, and he told me I couldn't go to Disneyland because someone might try to take my picture with Mickey Mouse!

But by the time she was released to her parents' custody, she had developed enough strength to assert herself again. She refused to comply with Bailey's attempt to further confine her and insisted on trying to develop a normal life again. "Being out on bail finally put me back into a normal environment where I could have normal interactions with people. Until I could socially interact again, I was not able to assert myself or function the way other people do. That's when I stopped seeing a psychiatrist, even though my family protested, but I figured I could rely on myself then. I wanted to make it on my own."

She went home to people who love her—her parents, her sisters, and friends. She no longer saw many of her old friends from school. "They weren't part of what happened to me. They didn't have to change as the rest of us did. It's hard to relate to them now, and a lot of people have this thing—they actually are afraid to be around me. Some of my old friends are afraid, their families are afraid, so I just can't put up with them!" With family and friends she began to connect the past with the present and the future. Her identity was established in that continuity. When I met with her after she had been returned to the Federal Correctional Institution in Pleasanton, California, she seemed more sure of herself than media reports had suggested. She had changed lawyers and she herself had taken over decisions and direction regarding the legal issues she faced. Clearly, the initiative and the decisions were hers then. Until she was granted clemency, she had to maintain a delicate balance between tolerating her confinement and knowing it was unjust, between seeking release and vindication and not wanting her life to be absorbed in negativism.

Feminism and the Left

From the SLA's inception, theories were developed that it was a government-sponsored covert plan to discredit and destroy the left and so-called revolutionary movements. Whether or not that was the case, leftist organizations did not denounce the atrocities carried out by the SLA, and consequently those acts were seen as a logical extension of male left revolutionary rhetoric. Tacit approval of the SLA was implied in the silence of groups with whom it was trying to establish a solidarity.

Political movements like the left, dominated by white middle-class males, derive their rhetoric from intellectual theories rather than lived experience of oppression. As a result, their politics are motivated more by their self-interest and personal power than by actions that would change the actual conditions of oppression. The SLA belonged to that group of political people whose connection to oppression was superficial and self-serving. They claimed to be in support of feminism, but they exploited the women's movement for their own purposes. The media accepted their line, and no one noticed that the SLA had actually violated, in the most dangerous and vicious way, the basic principles of feminism by *kidnapping a woman to punish her father* and justifying the action because she was from a privileged class. Behind the shabby rhetoric, in the SLA feminists saw *men against men over the body of a woman.*

Like so many left groups in the 1970s, the women of the SLA used feminism by emptying it of its politics and reducing it to a kind of self-improvement ideology, in order to gain recognition and legitimacy from the men in their group. Without a feminist politics the SLA could not recognize the threat Patricia Hearst's change in identity represented to the patriarchal establishment. To the FBI and the general public, she was dangerous and threatening, not simply because of some abstract identification with another class, but because as a *woman* she was defying—for all the world to see—the gender expectations of her sex-class. She had been a loving daughter, but after her change in identity she was a woman trampling on all the female virtues to which she had been so carefully socialized. She appeared openly to reject wealth, her family, her fiancé, and the protection of the FBI. There were few female roles that tradition begs us to play that Patricia didn't challenge as "Tania." What was assumed to be her ungratefulness and defiance angered the public and enraged the establishment.

It was not just because Patricia defied female gender expectations that this wrath was brought down on her; in a patriarchy set up to protect and thereby confine women, Patricia as Tania appeared to turn her back on rather elaborate offers of protection—her father's wealth and the FBI's support (even though accepting could have meant her death). Try as they might, the SLA women—Emily Harris, Camilla Hall, Patricia Soltysik, Angela Atwood, and Nancy Ling Perry—could never have rejected so much, for they never had so much combined patriarchal love, capitalist advantage, and personal support and protection offered to them. As a child of wealth, Patricia had inherited the Great American Dream for womanhood. The other women were only on the fringes of such a patrimony. But Patricia could have had it all. It was when the public thought that she rejected this inheritance, when she seemed to defy the offerings of patriarchal protection, that she brought down the wrath of the FBI in the form of an anti-feminist backlash. The backlash was directed against Patricia, and was meant as a warning to feminism.

Loyalty

From the time she was kidnapped, society, across the spectrum from right to left, expected Patricia to vindicate herself. To the right, vindication meant fighting to her death or at least being able to walk away from her captors and into the hands of the FBI, even after she witnessed the massacre in Los Angeles on television. In other words, both the right and the left expected her to extricate herself from her fear for her life while in the hands of her captors and hunted by the FBI, and to undo the dependency that had been cultivated with great calculation by her captors. To vindicate herself to the SLA, to the American left, and to the other self-proclaimed revolutionary movements, she was expected to espouse the cause of violent revolution and murder even unto death (her death). Had she refused to testify on her own behalf, she could have gained some support from the left. Had she in martyrdom submitted herself to the fate of her captors, she would at least have won pity from everyone else.

Considering all this, women are left to conclude that to be recognized as a victim one has to be dead, the condition of honor in masculinist society.

When we talked at the prison in Pleasanton, California, I asked Patricia how she felt about loyalty. Her response was immediate and firm: "To thine own self be true!" This is the "selfish state" she referred to earlier in our discussion, and I thought it marked her passage from victim to survivor. Yet it was not freedom. Freedom lies beyond mere survival and beyond prisons, and Patricia had not yet arrived there; she was still in prison, looking forward to being released and to beginning a life that would not be lived in reaction to the past.

President Jimmy Carter commuted Patricia Hearst's sentence on February 1, 1979. After she was released, she married her former bodyguard.

Human Rights and Global
Feminist Action

S trategies to confront sexual exploitation should be as global as
the economy is international and as the dimensions of women's
subordination are universal, and as radical as is the rootedness of
the prostitution of sexuality. As domination produces despair,
struggle for liberation is the act of hope. Hope shatters the conviction that domination is inevitable, especially in the case of sexual
exploitation, particularly in regard to prostitution.

The primary reason why I have been able to continue this work
(even, at times, against my personal will) is because of those
women whose feminist consciousness of domination has enabled
them to act on their knowledge, to transform the facts of women's
subordination into political struggle and personal healing—of self
and of others—for women. They are and have been the source of
my optimism. Sources of hope that transcend the brutal realities of
sexual exploitation can be found in women's projects around the
globe. This hope is found in collectives of women and, in some
places, in a singular feminist whose solitary voice breaks the barrier

of sound overpowering the voices of despair of those who refuse to speak of sexual exploitation as violation and thus perpetuate it. The voices of hope are diverse; they do not speak in one unison chord. Rather, they come together from their diversity, yet in a universal condition to unravel and expose sexual exploitation in all its global complexity. They are the foundation of a global feminism moving ever closer to the visionary understanding that sexual exploitation, beginning with prostitution, is not inevitable and therefore a world free from sexual exploitation is possible.

In often tentative ways, Western and Third World women are finding the bases of common struggles, transcending patriarchal separations of women into the opposing forces men have constructed to dominate and war against each other. Global feminist action against sexual exploitation is genuine international struggle for Western feminists when we first understand domination and struggle against sexual subordination in our own lives, cultures, and countries. It is therefore the obligation of Western feminists to take extra steps toward making connections, listening and learning, and finding the common base for collective action against sexual exploitation. A global struggle is required to confront the international industrialization of women through Western sexual and economic hegemony over the Third World, which is acted out by military men, tourists and businessmen, diplomats and governments, and which perpetuates the sexual exploitation of women, particularly in prostitution.

International feminism gives voice and presence to that which has been unspoken in the global oppression of women. Where women are actively silenced from speaking the unspeakable, particularly in areas of the world where women may be at great risk in claiming their human right to be free of sexual exploitation, global feminism gives international presence to issues that otherwise would be buried by political repression.

The Silence of Forgetting

The problem remains for feminism to speak about sex and its socio-political construction into female dehumanization. In one professional meeting after another, in one conference after another, I have introduced the problem of silencing of sex when sex itself is exploitation, is harm, destroys. When I organized a conference, "The Politics of Sexuality" at Penn State in 1991, in order to explore this issue with feminists who have confronted the problem more directly and forcefully than anyone else, I found that even there, sex itself was not discussed. Sex as violence was discussed, but sex itself—the condition of subordination of women that is both bodied in femaleness and enacted in sexual experience—was silenced even in a feminist context most conducive to discussion of it. Adding violence on to sex makes sexual exploitation speakable, but it silences sexual oppression—the sexual relations of power that produce a condition of sexual exploitation. The fact is that in more than 20 years of feminist organizing against "violence against women" and against pornography, we have not yet created the language, the conceptual base from which to speak of sex itself as violation of women, whether or not there is consent, as there is usually presumed to be in prostitution. Andrea Dworkin has broken ground in this area in her book *Intercourse*.[1]

The political silencing of sex as exploitation begins in its privatized condition in marriage and extends to the public normalization of prostitution, especially in the West. Normalizing prostitution socially reaffirms women's not remembering. We know that when the self, the body, and one's experience are sufficiently traumatized, those acts that hurt cannot be contained in memory. The promotion of pornography and the legitimization of prostitution sustain women's forgetting and politically reinforce the sexual relations of power.

Consider the enormous, yet-unknown female population who

have been victims of incest abuse, who were sexualized by adult males—their "protectors"—before they had even developed their own identities as human beings, and who do not remember because the utter violation is so severe that the human soul has not the capacity to endure it in the memory of those women. If no one says to them, "This is wrong; no human being, no girl should ever be treated this way," there is nothing to trigger memory of it that has been buried in an intensively sexualized society.

We cannot begin to calculate the numbers of women who promote pornography, defend prostitution, or oppose feminist naming of sex as exploitation. We may never know how many among these women do not remember and cannot yet know that they were sexualized as children by uncles, fathers, stepfathers, grandfathers. There are women who actively pursue objectified sex, who promote kinky sex, who promote prostitution (usually of other women, infrequently of themselves), and who defend and promote pornography. Given the patriarchal relations of power, it is not surprising that they are taken as representative of what women want and what women should be doing in their bodies.

I can no longer count the number of times my work has been challenged and censored by academic women who later reveal to me privately, but *never say publicly,* what they ultimately could not remember or did not even know they dared not speak. Their own experience of sexual abuse as children or in a marriage or with a lover, rendered into silence, prods their censorship of women who dare to break that silence. This fact of women's sexual exploitation gives new meaning to "divide and conquer," the well-known strategy of oppressors. In the private, silent, unspoken, sometimes unremembered, often dissociated experience of sexual exploitation, girls and women are saddled with a bonding to male sexual demands that turns women against other women, not their unnamed oppressors, their unidentified violators.

Some women, a few (and they are the tip of an iceberg), are beginning to remember. Even fewer are daring to speak publicly.

They are struggling through the hell of what has been unspeakable, unknowable violation—of knowing the unspeakable, of reliving the unknowable. As they are struggling, with courage that sometimes tests the limits of human imagination and endurance, and as they are coming to grips with their past, we as a feminist movement have been growing enormously because of their remembering, their struggle, their courage—for in their remembering they name the sex that is sexual exploitation. The sexual relations of power are revealed to them and to us for what they really are: oppression that perpetrates the violation of women's human dignity and human rights.

Sexual exploitation is in and on our bodies, and its severity not only fragments the self, reducing human wholeness through objectification, but also often becoming an "out-of-body" experience, something that cannot even be contained in human memory. Not remembering does not give voice and speech to violation. Thus not remembering is more than a traumatic consequence of individual acts of domination. Not naming, or in some cases not remembering, being sexed into subordination and consequently dehumanized leads directly to the displacement of sex from being a part of human experience to being the cornerstone of the sexual politics of oppression. At the crux of this displacement is the production of a separate throw-away class of women—prostitutes, the women who knowingly do the sex of sexual exploitation, who are represented as the validation of sex that is exploited.

In the West, feminism has been pushed to defend its raison d'être by establishing force in relation to any sexual exploitation. But violence is only one aspect of oppression, and opposing violence alone diminishes the possibility of a liberation movement. It contains feminism within a reform of sexual exploitation, and sustains the sense of inevitability of prostitution. Emphasizing force as the condition that makes sexual exploitation a violation silences sexual oppression. Most importantly, it silences the millions of women who are not coerced into prostitution and who are deeply harmed by it. And it silences those victims of sexual exploitation who have lost their memory of experiences so trau-matizing that they cannot be remembered.

Remembering, Healing, Consciousness

If we are to speak of women as human beings, they must be enabled to enjoy full human rights. The *intraindividual* effects of sexual commodification and other sexual exploitations that pre-vent their enjoyment of human rights must be discovered, re-vealed, confronted, and overcome. With all of the new syndromes and 12-step healing programs, nothing can replace or surpass the effect of feminist consciousness raising in personal healing and collective struggle. It is the basis for women reclaiming themselves from sexual expropriation. Because feminist consciousness is criti-cal, it invokes women's active engagement in both personal and political struggle and sustains our ongoing resistance to domina-tion, creating an ongoing realization of the possibilities of revolu-tionary change. Feminist consciousness is the key to knowing the possibility of a life beyond exploitation.

From feminist consciousness of sexual relations of power, per-sonal healing begins with political and social rejection of sexual exploitation, especially prostitution and pornography. Where there has been multilayered abuse as in the experience of refugee women, as in the condition of women subjected to state as well as sexual terrorism over time, consciousness of state power may well delay awareness of sexual power, and seeking safety from political torture may precede the recognition that safety also means protec-tion of one's sexual/bodily integrity. Similarly, in almost all cases of sexual exploitation of women who are mothers, preoccupation with children's safety will precede coming to terms with one's own sexual subjugation. Women are the first to be exploited and the last to be healed.

Although individual therapy programs focused on personal healing may lead some women to political consciousness of sexual relations of power, I suggest that critical consciousness of sexual subjugation, as in "consciousness raising," is a fundamental condition to personal healing because, among other things, it invokes collective struggle, breaking the isolation imposed through domination. It is virtually impossible to fully recover from the damage of sexual exploitation if one does not "know" the sexual relations of power that produced the harm in the first place. Knowing the sexual power that reduces one to a sexual object only makes sense in the context of a struggle that refuses sexual exploitation, confronts sexual relations of power, and challenges the foundations of male domination. To remember and to know outside of that struggle sends a woman from a victimizer to a protector, meaning that she is never able to return fully to her own self. Feminist consciousness of power relations, then, is at the center of both personal healing and political struggle. But knowing has a deeper meaning than having a correct political analysis. Full knowledge requires facing the damages and confronting the source of suffering so that the legacy of domination no longer holds power over one's person in the form of enduring pain, being ashamed of or at odds with oneself, turning anger on other women in horizontal hostility, or continuing the self-hatred engendered in the original harms.

To illustrate the possibilities of feminist programs and the limitations they confront, I will present 3 programs, the Prostitution Group in Sweden, the Council for Prostitution Alternatives in the United States, and Buklod in the Philippines. (*Buklod,* which means "bonding," is the name the Filipina bar women gave to the seminars that brought them together.) What is common to these programs is that they rest upon consciousness raising as the basis for women's healing, for their claiming of their selves in order to become active agents of their own lives.

The Prostitution Group in Göteborg, Sweden, a city of approximately 500,000, consists of 4 social workers, 2 women and 2 men who go out on the streets every evening to meet the women there, talk with them, and invite them to coffee and their project. They see from 350 to 500 prostitutes a year in a city with 15,000 to 25,000 johns or customers. Elisabet Petterson, who has been working in the project since it began in 1982, finds that a crucial element in women leaving prostitution is "to be there for them and to listen." Yet there is more. The single most important factor is care. "They are beautiful women. They are kind, too kind because they can't say no to customers." When a girl or woman comes off the streets into the group, she works with a particular social worker, who is the one in the group who has a particular feeling of care for that woman. The Prostitution Group realizes that care must be expressed by the social worker to make a good match with the woman. In addition to counseling, the social worker involves the woman in training and social health programs.

Girls who are minors (under the age of 20 in Sweden) can be forcibly removed from prostitution with support of the state. The Prostitution Group uses this authority to get girls out of prostitution even when they initially are reluctant to leave. As Elisabet reported, often someone from the Prostitution Group is the first one ever to say "no" to the girls. They frequently come from families that have not established boundaries for them and where no one has ever said, "No, you can't do this." The combination of firm direction, personal caring, and listening seem to be the critical ingredients to keep the girls from going back into prostitution.

At Buklod in Olongapo, seminars are held for women in the bars. The seminars are meant to empower women who typically have lost control over their lives because the bar managers or "papa-sans" dictate the terms of their existence. In meeting with the Buklod women, I was told by bar women and former prostitutes that when women first join the group they have been saying yes to everything their managers tell them to do. But after some time in the seminars,[2] they begin to assert themselves, little by little. They begin to make choices, to refuse some things and to decide which other things they are willing to do in the bar. But their choices are confined within the objective limits of what their poverty will permit. The Buklod seminars begin with remembering, as the coordinator, Emela Cabayong, explained: "We always ask them to make your own 'river of life.' And every woman talks about her story." Coming into the seminar, "you just remember the past when you are working in the bars," explained Pearline, who came to Buklod from the bars. But as women explore their lives together in the seminars, they begin to "remember the past when you were a little kid." There is much crying as they think back to the lives they had before the bars. Stories of childhood joys and of the horrors of incest abuse come out. Pearline explained, "You need to recall because you don't know why you work in the bars."

Connecting to the past, remembering, telling stories, crying, and joking—it all goes together and healing begins. "Healing is in the process," Emela explained, because, as Pearline said, "the most important thing in the seminar is that you come to understand your situation."

Fifty to 75 women, some new ones, others who keep coming back, attend each seminar, of which there have been hundreds. A kind of community building goes on there, and as the women strengthen their relationships to each other, relaxing, joking, and playing games, their interactions in the bars begin to change. Many of the women, even though they are in the healing process, go from the Buklod meetings to the bars. Buklod sponsors training programs to teach women sewing and other crafts, but this work has not yet been developed to a level that sustains them economically.

Something changes after attendance at Buklod seminars. Consciousness stirs something, and women transcend the objectification of their bar lives to become human beings with histories, places in time, lives and relationships beyond prostitution. They come to know themselves as they learn that they are not only that which prostitution does to them. They begin to say no, although sometimes, because of their dire economic situations, they can only afford to say no to some things. "The papa-san told me to scrub the floor and I said, 'Why should I?' He gets mad at me." In another case, one woman decided not to go to the bar on New Year's Eve. "It's a time to relax," she said. This was a decision, a choice, a self-motivated action that likely would not have occurred before, when she did not even think of herself as someone who should have a "time to relax."

The bar managers are unused to such truculence in "their" women. "Before, Linda and I always go with American guys," Pearline explained. After attending the seminars, they stopped. "At least you know how to talk to managers." The women begin to look for ways to do something else—perhaps tend bar instead of going with the customers. But here the system beats them out because "you don't earn enough money tending bar to support your child." These distinctions are finely tuned, reasoned out from within the increasing selfhood that women reclaim.

Unlike the Prostitution Group in Sweden, "We cannot tell the women to stop [prostitution]," Emela explained, because Buklod cannot provide the economic means for them to survive. The gendering of poverty provides the work upon which these women survive while being destroyed, de-constructed, de-selved. For these women, the dilemma of prostitution is complexly multilayered. They come from massive poverty amidst the new material gains in rapid industrialization; they have been sexually abused as children or married in their teens and abandoned with their own children. Under the conditions of underdevelopment, women see marriage as their only possibility, and when they are cast adrift there are few other possibilities outside of the sex industries. This evokes a sense of inevitability about prostitution and marriage. That inevitability is expressed in the brochure for Buklod, which explains that "forcing or helping individual women to leave prostitution is the least effective way of addressing the problem. For every woman who leaves the bar, there will be at least five willing to take her place." This desperation is precisely what the sex industry counts on and the proprostitution movements legitimize.

Consequently, the main emphasis of this program is on personal empowerment in victimizing situations.

What about welfare or social assistance? "The government doesn't care about us," many of the women said to us over and over again. While they see Olongapo being remodeled to develop industries, they see themselves rejected, ignored, invisible in the plans for conversion of the bases and the prostitution towns that served the U.S. military when it was there. If tourist men replace the military men as they have in other prostitution areas, the women will continue to be enlisted for sexual service.

There is no welfare system, no source of support for food, for rent, or for the many children fathered by many of the American military men who took the women out on "bar fines" to live with them during their stay in the Philippines. In the bar-fine system, the GI paid the bar for the time he was away with the woman. The bar established bargain rates by the week, the month, etc. This system made it possible to transfer human life as sexual property. Living together on a bar fine, the men usually treated the women as girlfriends. Frequently the women became pregnant and bore children.

When I visited there in 1993, the American military had left. As the inevitability of prostitution is unchallenged, the women were still clinging to the belief that their "boyfriends" who were the fathers of their children would come back. Inevitability of sexual exploitation in prostitution interconnects with the inevitability of marriage and the perpetuation of female subordination. Ever since the existence of U.S. bases, marrying an American has been seen as a way out of poverty for women. But for the military men, Philippine women were merely there for their sexual use. "I got a passport but he never sent the ticket," we were told, or "I get a postcard sometimes," maybe once in 6 months. The "luckier" ones receive small amounts of money, and that helps. But receiving cash in an envelope without a letter, without a way to locate the "boyfriend," is a reality that cuts deeply and that women try not to know. The tension of economic dependence on the bar system prevents them from attaining consciousness of independence and perpetuates the dreams of going to the United States as a GI's wife. Not surprisingly, "love is bullshit" became a common saying among bar women in Olongapo.[3]

In addition to Buklod, there are several centers organized by Sister Soledad Perpinan, leader of the Third World Movement Against the Exploitation of Women. She has organized training programs, drop-in centers, and shelters in Subic and Manila in Angles, which adjoins former Clark Air Force Base. These centers provide shelter, long-term living arrangements, retraining, and self-sustaining-employment training in sewing, typing, and soap making. Visiting a new center recently opened by Sister Sol in Manila, we saw the patio of the house where she plans to open a candle-making factory.

It is a beginning. In these small projects, the women will not make more than they made in prostitution, but they are aware that they will have themselves. When women go from rural poverty to being exploited labor in new factory systems to making more money in prostitution, often they are unaware of what they are losing of themselves and of their rights at each stage. But these projects are making them aware of what they have lost and what they can regain. And out of these programs larger projects may be developed. They are already envisioned. They only lack economic aid. For now, economic aid to prostitute women has been focused on condom distribution, a necessary strategy but one which perpetuates prostitution. Only in a world where prostitution is not considered inevitable, natural, or a woman's choice can women begin to think of creating real choices by building such things as cooperative industries.

But the fact that prostitution is increasingly treated as merely another form of labor reminds us that slavery too is considered labor, not slavery, by slave masters and systems that support slavery. "Never once did you deserve that abuse" is the first and most consistent message of the Council for Prostitution Alternatives (CPA) in Portland, Oregon. The first step, according to Susan Hunter, the director, is that "you must reframe prostitution" because "most women come in the door with a threshold and tolerance for abuse so high that they will set themselves up for it."

The CPA program is based on consciousness raising. It operates from the understanding that in order to reframe prostitution, the women must "look at all aspects of their lives from a new form." CPA, a project that continually struggles to survive with minimal resources, is wealthy compared to Buklod and impoverished compared to the standard of living in the United States. CPA has 15 to 20 apartments available to provide women with a safe place to leave prostitution. These apartments are used mostly by single women, who do not have access to welfare through Aid to Dependent Children. CPA helps women with children get enrolled in welfare. One of the first problems they confront is that the welfare system tries to treat prostitution as a form of work instead of as violation and abuse. If successful, the system can lower the welfare payments or eliminate the benefits entirely on the basis of income from prostitution.

"Women would leave in droves if more services were available for them," says Susan Hunter, echoing Pearline and Emela in the Philippines. While Buklod cannot draw upon the resources of a social-services system to help women get a "fresh start," CPA is able to insist that women who fully enter their program cut themselves off from the prostitution world that is always drawing them back. While they work with women coming in and out of prostitution, for the women who are ready to leave permanently, CPA draws up a contract in which the women agree to

Not having contact with anyone who harms me emotionally, physically, or sexually.

Participate in an alcohol/drug treatment program if I have Alc/Drug problems.

Help make a plan to take care of my needs and work on my personal goals.

Keeping appointments in my plan.[4]

Consciousness raising continues in individual counseling and in group sessions as women begin to reconstruct their health, their work lives, and their social world.

In the last 5 years, programs to support women getting out of prostitution have proliferated around the globe. Maria Lourdes Barreto, president of Women Prostitutes of Belen de Para in northern Brazil, is emphatic: "We don't want women to become prostitutes but we do want women in prostitution to know that they have autonomy, the right to discuss, to solve their problems, to do whatever they want."[5] She is fighting for citizenship rights for prostitute women.

In the United States, critical feminist consciousness developing from prostitution women began when Evelina Giobbe founded Women Hurt In Systems of Prostitution Engaged in Revolt. WHISPER is now a Minnesota-based organization that conducts educational forums on prostitution and advocates for women in prostitution.

While projects offering women in prostitution shelter and retraining so they can leave prostitution are new in the United States as of the last decade, they have a much longer history in other parts of the world. In France, Equipe d'Action Contre le Prostitution and Le Nid and Le Cri have not only provided support to individual women but their representatives have also been active in the International Abolitionist Federation, a movement against prostitution on the basis that it violates human rights. In the Third World, EMPOWER in Thailand and El Pozo in Peru are prominent among the hundreds of developing projects that enable women to see a way out of prostitution. In the summer of 1992, Dr. Renu Rejbhandari set up a program to train former prostitute women in bamboo crafts in Kathmandu, Nepal. The

Women's Rehabilitation Centre that she organized taught women skills that enabled them to earn their own incomes while teaching them about sexually transmitted diseases and AIDS. After 45 days of training, "Some of them are working on a salary basis in Shikerbensi, and some are now training others at the training center."[6]

In the last decade, programs by men for men to prevent violence against women have developed. Although we have yet to see men of conscience actually do work to prevent men from buying women, there are many programs that are laying the foundation for such action. EMERGE is a counseling program in the Boston area that is organized by men and operates from a feminist perspective to stop men from beating women. Common Purpose is a men's counseling program that works primarily with African American and Latino men in the Boston area. It involves them in developing "Safe Behavior" plans, and Common Purpose works with social institutions to "hold batterers accountable." Based in San Francisco, the Ending Men's Violence Task Group of the National Organization for Men Against Sexism is "an activist network for pro-feminist projects and individuals who are working with men to end men's violence." They work with men who batter, rape, and consume pornography. Men Against Pornography, based in Brooklyn, have issued statements of accountability "for profeminist men's activism against pornography and pro-prostitution." In Japan, according to Yayori Matsui, some men are reacting to the image of Japanese men as sex exploiters, particularly in sex tourism. In 1989, a Men's Group Against Prostitution in Asia was organized to focus on consciousness raising among men. The group publishes a newsletter, holds symposiums, and has developed a slide show on "Prostitution in Asia and Japanese Men." In 1991 a Men's Lib Study Group was formed in Osaka to consider men's sexuality and prostitution.[7] This network of men has developed and expanded over the last decade, and the number of men involved in it, though small, reflects the few who are willing to consciously forego the power men gain, individually and collectively, from the sexual exploitation of women.

Therapy: The Individual Approach

Feminism is a persistent movement of women toward liberation that insists on alternatives, ways out, escapes for women from violence and abuse, from exploitation and oppression. For 25 years feminism has pioneered two interdependent projects—projects in the sense that they are personal/political engagements in social action oriented toward change: consciousness raising and safe space. Consciousness raising brings the personal out of its individual isolation and into political awareness and analysis of oppression. Safe space takes the forms of crisis programs, shelters, and group projects where women can escape from abuse or even just find the context in which they can be themselves, explore who they are and what they want, engage in consciousness raising while the pain that patriarchal domination invokes in women's lives is kept off limits. Furthermore, consciousness raising and safe space build alternatives for women that allow women to stand outside of the most direct experience of oppression and consider personally and collectively other possibilities—for their own lives, for women as a class.

Feminist-movement projects of consciousness raising and of safe space have been individualized into psychological therapies developed specifically to confront the harms to women from sexual exploitation. Feminist research, therapy, and social action with incest victims is a more formalized, clinical, and individualized approach to what consciousness raising and counseling provide for women leaving prostitution. The caveat for women in Western societies, particularly in the United States with its intense emphasis on individualism, is that this dual feminist project can easily be reduced from consciousness raising to individual therapy and social services dissociated from the condition of oppression.

Furthermore, the multiplication of "syndromes" and various 12-step programs, however effective they are in naming conditions that have been invisible, tend to "blame the victim" in that change is focused on the individual victim and not on the perpetrators—the individuals and systems that perpetuate the sexual exploitation of woman. The victim blaming in syndromizing women's experiences of exploitation ultimately reverts to biologizing exploitation. When consciousness raising and safe space are depoliticized, their goals and effectiveness shift from developing women's *autonomy and connectivity with other women* to making women feel better. And frequently, as they begin to feel better, if there is no development of political consciousness of their experiences, they turn their newly discovered anger against other women. That is how apolitical therapy perpetuates the separations of women from each other invoked by sex colonization.

Judith Herman is among the feminist psychologists who have sustained the connection between the personal and the political in her development of therapies based on feminist consciousness raising and safe-space work. Herman's work is notable in the way its individual therapy is shaped from a consciousness of sexual politics. She has extended the post-traumatic stress disorder to include situations in which women are subjected to "totalitarian control over a prolonged period." Her identification of a complex post-traumatic stress disorder names a condition that women face in marriage, in families, in prostitution.

Feminist consciousness is evident in the three stages of recovery identified by Herman: safety, remembrance and mourning, and reconnection. Her work is developed from the late-nineteenth-century identification of stages of recovery in hysteria, from more recent work on combat trauma, and from the identification of complicated post-traumatic stress disorder, as well as from research that recognizes the particular effect of multiple personality disorders—especially as a product of incest abuse.[8]

The first stage, safety, involves gaining control over one's body and one's environment and moving toward self-care. It means recovering a safe place. In the second stage, remembrance and mourning, "the survivor tells the story of the trauma. She tells it completely, in depth and in detail. This work of reconstruction actually transforms the traumatic memory, so that it can be integrated into the survivor's life."[9] Telling one's story, putting it into words in a context that is safe, secure, and supportive, "can actually produce a change in the abnormal processing of the traumatic memory."[10] For many victims of incest abuse, this means actually remembering that which has not been contained in human memory. And Herman is clear that reconstructing memory is not merely a mental activity: "The survivor cannot reconstruct a sense of meaning by the exercise of thought alone. The remedy for injustice also requires action. The survivor must decide what is to be done."[11]

In Herman's third stage, "the survivor reclaims her world."[12] For the incest survivor this means disruption of family relations. She develops new relationships and learns to take power (empowerment) at a personal level. Her desire and her own initiative come into play.[13] She is no longer living to please another as she learned to do when subjected to incest abuse or other sexual exploitation.

Feminist research and therapy on incest abuse has effectively revealed the harm that sexual exploitation causes women. It has pioneered approaches that enable women to move beyond the limits that the victimization of sexual exploitation has imposed on their lives and to gain autonomy and learn to construct their own lives through genuine choice and real, personally felt desire.

What we have learned from incest victims' survival brings into clearer focus both the similarities and the stark contrast for the prostitute woman. And given that prostitution is the patriarchal model for sexual exploitation, women's survival of it reveals the far-ranging damages of sexual exploitation. For a woman leaving prostitution and beginning to rebuild her life, society either condemns her for her prostitution or normalizes it as work. How then in either context can she confront the trauma of sexual exploitation as trauma? To be engaged in survival and healing, prostitute women must learn to understand their experiences in a way that the society has refused to acknowledge—they must understand that prostitution itself is abuse. CPA engages women who are leaving prostitution in a "long-term stabilization, a re-orientation where they learn to reframe the experience of prostitution as abuse, and pursue their healing and recovery."[14] For a prostitute woman, this means totally severing herself from all of her experiences and the people she knew in the prostitution world. Unlike the incest victim, who may have to break off relations with a father, a grandfather, and possibly other close family members, the prostitute woman must sever *all* ties with her social world if she is to be able to find a new life that will not draw her back into prostitution. Moreover, upon leaving prostitution she has no income, she may be facing criminal charges on prostitution itself in countries where it is illegal, and/or she may be facing charges related to prostitution. CPA has found that providing a safe place for women in prostitution may require not only offering housing and a support group but also supporting women in going to court to face their charges and to clear themselves.[15] Before courts and social workers, women leaving prostitution must demand justice neither as a criminal pleading for mercy nor as a "worker" seeking legitimization.

What of the politics of therapy?

The intra-individual psychological approach reflects the individualistic values and orientation of Western society. Feminism has revealed that political action can be the source of profound individual and personal change. The approach of feminist psychologists is treatment from inner to outer, from the individual to the society, from personal change to political action.

From the standpoint of feminist psychology, social action is the culminating phase of the healing process and growth in individual and small-group therapy. "Survivors discover that they can transform the meaning of their personal tragedy by making it a basis for social action," as Herman points out. "Social action offers the survivor a source of power that draws upon her own initiative, energy, and resourcefulness but that magnifies these qualities far beyond her own capabilities." [16] This is evident in the numbers of women who, on recovering from sexual exploitation, become counselors or other kinds of workers in projects designed to help other women. Social action—feminist political struggle—engages the individual healing from private therapy in new sustaining bonds that begin "with the discovery that one is not alone" and leads to "a complex mirroring process" in which, "as each participant extends herself to others, she becomes more capable of receiving the gifts that others have to offer." [17] Sociologically, as the society is constructed through social interaction, that is the means by which we, as humans, socially construct our selves and women in these situations reconstruct their lives. The directionality from outer to inner, from society to self, of sociological analysis is the foundation of the feminist analysis I am presenting. It connects global feminism and women's personal survival of sexual exploitation, particularly prostitution. When global feminism begins with social action, it then becomes possible for women both to think of confronting their own experience of sexual exploitation and to confront its institutionalization, ultimately in prostitution and pornography. It does not necessarily work the other way around. Beginning with individualized therapy does not lead either to political consciousness or to social action.

Radical Reform

Ironically, the very individualistic ideology that gave rise to personal therapy and has made enormous gains in supporting women through their own recovery from sexual abuse, especially incest assault, is the ideology of individualism that also treats prostitution as a woman's choice, legitimizing their sexual objectification in economic exchange. The optimism of feminist action is more than difficult to sustain in the face of global normalization of prostitution and pornography—the international reduction of woman to whore, in the home, in colleges, in brothels, on the streets. In the global normalization of prostitution, the industry impacts most severely on women in the developing world, where states provide little or nothing in the way of social services to enable women to leave prostitution. Given the massive industrialization of women for prostitution in some parts of the globe, to assume that change can occur only through individual therapy-healing and will eventually lead to social action, casts a cloud of doom over the possibility of change. This hopelessness is already manifest in many programs that are trying to make the lives of women in prostitution easier or safer but only with the limited conviction that because the industries are too enormous and prostitution is inevitable, there is nothing more than that to be done about prostitution.

In that context, increasingly many women in prostitution who would leave if they could, as well as many human-rights and women's rights advocates, refer to prostitution as "sex work" or "sexual labor." "Sex work" is new language, introduced to normalize prostitution on the basis of the conviction that prostitute women will never gain any respect unless prostitution itself is accepted as normal, legitimate activity. It is also the language of individualized choice, of pluralistic options either to pursue prostitution as a form of work or to seek individual therapy to recover from it as sexual abuse—as if the same act can have these two different meanings.

When prostitution is referred to as "sex work" by women in prostitution who would leave if they could, the term is an indicator of their hopelessness. "Sex work" language has been adopted out of despair, not because these women promote prostitution but because it seems impossible to conceive of any other way to treat prostitute women with dignity and respect than through normalizing their exploitation. In many Third World countries, that hopelessness and despair is enforced by the economic dependence of Third World countries on the West. Western hegemony promotes the prostitution in the exploitation of women's poverty. Western aid provides condoms to women on the assumption that prostitution will persist. Western sexual liberalism and its rationalization of prostitution as "sex work" or "sexual labor" ideologically contextualizes Western aid to Third World women in prostitution, which more deeply aggravates sexual exploitation in prostitution by locking women in with funds that could be used to help them get out. By contrast, income-generating projects that would afford women the decent labor that I have so often heard them ask for are not focused on prostitute women. Such projects would enable women to leave prostitution and would *require that the state invest in prostitute women's futures.* But Western foundation funding has provided little in the way of resources that will assist women in leaving prostitution. Thus, hopelessness that women can respond to their poverty through any other means than prostitution is sustained by these programs.

Feminism reframes women's despair resulting from individual women's experiences of prostitution and from the apparent inevitability of prostitution as it is massively imposed by sex industrialization. This new feminist work is only possible because within the last decade, women in prostitution have begun to confront this condition themselves. They are the new voices of hope, the sources of a new activism. They not only have left prostitution and reshaped their lives but have also begun to speak out against it, revealing their experiences of it, confronting the exploitation of it, and helping other women leave it. In 1980, in Grenoble, France, 4 women in prostitution bravely faced down their pimps in a court trial that broke up a gang of 17 pimps and awarded a judgment in favor of the women. Women's projects in many countries are providing support for women leaving prostitution, support eagerly sought by prostitute women. In the United States Evelina Giobbe launched WHISPER on the conviction that prostitution itself must be (and therefore can be) eliminated. Global feminist action against sex industries is the first step in which women begin to dissolve the patriarchal dichotomy of women and prostitute, self and other. Further, for Western women *genuine* international feminist struggle must be responsive to the exploitation of women in the West and the hegemonic imposition of sexual colonization on women by the West in the Third World. Not only does the West promote exploitation of women through prostitution, but also it robs states of their resources, which leaves little for states to use, even if they were willing to do so, for programs that support women leaving prostitution. The conviction that prostitution is not inevitable, that sexual exploitation does not have to be tolerated and should not be sustained, is the foundation of radical reform.

In the late 1970s, writing *Female Sexual Slavery* before a feminist movement developed to confront prostitution, I proposed decriminalization as the appropriate legal strategy to confront the sexual enslavement of women. Concerned with women's victimization by police under conditions where prostitution is criminalized, and with pimping that produces slavery of women in prostitution, I saw the urgent need to take the laws off prostitute women, as the abolitionists have argued, without promoting prostitution as the regulationists do. But at that time my proposal to decriminalize prostitution implicitly meant decriminalizing men who buy women's bodies. The error in proposing blanket decriminalization was that it decriminalizes the customers as well as the prostitute, leaving the customer, the direct perpetrator of sexual exploitation, virtually sanctioned.

Taking prostitution as the model of the sexual exploitation of women, I proposed in a meeting called by UNESCO in 1986, that prostitute women should not only be decriminalized; they should also be recognized as victims of sexual exploitation *by the customer*. When customers are legally identified, sanctioned, fined, and publicly exposed for buying women's bodies, then the sex they are buying is recognized as an act of aggression, a violation of women, whether or not the women consent. Punishing customers makes all prostitution illegal but does not reduce prostitutes to criminals. This approach is neither prohibitionist nor abolitionist. It is a feminist human-rights approach that does not separate prostitution from other forms of female sexual exploitation.

Identifying necessary legal changes makes it possible to set new feminist standards, but it is not as easy to change the objective realities and experiences of that exploitation. In actuality, legally enacting the criminalization of customers will immediately reduce or eliminate prostitute women's income. In the West, where there may be possibilities for women to receive welfare or find some kind of work to sustain them as they begin to transform their lives, cutting off women's income from prostitution has a different meaning than it does in countries where there are no welfare or social-service systems. In massive poverty, severe and severely gendered, prostitution may be the only source of income for many women. That means that economic development programs and services aimed at prostitute women must begin with economic-alternative strategies and support.

The alternative to desperate conditions is not to validate them. Rather, legal proposals to criminalize customers, based on the recognition that prostitution violates and harms women, must be developed in such a way as to include social-service, health and counseling, and job retraining programs. Where states would be closing down brothels if customers were criminalized, the economic resources poured into the former prostitution areas could be turned toward producing gainful employment for women. Envisioning a liberated future *invokes the intention to claim it.*

Too idealistic? Unrealistic?

Recognizing the "disastrous social consequences and noxious effects of prostitution," identifying prostitution as one of its top 10 social problems to address, on January 29, 1993, the government of the Socialist Republic of Vietnam issued Decision 5 on the Prevention and Restriction of Prostitution in Vietnam.* The

---

*In January 1993, as part of a faculty seminar I organized with Vietnamese women, I presented the elements of a new U.N. Convention Against Sexual Exploitation, which provided some foundation for Decision 5.

decision begins, "Prostitution under whatever form it might be, should be decidedly eradicated." The program includes an educational campaign utilizing the press and media to focus on young people (not unlike the media campaigns against drugs in the United States or the successful media campaign addressing prostitution in the Malmo project in Sweden). Not only should funding be provided to support programs that punish pimps and kidnappers and "brothel owners of any sort" but the state is also particularly concerned that "civil servant playboys should be subject to disciplinary measures, their names notified to relevant authorities and published in mass-media." Everyone else buying prostitutes will be reported to local authorities.

The Vietnamese measures for supporting prostitute women are more far reaching than any that have yet been conceived by state authorities. These strategies have been carved out in the midst of massive poverty, after decades of war and 19 years of the U.S. embargo that was only lifted in 1994. But until the late 1980s it was honored by all but the Soviet bloc countries and thereby severely diminished Vietnam's economic development. Nevertheless, the government has initiated the following program:

Prostitutes who are willing to lead a normal life will be given a certain sum of money by the Government for a fresh start. Any enterprise (private or state-owned) which offers employment to prostitutes will be allotted funds consistent with every specific case. Credits can be given to reformation centres to create work-places destined for productive labor.

Furthermore, prostitutes infected with venereal disease will be afforded food, accommodations, and medical care until they have completely recovered. And "subsistence allowances can be made for prostitutes coming from poor families lacking the necessities of life [for] a period of 3 months." [18]

Vietnam recognizes that even in the poorest countries of the world, not all women in prostitution are there because of poverty. Therefore, this new law will provide the kind of programming, or "re-education," that was made available to women at the end of the war. Women who remain in prostitution, despite the ban on it and the resources and support offered to leave it, will be "gathered in special centres for reformation for at least a minimum of 6 months."

The rise of women's consciousness of gender issues[19] with the socialist approach to prostitution has led directly to the development of this new social policy. This plan for the eradication of prostitution does not treat prostitutes as responsible for their victimization, but makes the socialist state responsible for prostitute women's future and welfare. By early 1994, with normalization of economic relations between the United States and Vietnam that promises a boost to the Vietnamese economy but may also lead to increased prostitution, the government of Vietnam established a committee to implement Decision 5 and opened new education and training centers for women in prostitution. The vigorous and far-reaching program "to eradicate prostitution" could reverse the trend in the marketing of women under industrialization if resources for supporting women leaving prostitution are coupled with penalization of sex industrialists as well as customers promoting it. This far-reaching protection to women in prostitution, the fact that it has been conceptualized in the face of a seemingly hopeless situation, constitutes a first advance, a step not yet envisioned elsewhere.

The United Nations: The Possibility of Women's Human Rights?

To confront the sexual exploitation of women globally, I have turned to the Universal Bill of Human Rights, which condemns the "contempt for human rights" that has "resulted in barbarous acts which have outraged the conscience of mankind," in order to demand that sexual exploitation be treated as a contempt for human rights, a barbarous act. Human-rights instruments are premised on a utopian vision, the "advent of a world in which

human beings shall enjoy freedom of speech and belief and freedom from fear and want," and on collective consciousness, "the
highest aspirations of the common people." Human-rights philosophy matches radical feminist moral outrage, recognizing *any acts*
that are destructive to human beings—anything that dehumanizes
the human condition—as barbarous.

More than a technical adherence to justice and equality, human-rights philosophy as expressed in the United Nations conventions expresses moral outrage against dehumanization of both
human persons *and* the human condition. It encompasses oppression of peoples as well as violation of individuals. Marxist academics have criticized human rights as an individualistic ideology
of capitalism. And it is true that human rights have been interpreted narrowly and applied exclusively within the framework of
liberal individualism especially in countries like the United States.
But internationally, they have been effectively used by exploited
peoples under colonialism, under apartheid, and in totalitarian
regimes to confront and expose domination.

"The purpose of recognizing and safeguarding human rights is
to ensure the possibility of living fully and completely, in dignity
and freedom." [20] "Human rights are the legal expression of human life." [21] Article 1 of the Universal Declaration of Human
Rights affirms that "all human beings are born free and equal
in dignity and rights." While prohibiting slavery, the Universal
Declaration goes further to protect the human being, stating that
"no person shall be subjected to torture or cruel, inhuman, or
degrading treatment or punishment" (article 5).

Recognizing that human persons are not bodies separable from
the social fabric, institutional realities, and class conditions, human rights establish the inseparability of the individual from the
collective condition. Therefore human rights are inalienable to
both the human person and the human condition; responsibility
for them rests *both* on individuals and on states, [22] as the Charter
of the United Nations declares when it affirms "the dignity and
worth of the human person, in the equal rights of men and

women, and of nations large and small." Human rights adhere to all human beings and cannot be privileged for one class, group, or state power over another. Moreover, they exist because human beings exist and need no other justification. The fact that women have been left out of human rights and, more than any other group, must establish factual justification for being accorded human rights, returns to the question in patriarchy, "Are women human beings?"

In its applicability to feminism and women's right to dignity, the universality of human rights is a foundation for global feminist struggle based on the common dimensions of women's oppression. Recognizing that human rights are indivisible and inalienable and located in human dignity gives renewed meaning to struggles for legal equality that are subverted as sexual exploitation is treated as something outside of and different than violation of the right to equality.

As patriarchal oppression, specifically sexual exploitation, is a universalized condition of domination, ideally there should be a good fit between feminism and human rights. International human rights for women based on the reality of feminism, a global movement of women's liberation, is built from the commonalities of women's condition across state boundaries, class conditions, races, and ethnicities. Yet, recognizing that women are diverse in their individualities, races, and cultures, feminism rejects the reduction of women to one universalized essential, and claiming women's right to control their own bodies, feminism upholds the inalienability of the individual. Universal human rights holds the potential for recognizing that the power individual men gain from sexual exploitation is only possible because of a class condition in which men as a group gain advancement and benefit from the way they use women sexually. As feminists have established, if men did not gain collectively from the individual and collective sexual exploitation of women, then individual sexual exploitation would be harmful and destructive to individual women, but it could not hold down women as a class.

A *New* Feminist *Human Rights*

My work has focused on joining the fundamental principles of human rights with the politics of radical feminism in order to confront the massive global proliferation of prostitution, especially the dramatic increase in trafficking in women, and to recognize that these abuses are perpetrated by international sex industries that promote the legitimization of prostitution and pornography.

In 1991, as the director of the Coalition Against Trafficking in Women (a nongovernmental organization in consultative status with the Economic and Social Council [ECOSOC] of the UN), in collaboration with Wassyla Tamzali of UNESCO, I convened a working group at Pennsylvania State University to analyze the 1949 Convention for the Suppression of the Traffic in Persons and of the Exploitation of the Prostitution of Others and to consider the contemporary dimensions of sexual exploitation globally. The working group concluded that worldwide sexual exploitation is the foundation of human-rights violations of women in prostitution, through pornography, and in all forms of sexual abuse and violence. From this meeting an international human-rights instrument was developed, the Convention Against Sexual Exploitation.

Following the meeting, the Coalition Against Trafficking in Women and UNESCO sponsored a series of meetings to develop a new human-rights instrument and to propose that the Secretary-General of the United Nations promulgate a new Convention against Sexual Exploitation. (See appendix for complete text.) Within the Coalition, working with Dorchen Leidholdt, we have turned to grassroots women's movements for consultation, input, recommendations, and revisions in order to refine the document so that it will address women's needs in each world region.

In the "Elements of a New Convention," formulated at the Penn State meeting, sexual exploitation is recognized as a violation of human dignity, and therefore it is "a fundamental human right to be free from sexual exploitation in all of its forms."[23] In the Penn State meeting, we defined sexual exploitation as "a practice by which person(s) achieve sexual gratification or financial gain or advancement through the abuse of a person's sexuality by abrogating that person's human right to dignity, equality, autonomy, and physical and mental well-being."[24] Formulated by Professor Susan Edwards of the University of Buckingham in England, this definition establishes the basis of sexual power as gain, which can be as specific as sexual gratification or as concretely material as financial profit. This Convention treats sexual exploitation as a class condition and as individual violation, stating that the "sexual exploitation of any woman is the sexual degradation of all women," depriving women of freedom of movement, threatening women's safety and security, and thus creating the conditions of sexual terrorism. As such, sexual exploitation violates human dignity and equal rights, invoking cruel, inhuman, and degrading treatment.

Over many months and in numerous meetings, this Convention was developed and refined in consultation with United Nations nongovernmental organizations and feminist projects as well as women's groups in Asia, Latin America, Europe, and North America. As a product of worldwide grassroots feminism, it is framed to reveal how sexual exploitation aggravates the harm of other existing inequalities, often taking the form of sexual slavery, torture, mutilation, and death. The proposed Convention recognizes that sexual exploitation takes the form of denial of life through female infanticide, murder of women by reason of their gender, including wife/widow murder, woman battering, pornography, prostitution, genital mutilation, female seclusion, dowry and bride price, sexual harassment, rape, incest and sexual abuse, and torture, including sadistic and mutilating practices. Therefore, the Convention calls upon States Parties to punish all perpetrators of sexual exploitation and to redress the wrongs done to their victims through penal, civil, labor, and administrative sanctions.

In defining sexual exploitation, states must consider that it is an aggravating circumstance and not a defense of sexual exploitation that the perpetrator is the husband, father, other relative, or employer of the victim.

The proposed Convention builds upon the legacy of international human-rights law developed in the United Nations 1949 Convention, which found that prostitution is "incompatible with the dignity and worth of the human person." According to the Universal Declaration of Human Rights (article 30), "Nothing in this declaration may be interpreted as implying for any state, group, or person any right to engage in any activity or to perform any act aimed at the destruction of any of the rights and freedoms set forth herein." Accordingly, there is no "right to prostitute."

Rejecting distinctions between "free" and "forced" prostitution as legitimizing prostitution, the proposed Convention recognizes that the act of prostitution is the use of a woman's body as a commodity to be bought and sold, to be exchanged, not always for money, including casual or "occasional" prostitution as well as prostitution in brothels, military prostitution, pornography, sex tourism, and mail-order-bride markets. The Convention calls upon states to penalize the customers, recognizing them as perpetrators to be criminalized while rejecting any form of penalization of the prostitute. Therefore States Parties would be required to agree to reject any policy or law that legitimizes prostitution of any person, male or female, adult or child, so-called first or third world; that distinguishes between free and forced prostitution; or that in any way legalizes or regulates prostitution as a profession or occupation. Recognizing that the pornography industry enlarges the demand for, promotes, and is actively engaged in sexual exploitation, States Parties would be required to enact regulations that hold liable the producers and distributors of pornography.

Global industrialization of prostitution is both a consequence of sex-discriminatory economic development policies and the basis of unofficial economic development in some regions. The Convention calls upon States Parties to reject policies and practices of economic development that channel women into conditions of sexual exploitation, eroding women's traditional economic base where it has existed. They shall insure that economic-development policies provide for the full economic development of women through their integration into dignified paid labor at a decent standard of living, from which they have been deprived through sexual exploitation, including, especially, prostitution. Therefore they shall prohibit sex tourism and penalize those who organize it as procurers and promoters of prostitution (pimps) in both the countries from which customers travel and the countries to which they go for sex tourism.

Furthermore, persons or enterprises will be prohibited from promoting, profiting from, or engaging in any business involving the matching of women in marriage to foreign nationals on a mail-order basis (mail-order-bride selling). To prevent sexual exploitation in prostitution on and around military bases, military personnel will be prohibited from engaging in the prostitution of women and children in communities where bases are located. Special observers will be designated to prevent the sexual exploitation of women and children in refugee camps, and special provisions will be enacted to protect women from sexual exploitation during wartime, including times of ethnic conflict, civil war, and foreign intervention.

There are certain types of work involved in the immigration process, such as domestic labor and entertainment, that are conducive to sexual exploitation and may lead to prostitution. The proposed Convention would require States Parties to take all appropriate measures to provide victims of sexual exploitation, including prostitution and traffic in women, with refuge and protection and to repatriate those who desire to be repatriated. Employers who sexually exploit women in the migrating process will be held criminally liable.

Women subjected to sexual exploitation are frequently homeless and, often, stateless when they escape. The "vagabonds" of feudalism, they are controlled neither by husband nor by brothels, and often their human rights as homeless and stateless persons are not recognized by the country into which they have been trafficked. Under the Convention, refugee status shall be granted to all victims of sexual exploitation, whether they have entered the country legally or illegally. States Parties will ensure that valid written contracts of employment are entered into and will provide for monitoring of the provisions of those contracts. According to the proposed Convention, States Parties will protect the right of all women to retain their own passports and travel documents, which will help prevent the sale of women into prostitution or their sexual use by another person.

Recognizing that sexual exploitation is injurious to women's physical and mental health and well-being and that it constitutes a major health problem for women, under this Convention States Parties will be expected to provide specialized health services, to fund centers for prostitution alternatives that are voluntary and confidential, and to provide treatment and testing for STDs and HIV, substance-abuse rehabilitation, counseling, day care, housing, income support, preferential access to credit loans to begin small-scale businesses, and skills-training programs. Support, such as shelters in which women work with women who have been exploited to provide alternatives, will be provided to create and establish services for victims of sexual exploitation, including prostitution.

When a convention is adopted by the United Nations, States Parties are invited to ratify it. Their ratification carries the assumption that they are or will become in compliance with the convention in their own laws and practices. To implement this Convention, the United Nations will establish a Committee Against Sexual Exploitation, which will be authorized to make confidential inquiries into any reliable accounts of systematic sexual exploitation as defined above and to submit its findings to the State Party concerned with the aim of reaching an equitable solution. The Committee would receive and review individual complaints from victims of sexual exploitation, which it will bring to the attention of the concerned State Party. The State Party will be required to respond within 6 months.

Are Women People?

Conventions are international treaties. The proposed Convention Against Sexual Exploitation would not be the first United Nations convention to explicitly address women's rights. The Convention on the Political Rights of Women was adopted as early as 1952 and was preceded by the convention on prostitution (1949) discussed earlier. These were followed by several conventions and official U.N. declarations to protect women's rights in marriage (1957) and to protect women and children in armed conflict (declaration of 1974).

Furthermore the international treaties of the mid-1960s, promulgated in response to Third World struggles against and liberation from European colonization, advance the right of peoples to self-determination in Economic, Social and Cultural Rights (1966) and Civil and Political Rights (1966). Both covenants recognize women's rights insofar as they explicitly are in force "without distinction of any kind, such as race, colour, sex, language, religion, political or other opinion, national or social origin, property, birth or other status."

And as women know very well, adding women to codified rights is not the same as actually protecting and promoting those rights for women. That is why, with this long and elaborate history of women's rights codified but largely ignored by the United Nations, many of us held high hopes for the Convention on the Elimination of All Forms of Discrimination Against Women (CEDAW) adopted in 1979 and ratified by nation states beginning in 1980.

But as often happens when legislation turns to women, something is lost. The loss is first evident in the absence of moral outrage against violation of women. One of the effects of the long-term sexual colonization of women's bodies, of the advocacy of this colonization by sexual liberals, and of its institutionalization by sex industries, is that many women can barely grasp our right to moral outrage against sexual dehumanization. When the United Nations turns to women, emphasis on human rights is narrowed and its commitments seem to fizzle. In terms of human rights commitment, CEDAW is no match for the powerful International Convention on the Elimination of All Forms of Racial Discrimination, which recognizes that "the existence of racial barriers is repugnant to the ideal of any human society" and, consequently, that "any doctrine of superiority based on racial differentiation is scientifically false, morally condemnable, socially unjust and dangerous, and that there is no justification for racial discrimination, in theory or in practice, anywhere." By contrast, sexism is only "discrimination against women" which "shall mean any distinction, exclusion or restriction made on the basis of sex" (article 1). Absent is the passionate denunciation of injustice found in other struggles against oppression, precisely because sexism is taken as a condition of inequality but not of oppression. The fuller, subtler, and more profound meaning of human rights is diminished to legal discriminations, technical inequalities that require rebalancing. Removed from the context of collective discrimination against a separate people, the moral outrage against women's condition and the exploitation of women is toned down, reduced to a matter of individual violation. This reverts the exploitation of women to a matter of technical equality regarding "any distinction, exclusion or restriction made on the basis of sex." Although broad in scope, and a significant gain for women who otherwise had almost disappeared from the generic "human" of human rights, this Convention stops short of actually encompassing the full meaning of human rights. Not surprisingly, in the United Nations "women's rights" have been treated as a different venue, with a separate division and in a different location from "human rights."

The losses women suffered in CEDAW, adopted in the midst of

a global women's movement which raised sexual violence and exploitation to issues of primary importance, are that in relation to sexual exploitation it did not cover or include violence against women and it simply reaffirmed the 1949 Convention on prostitution, a law that would have been useful had it been promulgated in 1890 but by the 1980s no longer addressed global sex industrialization and the normalization of prostitution.

This led to new and potentially important work in the 1990s on the development of a U.N. Declaration on the Elimination of Violence Against Women, which is meant to expand the limited scope of CEDAW. The Declaration is broad in its definition of violence against women, including "any act of gender-based violence that results in, or is likely to result in, physical, sexual or psychological harm or suffering to women" (article 1). However, violence against women takes place in a context of patriarchal oppression, and sexual violence is one dimension in a broad scope of sexual exploitation. In writings and reports about this new Declaration, there are radical proclamations about male power and subordination of women but they do not find their way into the official U.N. Declaration. Most importantly, the broad scope of sexual exploitation as it includes pornography and prostitution is omitted. Not thousands but millions of women, daily, hourly, through lifetimes subjected to sexual exploitation are excluded from the violence against women declaration that so many other women rightly are thankful to have won. Intensive lobbying of the U.N. Commission on the Status of Women, which approved the draft Declaration, and particularly from the representatives of the government of the Netherlands, prevented inclusion of prostitution and pornography as forms of sexual exploitation even when it was proposed by nongovernmental organizations later.

The omission was not an oversight. The Declaration was drafted *after* the elements of the new Convention Against Sexual Exploitation were formulated, presented to the U.N. Human Rights Nongovernmental Organizations, forwarded to the U.N.

Centre for Human Rights in Geneva to be considered for the World Conference on Human Rights scheduled for Vienna, June 1993, and then was published in conjunction with UNESCO in 1991. Months later, after the elements of the Convention Against Sexual Exploitation from the Penn State experts group meeting were made public, a meeting was convened in Vienna that led to the drafting of the Declaration on the Elimination of Violence Against Women. Held by the U.N. Division for the Advancement of Women, neither UNESCO representatives nor nongovernmental organizations involved in initiating the proposed Convention Against Sexual Exploitation were included. Allowing for the unlikely possibility of oversight, shortly after the Vienna meeting I met with directors of several human rights and women's rights organizations involved in the Vienna meeting regarding the draft Declaration to discuss its omissions and the proposed Convention. One stated that prostitution was irrelevant to human rights while another acknowledged that it was at the base of women's equality but said "we can't touch it."

It was not only within the Division on the Advancement of Women that prostitution and the normalization of sexual exploitation was discarded as a human rights violation in the United Nations. The World Health Organization had already committed its policies to the proprostitution lobby by placing a representative of that lobby in charge of the WHO policy on prostitution and AIDS, which, not surprisingly, led WHO to issue policy that in effect promotes prostitution by only addressing AIDS in prostitution through condom distribution. And for the new European community, the Council of Europe held a seminar in 1991 with a preplanned agenda that favored the proprostitution policy of the Netherlands.

Yet, this history of the United Nations and its concern for women's human rights is incomplete without recounting its relationship to the United Nations World Conference on Human Rights. In its early stages of planning, the Centre for Human Rights did not even plan to have a nongovernmental component to its world conference in 1993. When it finally conceded to open the world conference to nongovernmental organizations and human rights advocates, it did so by closing down their access to the official conference of government representatives, ensuring that nongovernmental activists would have no direct involvement in determining the outcomes of the World Conference on Human Rights. As women, indigenous peoples, and other oppressed groups gained easy access to the nongovernmental meeting, most were so grateful to have some public international forum to speak what had been silenced in their experiences of human rights violations, that the extent to which the formal government meeting excluded most of their issues went by unnoticed. Having participated in other U.N. world conferences, I was keenly aware of a shift or change in U.N. policy toward nongovernmental organizations whose consultative status in the past meant that they had some access to and involvement in the meetings of government representatives. Instead, in preplanned programs of regional meetings, a draft for the final report of the World Conference was developed before the Conference took place.

Although it had been presented to U.N. meetings many times, and it had been recommended from nongovernmental consultations to be considered in the World Conference on Human Rights, the proposed Convention Against Sexual Exploitation was excluded. In fact, while women used the nongovernmental format to educate participants to the abuses women suffer globally, nothing in the form of new or additional protections was asked of the United Nations. The United Nations received extensive media coverage for allowing women to expose our human rights violations. But the United Nations has not been asked to take action on them. While the proposed Convention Against Sexual Exploitation would involve the United Nations in a treaty with nation states that required not only monitoring of human rights violations but action against them and programmatic support for women, it appears that educational campaigns toward delegitimizing violence against women is as far as the U.N. Division on the

Advancement of Women wants to go. A 1993 background paper of the U.N. Division for the Advancement of Women outlines the position on delegitimizing violence against women. Distinguishing between violence in the family and in the community, the paper concludes that controlling violence in the family by law is problematic. "There are legitimate questions of how far the States should or even can intrude into family life. . . . There is no consensus about whether jailing violators provides an effective deterrent."[25] So as the position turns away from criminalizing wife-beaters and incest abusers for the sake of protecting privatized power relations, it is the same position that is articulated when violence and harassment is public. Criminalization of crimes against women in the community is rejected in favor of educational campaigns to delegitimize violence because testimony about sexual assault and sexual harassment involves "different perceptions by the parties involved [that] tend to cloud the issue. The problem of 'he said, she said', where the extent of which what was perceived as harassment by one party, was perceived as innocent badinage by the other, makes adjudication difficult." And the conclusion is the same for the community as it is in private: "eradication of practices may require sensitization and education rather than legal remedies."[26] Likewise, civil as well as criminal law is disfavored in this approach.

This anti-criminalization strategy has been used repeatedly in the United States against the women's movement, first when we called for new laws and harsher penalties for rape in the early 1970s and since then with each campaign against sexual exploitation. It usually comes with the admonition that using law to criminalize perpetrators of prostitution, pornography, rape or wife abuse will "put power in the hands of the state." No oppressed group ever puts power in the hands of the state. But oppressed groups often put enormous pressure on the state to use its power to protect them, and in many cases, states have been brought down because they would not ultimately meet the demands of the oppressed group for justice. In a long struggle, that is how power has been redefined, as it is being done now in South Africa, for example. Neither the U.N. nor international human rights groups have asked victims of apartheid, or colonialization, or racism not to seek justice in and protection from courts, not to force the hand of law to work in their behalf. But that is what the United Nations appears to expect women to do now. This anti-criminalization approach to crimes against women can be contrasted to a combined action of Voices of Thai Women and the Foundation for Women that has led them to a demand that the government abolish the Prostitution Suppression Act, which solely blames women for prostitution. "Prostitutes could not do business if there were no male clients," and therefore they are also calling for criminal action against "brothelgoers, as supporters of the flesh trade." And that, among other protections, is what the proposed Convention Against Sexual Exploitation would accomplish globally.

Behind the new U.N. declaration on violence against women is a callous disregard for actions of women in their struggles against domination and for the well-being of women globally covered by militant sounding rhetoric about "male power, privilege, and control." In the final analysis, when the rhetoric is stripped away what is left are unfunded educational campaigns that presumably in one century or another will stop men from beating, raping, and sexually exploiting women because they have been educated to stop doing that which brings them power, privilege, and gain.

What is evident in the power wielding to determine whose definition of violence and exploitation will prevail is a well-oiled collusion between Western, primarily U.S.-based, women's and human rights groups and the United Nations, especially the Division for the Advancement of Women. It is the newest international hegemony over women, particularly women in the Third World. This hegemony is brokered by the U.S. manipulation of global human rights for the purposes of its own dominance in the global economy. Using international human rights to control and manipulate other countries began in the United States under President Carter but became an intensified strategy of Ronald Reagan. While he was manipulating human rights globally he was responsible for the escalation of human misery, especially for women, in the United States, retracting welfare rights and food stamps and regressing affirmative action and civil rights.

As the United States has increasingly entered into the international human rights scene governmentally, it has lobbied to narrow the platform of human rights away from collective rights of peoples, particularly the protected Economic, Social and Cultural Rights, which require such rights as the "right to work," and toward individual rights. That is why the U.S. government has joined U.S.-based human rights groups in supporting the CEDAW approach to violence against women that does not ask governments to penalize perpetrators and narrows women's claims from that of a class seeking their self-determination, women *as a people,* to educational campaigns in a rhetoric of individual rights that are not even protected.

Meanwhile, the proposed Convention Against Sexual Exploitation represents women collectively and individually, requiring protections, sanctions, and support programs for victims. And it is the least we should expect.

Intolerance

A world without prostitution. . . .

To imagine it is like imagining a world without slavery in the United States in the 1820s. At the height of U.S. slavery, it was inconceivable to all except a few that slavery could be eradicated. Those few fiery and determined abolitionists, many of whom were feminists, refused to concede to the prevailing ideology that slavery was inevitable. They refused to be morally compromised or defeated by arguments that traced slavery back to the beginning of recorded history. At times abolitionism was considered a vanguard movement, and at other times it was considered a retrograde movement consisting of a collection of oddities who could not fit in elsewhere in the society and who protested the near-sacred U.S. Constitution, which rationalized slavery. The core group of determined abolitionists persisted despite the unpopularity of their message.

This has been the pattern globally. By 1927 the international Slavery Convention entered into force declaring what had been unthinkable a century before: "the firm intention of putting an end to the traffic in African slaves" and hence "to bring about, progressively and as soon as possible, the complete abolition of slavery in all of its forms" (article 2b).

To imagine a world without prostitution is to conceive of eliminating the sexual exploitation of all women. Unless we can go that way, rape-crisis work and protection for abused women will lead only to what I call the "Evian solution," that is, will reduce our work to a drop in a bucket, to something akin to sending a case of Evian water to a drought-stricken country.

New laws, national and international, cannot replace responsive action. But they are an important part of the strategy, because they establish the base and standards for the liberation of women. As legal change will always fall short of feminist demands, we must pursue it while also knowing that it will never be sufficient. Activism must be shaped from feminist consciousness of domination as it must reveal *women's refusal to co-exist on this planet with sexual exploitation.*

Prostitution makes all women vulnerable, exposed to danger, open to attack. To be vulnerable is, by definition, to be "able to be hurt or wounded or injured." Such vulnerability is publicly institutionalized sexual exploitation. Sexual exploitation is privately institutionalized in marriage.

The point is that women's vulnerability to sexual exploitation is an institutionalized social system. From distancing to disengagement, women lose the boundaries that identify them to themselves as separate, distinct, and autonomous. Instead, to survive they must segment themselves, must set up demarcations within themselves that break down the human self—a process that, in the worst cases, results in multiple personality disorders. That which is the human, personally identified self, when made vulnerable, meshes with the world outside the self. I am not speaking here of what makes women "relational," a popular theme in the psychology of women. Rather, I am referring to the way the self that is not bounded is made vulnerable; exposed and unprotected, it is robbed of the experience of direct action on its own accord and, as a result, choice is reduced to managing survival in dehumanized conditions.

Nor is women's vulnerability only individual. Pornography and the sexualization of women in society is a collective, social-class representation of women's vulnerability in which women are socially presented as vulnerable—open to sexual attack, able to be sexually hurt or wounded.

Vulnerability has been exploited into a condition of oppression—a condition taken to an extreme in the breakdown of the female self promoted by the sexual exploitation of women. Oppressors are protected from being vulnerable precisely because they, as a bonded (however diverse) class, are the ones responsible for creating vulnerability.

It is worse than ironic that "vulnerable" has been made into a positive term in the daily experience of sexual relations. The "sexual revolution" and 1960s guides like *The Power of Sexual Surrender* have made "being vulnerable" an expectation in sexual relations. "Being vulnerable" has stripped the idea of harm from the meaning of the word "vulnerable." "Being vulnerable" has come to mean being open, with no recognition that openness requires protection of human fragility.

The feminist challenge is not to promote the institutionalization of women's vulnerability and openness to sexual exploitation, which then becomes treated as sex and as sexy. Sex in this way is dehumanized and its use violates human rights. By contrast, the feminist challenge is to demand the neutralization of visible, media-promoted images of sexual exploitation and to restore the social image of woman to that of human being, an image not synonymous with whore. The feminist challenge is to confront all institutionalized sexual exploitation—made public in prostitution and privatized in homes, among couples, in marriage.

What is sexual equality if it does not begin with equality in sexual relations? That is the first and foremost condition for a sexual intimacy in which openness leads to a human experience of sex, in which interaction is passionate *with integrity*.

In this, the most profound level at which the personal is political, women will set the standards by which we will experience ourselves, by which we can and will be open, by which we know ourselves as open, desirous sexual beings.

In this sense, I do not envision a political struggle that culminates in a final revolution, a revolution that promises complete and final change while we live in the misery of the present condition until then. Neither is revolution, as I think of it here, reduced to "process," a series of psychological changes we go through stage by stage as individuals, falsely assuming that individual change repeated in many will lead to collective action.

For me, envisioning a reality beyond the seemingly intransigent, immutable conditions of patriarchal domination means being grounded in this world while positing another possible reality. It requires being located in women's (collective) experiences while knowing the material, concrete, unexploited, human possibility, a possibility that is within reach, a possibility already begun. This possibility is the meaning of feminist struggle against domination and for liberation—a possibility that has already been put in motion in the many projects and actions of feminists worldwide, yet a possibility that holds more potential for change than most women in these projects fully realize. To provide for any woman or girl the possible reality that there is another world, another kind of life than the sexual exploitation in prostitution, in incest, in rape, in marriage, and then to provide for the material realities of housing and health care, money, jobs, counseling, group awareness, and, indeed, love already is the manifestation of that other new reality.

The 1994 draft of the Convention Against Sexual Exploitation is presented here to convey the minimum conditions for a new international law and does not represent the fullest formulation of all the possibilities which continue to be discussed and formulated in each world region as this book goes to press. However because legal change for women is frequently undermined either by being sabotaged before it can be adopted or ruthlessly revised to less than minimal needs, this text provides a baseline for evaluating future actions on this Convention.

Appendix: Proposed Convention Against Sexual Exploitation

Draft of January 1994

The States Parties to the Present Convention,

Considering that, in accordance with the principles proclaimed in the Charter of the United Nations, recognition of the equal and unalienable rights of all members of the human family without distinction as to sex is the foundation of freedom, justice and peace in the world,

Recognizing that those rights derive from the inherent dignity of the human person,

Considering the obligation of States under the Charter, in particular Article 55, to promote universal respect for, and observance of, human rights and fundamental freedoms,

Having regard to Article 3 of the Universal Declaration of Human Rights and Articles 6 and 9 of the International Covenant on Civil

and Political Rights, both of which affirm the right of all persons
to life, liberty and the security of persons,
Having regard to Article 4 of the Universal Declaration of Human
Rights and Article 8 of the International Covenant on Civil and
Political Rights, both of which prohibit slavery and the slave trade
in all its forms,
Having regard to Article 5 of the Universal Declaration of Human
Rights and Article 7 of the International Covenant on Civil and
Political Rights both of which recognize the right of all persons to
be free from cruel, inhuman or degrading treatment or punishment,
Noting that the Universal Declaration of Human Rights affirms
the principle of the inadmissibility of discrimination and pro-
claims that all human beings are born free and equal in dignity
and rights and that everyone is entitled to all the rights and
freedoms set forth therein without discrimination of any kind,
including distinction based on sex,
Noting that States Parties to the International Covenant on Civil
and Political Rights undertake to secure the equal rights of women
and men to enjoy all economic, social, cultural, civil and political
rights,
Having regard to the 1949 Convention for the Suppression of
Traffic in Persons and the Exploitation of the Prostitution of
Others which states that prostitution and the accompanying evil
of the traffic in persons for the purpose of prostitution are incompatible with the dignity and worth of the human person and
endanger the welfare of the individual, the family, and the community,
Recognizing that the Convention Against Torture prohibits cruel,
inhuman and degrading treatment or punishment,
Having regard also to the Convention on the Elimination of all
Forms of Discrimination Against Women which obligates States
Parties to take all appropriate measures, including legislation, to
suppress all forms of traffic in women and exploitation of traffic
in women,

Having regard also to the Convention on the Rights of the Child which obligates States Parties to protect the child from all forms of sexual exploitation and sexual abuse and obligates the States Parties to take all appropriate national, bilateral and multilateral measures to prevent (a) the inducement or coercion of a child to engage in any unlawful sexual activity, (b) the exploitative use of children in prostitution or other unlawful sexual practices and (c) the exploitative use of children in pornographic performances and materials,

Noting that the International Convention on the Elimination of All Forms of Racial Discrimination condemns any attempt to justify or promote racial hatred in any form,

Noting that the General Assembly, in the International Convention on the Protection of the Rights of All Migrant Workers and Members of Their Families, reaffirmed the principles and standards set forth in the basic instruments regarding the international protection of human rights,

Concerned that women's human rights are seriously threatened by the massive and growing sexual exploitation of women,

Recognizing that sexuality is integral to the human being and that women have the right to sexual integrity and autonomy,

Recognizing further that sexual exploitation, including prostitution, abrogates these rights and subordinates women as a group, and therefore violates human dignity and the right of equality,

Concerned that sexual exploitation inflicts grave harm and often takes the extreme forms of sexual slavery, torture, mutilation and death,

Concerned that sexual violence and prostitution are not inevitable but are forms of sexual exploitation,

Recognizing that the sexual exploitation of any woman is the sexual degradation of all women, deprives women of freedom of movement, and threatens women's safety and security, thus creating the conditions of sexual terrorism,

Concerned that human sexual exploitation, including prostitution, has increasingly become an integral part of national practices which have deprived women of their human rights,

Recognizing the need for a new convention that will affirm and expand the definitions of sexual exploitation which includes violence against women and prostitution as a violation of women's human rights,

Considering that there is no convention presently in existence which addresses sexual exploitation of adults,

Desiring to make more effective the struggle against sexual exploitation,

Have agreed as follows:

Part I: General Provisions

Article 1. Definition of Sexual Exploitation

Sexual exploitation is a practice by which person(s) achieve sexual gratification, or financial gain, or advancement, through the abuse of a person's sexuality by abrogating that person's human right to dignity, equality, autonomy, and physical and mental well-being.

Article 2

Sexual exploitation takes the form of, but is not limited to:

a) The denial of life through female infanticide and the murder of women by reason of their gender, including wife and widow murder.

b) Subjection to cruel, inhuman and degrading treatment through the following: battering, pornography, prostitution, genital mutilation, female seclusion, dowry and bride price, forced sterilization and forced child-bearing, sexual harassment, rape, incest, sexual abuse, and trafficking.

c) Subjection to sexual abuse and torture, overt or covert, including sadistic, mutilating practices.

d) Temporary marriage or marriage of convenience for the purpose of sexual exploitation.

e) Sex predetermination.

Article 3

The following shall apply throughout this Convention:

a) Rape is sexual intercourse/sexual assault of any part of the body of a female of any age, by any means.

b) Sexual harassment is the imposition of any unwelcome sexual acts, gestures, speech or materials.

c) Prostitution is the use of a woman's body as a commodity to be bought, sold, exchanged, not always for money, and includes casual prostitution, street prostitution, prostitution sanctioned by socio-cultural practices, brothels, military prostitution, development prostitution, pornography, sex tourism, and mail-order-bride markets.

d) Everything that is herein said about the sexual exploitation of women applies to men and boys in situations of sexual exploitation.

Part II: Sexual Exploitation

Article 4

States Parties condemn sexual exploitation of women and children in all of its forms and agree to formulate policies and practices affecting society to insure freedom from sexual exploitation by protecting control of one's body, sexual integrity, and sexual autonomy.

a) States Parties recognize that some groups of women are rendered particularly vulnerable to sexual exploitation, such as minority and indigenous women, women subjected to racial discrimination, rural women and women in the migrating process, ethnically and socially marginalized women, women workers particularly in free trade zones, women in the sex entertainment industry, female children, elderly women, women with disabilities that are physical and mental, including learning disabilities and mental retardation, and disabilities caused by substance abuse.

b) States Parties recognize that women are rendered particularly vulnerable to sexual exploitation in the following situations: armed conflict, natural catastrophe, poverty, incarceration, including that of political prisoners and females in immigration and juvenile detention centers, institutional care, certain family contexts, including that of child sexual abuse, domestic violence, forced and child marriages, homelessness, and refugee status.

Article 5

States Parties shall punish perpetrators of sexual exploitation and redress the harm done to victims by developing penal, civil, labor and administrative sanctions. Victims shall be provided with assistance to prosecute their perpetrators. In the formulation and/or application of statutory, common, and customary law:

a)   A woman's prior sexual history, including history in prostitution, cannot be used against her in any legal action.

b)   Honor shall not be used to justify or defend against any act of sexual exploitation or violence against women.

c)   It is an aggravating circumstance and not a defense of sexual exploitation that the perpetrator is the husband, father, other relative, or employer of the victim.

d)   A woman's status as an illegal immigrant or stateless person shall not be used against her.

Article 6

States Parties reject any policy or law that legitimates prostitution of any person, female or male, adult or child; that legalizes or regulates prostitution in any way including as a profession, occupation, or as entertainment; and agree to adopt appropriate legislation that recognizes prostitution as an acute form of sexual exploitation, including the following:

a) Punishment of any person who procures, entices, or leads away by any means for the purposes of prostitution, another person, even with the consent of that person; exploits the prostitution of another person, even with the consent of that person; keeps or manages, or knowingly finances or takes part in the financing of a brothel; knowingly rents or lets a building or other place for the purpose of the prostitution of others.

b) Penalization of the customers, recognizing them as perpetrators to be criminalized while rejecting any form of penalization of the prostitute.

c) Where criminal sanctions exist against victims of sexual exploitation, States Parties shall repeal such sanctions.

d) Holding liable the producers, sellers, and distributors of pornography, recognizing that the pornography industry enlarges the demand for, promotes, and is actively engaged in sexual exploitation.

Part III: Global Situations of Sexual Exploitation

Article 7

States Parties agree:

a) To reject State economic development policies and practices which channel women into conditions of sexual exploitation.

b) To insure that State policies and practices provide for the full economic development of women through their integration in dignified paid labor at a decent standard of living from which they have been deprived.

c) To adopt legislative and other measures to prohibit sex

tourism and to penalize those who organize tourism for the purpose of sexual exploitation, penalizing the organization of it as a practice of procuring and promoting prostitution. Such measures shall be adopted and implemented in both the countries from which the customers come and the countries to which they go.

d)　To provide educational programs to change social and cultural patterns that promote the sexual exploitation of women.

Article 8

States Parties agree:

a)　To adopt measures to prevent and prohibit the trafficking in women for the purpose of sexual exploitation, in particular, prostitution.

b)　To enact such regulations as are necessary for the protection of immigrant and emigrant women and children, both at the place of arrival and departure, and while en route.

c)　To arrange for appropriate publicity warning the public of the dangers of the traffic in women and children.

d)　To ensure supervision of railway stations, airports, seaports and en route, and of other public places, in order to prevent international traffic in women and children for the purpose of prostitution.

e)　To ensure that the appropriate authorities are informed of the arrival of persons who appear, *prima facie,* to be principals and accomplices in or victims of such traffic.

Article 9

States Parties recognize that there are certain types of work in the immigration process, such as domestic labor and entertainment, that are conducive to sexual exploitation and may lead to prostitution and shall take all appropriate measures to provide adequate protection to such victims of sexual exploitation including:

a) Refuge, refugee status and protection, and repatriation of those who desire to be repatriated, whether victims of sexual exploitation have entered a country legally or illegally.

b) Protection to insure that valid written contracts of employment are entered into, monitoring of the provisions of the contract, and protection of the migrant worker from sexual exploitation and abuse in the host country.

c) The right to retain one's own passport and travel documents so that no person can be sold into prostitution or subjected to sexual favours by any other person.

d) The right to shelter, medical care, counselling and other support services.

e) The right of migrant women to be protected under existing labor laws of the recipient countries.

Article 10

States Parties shall insure that:

a) All employers who sexually exploit or abuse migrant workers are held criminally and civilly liable.

b) Persons or enterprises will be prohibited from and punished for promoting, profiting from, or engaging in any business involving the matching of women in marriage to foreign nationals, for example, mail-order-bride selling and pseudo-marriages.

c) Under no circumstances can States construe this article to prevent women from migrating or travelling abroad.

d) Their military, enforcement, and related civilian personnel, whether on or off base in foreign territory or in their own countries, shall be held legally liable and punished for engaging in prostitution of women and children.

e) Their representatives, diplomatic officials, and related personnel shall be held criminally and civilly liable for sexual exploitation.

Article 11

States Parties shall adopt special provisions to prevent the sexual exploitation of women during all wartime conditions, including those of ethnic and communal conflict, civil war, riots, and foreign intervention, and to protect women and children from sexual exploitation in refugee camps and evacuation centers. States Parties recognize the necessity for a special team of observers composed of a majority of women to monitor violations of human rights in the area of sexual exploitation and trafficking.

Part IV: Support Services

Article 12

States Parties agree to take appropriate measures to provide:

a) Restitution to victims of sexual exploitation, and to insure that, notwithstanding the victims' immigration status, their reports of sexual exploitation receive a fair hearing.

b) Women with educational programs and work in order to increase women's economic opportunities and enhance women's worth and status, thereby diminishing the necessity for women to turn to prostitution, notwithstanding the victims' immigration status.

Article 13

States Parties shall create and establish services for victims of sexual exploitation, including prostitution, such as shelters and other social services, and shall fund specialized health services and centers for prostitution alternatives that are voluntary and confidential and would provide the following:

a) Prevention, treatment of, and testing for STDs and HIV.

b) Substance-abuse rehabilitation programs.

c) Training of medical staff to recognize sexual exploitation, including rape and prostitution, to give appropriate treatment, and to make referrals to appropriate services as well as to gather medical evidence for prosecution of crimes of sexual exploitation.

d) Free and elective counselling and education services.

e) Child care facilities and housing assistance.

f) Income support.

g) Preferential access to credit and loans to begin small-scale business.

h) Non-sexist skills-training programs.

Part V: Procedural Measures

Article 14

State Parties undertake to make the principles and provisions of the Convention widely known by appropriate and active means to adults and children alike.

Article 15

a) For the purpose of examining the progress made by States Parties in achieving the realization of the obligations undertaken in the present Convention, there shall be established a Committee on the Elimination of Sexual Exploitation which shall carry out the functions herein provided. The Committee shall consist of ten persons, consideration being given to equitable distribution of representatives from those countries from which and into which the women are trafficked into sexual exploitation. The members of the Committee shall be elected by States Parties from among their nationals and shall serve in their personal capacity, consideration also being given to equitable geographical distribution, as well as to the principal legal systems.

b) The members of the Committee shall be elected by secret

ballot from a list of persons nominated by States Parties. Each State Party may nominate one person from among its nationals.

c) Elections of the members of the Committee shall be held at biennial meetings of States Parties convened by the Secretary-General of the United Nations. At those meetings, for which two-thirds of the States Parties shall constitute a quorum, the persons elected to the Committee shall be those who obtain the largest number of votes and an absolute majority of the votes of the representatives of States Parties present and voting.

d) The initial election shall be held no later than six months after the date of the entry into force of this Convention. At least four months before the date of each election, the Secretary-General of the United Nations shall address a letter to the States Parties inviting them to submit their nominations within three months. The Secretary-General shall prepare a list in alphabetical order of all persons thus nominated, indicating the States Parties which have nominated them, and shall submit it to the States Parties.

e) The members of the Committee shall be elected for a term of four years. They shall be eligible for re-election if renominated. However, the term of five of the members elected at the first election shall expire at the end of two years; immediately after the first election the names of these five members shall be chosen by lot by the chairperson of the meeting referred to in paragraph c of this article.

f) If a member of the Committee dies or resigns or for any other cause can no longer perform her Committee duties, the State Party which nominated her shall appoint another expert from among its nationals to serve for the remainder of her term, subject to the approval of the majority of the States Parties. The approval shall be considered given unless half or more of the States Parties respond negatively within six weeks after having been informed by the Secretary-General of the United Nations of the proposed appointment.

g) States Parties shall be responsible for the expenses of the members of the Committee while they are in performance of Committee duties.

Article 16

a) The Committee shall elect its officers for a term of two years. They may be re-elected.

b) The Committee shall establish its own rules of procedure, but these rules shall provide, inter alia, that:

1) Six members shall constitute a quorum;

2) Decisions of the Committee shall be made by a majority vote of the members present.

c) The Secretary-General of the United Nations shall provide the necessary staff and facilities for the effective performance of the functions of the Committee under this Convention.

d) The Secretary-General of the United Nations shall convene the initial meeting of the Committee. After its initial meeting, the Committee shall meet at such times as shall be provided in its rules of procedure.

e) The States Parties shall be responsible for expenses incurred in connection with the holding of meetings of the States Parties and of the Committee, including reimbursement to the United Nations for any expenses, such as the cost of staff and facilities, incurred by the United Nations pursuant to paragraph c of this article.

Article 17

a) The States Parties shall submit to the Committee, through the Secretary-General of the United Nations, reports on the measures they have taken to give effect to their undertakings under this Convention, within one year after the entry into force of the Convention for the State Party concerned. Thereafter the States

Parties shall submit supplementary reports every four years on any new measures taken and such other reports as the Committee may request from States Parties, NGOs and other concerned parties.

b) The Secretary-General of the United Nations shall transmit the reports to all States Parties.

c) Each report shall be considered by the Committee which may make such general comments on the report as it may consider appropriate and shall forward these to the State Party concerned and concerned NGOs. That State Party and concerned NGOs may respond with any observations to the Committee.

d) The Committee may, at its discretion, include any comments made by it in accordance with paragraph c of this article, together with the observations thereon received from the State Party and any other concerned party, in its annual report made in accordance with this article. If so requested by the State Party concerned, the Committee also may include a copy of the report submitted under paragraph a of this article.

Article 18

a) If the Committee receives reliable information which appears to it to contain well-founded indications that sexual exploitation as defined above is being practiced in the territory of a State Party, the Committee shall invite that State Party to co-operate in the examination of the information and to this end to submit observations with regard to the information concerned.

b) Taking into account any observations which may have been submitted by the State Party concerned, as well as any other relevant information available to it, the Committee may, if it decides that this is warranted, designate one or more of its members to make a confidential inquiry and to report to the Committee urgently.

c) If an inquiry is made in accordance with paragraph b of this article, the Committee shall seek the co-operation of the State

Party and any NGOS concerned. In agreement with that State Party, such an inquiry may include a visit to its territory.

d) After examining the findings of its member or members submitted in accordance with paragraph b of this article, the Committee shall transmit these finding to the State Party and any concerned party together with any comments or suggestions which seem appropriate in view of the situation.

e) All the proceedings of the Committee referred to in paragraphs a–d of this article shall be confidential, and at all stages of the proceedings the co-operation of the State Party shall be sought. After such proceedings have been completed with regard to an inquiry made in accordance with paragraph b, the Committee may, after consultations with the State Party concerned, decide to include a summary account of the results of the proceedings in its annual report made in accordance with article 17. The report of such proceedings should be considered public documents.

Article 19

a) A State Party to this Convention may at any time declare under this article that it recognizes the competence of the Committee to receive and consider communications to the effect that a State Party claims that another State Party is not fulfilling its obligations under this Convention. Such communications may be received and considered according to the procedures laid down in this article only if submitted by a State Party which has made a declaration recognizing in regard to itself the competence of the Committee. No communication shall be dealt with by the Committee under this article if it concerns a State Party which has not made such a declaration. Communications received under this article shall be dealt with in accordance with the following procedure:

1) If a State Party considers that another State Party is not giving effect to the provisions of this Convention, it may, by written communication, bring the matter to the attention of that

State Party. Within three months after the receipt of the communication, the receiving State shall afford the State which sent the communication an explanation or any other statement in writing clarifying the matter, which should include, to the extent possible and pertinent, reference to domestic procedures and remedies taken, pending or available in the matter;

2) If the matter is not adjusted to the satisfaction of both States Parties concerned, within six months after the receipt by the receiving State of the initial communication, either State shall have the right to refer the matter to the Committee, by notice given to the Committee and to the other State;

3) The Committee shall deal with a matter referred to it under this article only after it has ascertained that all domestic remedies have been invoked and exhausted in the matter, in conformity with the generally recognized principles of international law. This shall not be the rule where the application of the remedies is unreasonably prolonged or is unlikely to bring effective relief to the person who is the victim of the violation of this Convention;

4) The Committee shall hold closed meetings when examining communications under this article;

5) Subject to the provisions of subparagraph 3, the Committee shall make available its good offices to the States Parties concerned with a view to an equitable solution of the matter on the basis of respect for the obligations provided for in this Convention. For this purpose, the Committee may, when appropriate, set up an *ad hoc* conciliation commission;

6) In any matter referred to it under this article, the Committee may call upon the States Parties concerned, referred to in subparagraph 2, to supply any relevant information;

7) The States Parties concerned, referred to in subparagraph 2, shall have the right to be represented when the matter is being considered by the Committee and to make submissions orally and/or in writing;

8) The Committee shall, within twelve months after the date of receipt of notice under subparagraph 2, submit a report:

(i) If a solution within the terms of subparagraph 1 is reached, the Committee shall confine its report to a brief statement of the facts and of the solution reached;

(ii) If a solution within the terms of subparagraph 1 is not reached, the Committee shall confine its report to a brief statement of the facts; the written submissions and record of the oral submissions made by the States Parties concerned shall be attached to the report.

In every matter, the report shall be communicated to the States Parties concerned;

b) The provisions of this article shall come into force when five States Parties to this Convention have made declarations under paragraph a of this article. Such declarations shall be deposited by the States Parties with the Secretary-General of the United Nations, who shall transmit copies thereof to the other States Parties. A declaration may be withdrawn at any time by notification to the Secretary-General. Such a withdrawal shall not prejudice the consideration of any matter which is the subject of a communication already transmitted under this article; no further communication by any State Party shall be received under this article after the notification of withdrawal of the declaration has been received by the Secretary-General, unless the State Party concerned has made a new declaration.

Article 20

a) A State Party to this Convention may at any time declare under this article that it recognizes the competence of the Committee to receive and consider communications from or on behalf of individuals subject to its jurisdiction who claim to be victims of a violation by a State Party of provisions of the Convention. No communication shall be received by the Committee if it concerns a State Party which has not made such a declaration.

b) The Committee shall consider inadmissible any communication under this article which is anonymous or which it considers to be an abuse of the right of submission of such communications or to be incompatible with the provisions of this Convention.

c) Subject to the provisions of paragraph b, the Committee shall bring any communications submitted to it under this article to the attention of the State Party to this Convention which has made a declaration under paragraph a and is alleged to be violating any provisions of the Convention. Within six months, the receiving State shall submit to the Committee written explanations or statements clarifying the matter and the remedy, if any, that may have been taken by that State.

d) The Committee shall consider communications received under this article in the light of all information made available to it by or on behalf of the individual and by the State Party concerned.

e) The Committee shall not consider any communications from an individual under this article unless it has ascertained that:

1) The same matter has not been, and is not being, examined under another procedure of international investigation or settlement;

2) The individual has exhausted all available domestic remedies; this shall not be the rule where the application of the remedies is unreasonably prolonged or is unlikely to bring effective relief to the person who is the victim of the violation of this Convention.

f) The Committee shall hold closed meetings when examining communications under this article.

g) The Committee shall forward its views to the State Party concerned and to the individual.

h) The provisions of this article shall come into force when five States Parties to this Convention have made declarations under paragraph a of this article. Such declarations shall be deposited by the States Parties with the Secretary-General of the United Nations, who shall transmit copies thereof to the other States Parties. A declaration may be withdrawn at any time by notification to the Secretary-General. Such a withdrawal shall not prejudice the consideration of any matter which is the subject of a communication already transmitted under this article; no further communication by or on behalf of an individual shall be received under this article after the notification of withdrawal of the declaration has been received by the Secretary-General, unless the State Party has made a new declaration.

Article 21

The members of the Committee and of the ad hoc conciliation commissions which may be appointed under article 19, paragraph a (5), shall be entitled to the facilities, privileges and immunities of experts on mission for the United Nations as laid down in the relevant sections of the Convention on the Privileges and Immunities of the United Nations.

Article 22

The Committee shall submit an annual report on its activities under this Convention to the States Parties and to the General Assembly of the United Nations.

Article 23

a) This Convention is open for signature by all States.

b) This Convention is subject to ratification. Instruments of ratification shall be deposited with the Secretary-General of the United Nations.

Article 24

This Convention is open to accession by all States. Accession shall be effected by the deposit of an instrument of accession with the Secretary-General of the United Nations.

Article 25

a) This Convention shall enter into force on the thirtieth day after the date of the deposit with the Secretary-General of the United Nations of the twentieth instrument of ratification or accession.

b) For each State ratifying this Convention or acceding to it after the deposit of the twentieth instrument of ratification or accession, the Convention shall enter into force on the thirtieth day after the date of the deposit of its own instrument of ratification or accession.

Article 26

a) Each State may, at the time of signature or ratification of this Convention or accession thereto, declare that it does not recognize the competence of the Committee provided for in Article 15.

b) Any State Party having made a reservation in accordance with paragraph a of this article may, at any time, withdraw this reservation by notification to the Secretary-General of the United Nations.

Article 27

a) Any State Party to this Convention may propose an amendment and file it with the Secretary-General of the United Nations. The Secretary-General shall thereupon communicate the proposed amendment to the States Parties with a request that they notify him or her whether they favour a conference of States Parties for the purpose of considering and voting upon the proposal. In the event that within four months from the date of such communication at least one-third of the States Parties favours such a conference, the Secretary-General shall convene the conference under the auspices of the United Nations. Any amendment adopted by a majority of the States Parties present and voting at the conference shall be submitted by the Secretary-General to all the States Parties for acceptance.

b) An amendment adopted in accordance with paragraph a of this article shall enter into force when two-thirds of the States Parties to this Convention have notified the Secretary-General of the United Nations that they have accepted it in accordance with their respective constitutional processes.

c) When amendments enter into force, they shall be binding on those States Parties which have accepted them, other States Parties still being bound by the provisions of this Convention and any earlier amendments which they have accepted.

Article 28

a) Any dispute between two or more States Parties concerning the interpretation or application of this Convention which cannot be settled through negotiation shall, at the request of one of them, be submitted to arbitration. If within six months from the date of the request for arbitration the Parties are unable to agree on the organization of the arbitration, any one of those Parties may refer the dispute to the International Court of Justice by request in conformity with the Statute of the Court.

b) Each State may, at the time of signature or ratification of this Convention or accession thereto, declare that it does not consider itself bound by paragraph a of this article. The other States Parties shall not be bound by paragraph a of this article with respect to any State Party having made such a reservation.

c) Any State Party having made a reservation in accordance with paragraph b of this article may at any time withdraw this reservation by notification to the Secretary-General of the United Nations.

Article 29

a) A State Party may denounce this Convention by written notification to the Secretary-General of the United Nations. Denunciation becomes effective one year after the date of receipt of the notification by the Secretary-General.

b) Such a denunciation shall not have the effect of releasing the State Party from its obligations under this Convention in regard to any act or omission which occurs prior to the date at which the denunciation becomes effective nor shall denunciation prejudice in any way the continued consideration of any matter which is already under consideration by the Committee prior to the date at which the denunciation becomes effective.

c) Following the date at which the denunciation of a State Party becomes effective, the Committee shall not commence consideration of any new matter regarding that State.

Article 30

The Secretary-General of the United Nations shall inform all States Members of the United Nations and all States which have signed this Convention or acceded to it of the following:

a) Signatures, ratifications, and accessions under Articles 23 and 24.

b) The date of entry into force of this Convention under Article 25 and the date of the entry into force of any amendments under Article 27.

c) Denunciations under Article 29.

Article 31

a) This Convention, of which the Arabic, Chinese, English, French, Russian and Spanish texts are equally authentic, shall be deposited with the Secretary-General of the United Nations.

b) The Secretary-General of the United Nations shall transmit certified copies of this Convention to all States.

Notes

Notes to Introduction

1. United Nations, Declaration on the Granting of Independence to Colonial Countries and Peoples, 1960. In *Human Rights: A Compilation of International Instruments* (New York: United Nations, 1988), 49.
2. Norman K. Denzin, *The Research Act* (Englewood Cliffs, N.J.: Prentice-Hall, 1970), 93.
3. See Herbert Blumer, *Symbolic Interactionism* (Englewood Cliffs, N.J.: Prentice-Hall, 1969).
4. See Emile Durkheim, *The Rules of the Sociological Method*, 1964 ed. (New York: Free Press, 1938), 1–9, for presentation of social facts. Social reality has its own objective basis not reducible to individuals. Social facts are external to individual consciousness, sui generis social. Social facts are normative in that they have the power of coercion. Social facts are collective; that is, they are found in the whole because it can be found in parts. These are the inter-individual conditions for the production of social reality.

Notes to Chapter 1

1. The sex industry has become specialized, with some sex practices that are purchased in one region being unavailable in others. The

sex towns that serviced Subic Naval Base in the Philippines were sometimes differentiated by what was sold. Three-holers were known to be particularly available in Subic, a town poorer than Olongapo and further from the base. See Saundra Pollack Sturdevant and Brenda Stoltzfus, *Let the Good Times Roll: Prostitution and the U.S. Military in Asia* (New York: New Press, 1992), 122–23.

2. See Patricia J. Williams, *The Alchemy of Race and Rights: Diary of a Law Professor* (Cambridge, Mass.: Harvard University Press, 1991), 87.

3. William H. Masters and Virginia E. Johnson, *Human Sexual Response* (Boston: Little Brown, 1966) and *Human Sexual Inadequacy* (Boston: Little Brown, 1970) are examples of sex revealed as a physiological process, a biological function which if it is not functioning properly can be restored, *for men,* with the use of women "surrogates"; that is, any woman can be made available to replace any other women for sexual functions men require when they need to be serviced.

4. Morris Berman, *Coming to Our Senses: Body and Spirit in the Hidden History of the West* (New York: Bantam, 1989), 23, points out that cultural history is encoded in our bodies.

5. Ibid., 57.

6. Ibid., 58.

7. Ibid., 35.

8. Dr. Suzanne Képès, "The Repercussions of the Condition of Prostitutes on Their Physical and Mental Health," in *Prostitution: A World Problem, a Threat to Humanity,* Record of the Congress, 29th International Congress, International Abolitionist Federation, (Germany: Verband der Mitternachtsmissionen e.V. und Diakonisches Werk der Evangelischen Kirche in Deutschland e.V., 1989), 61.

9. Ibid., 62.

10. Ibid.

11. Ibid., 63.

12. Berman, 20.

13. R. D. Laing, *The Politics of Experience* (Middlesex: Penguin, 1967), 24.

14. Cecilie Hoigard and Liv Finstad, *Backstreets: Prostitution, Money and Love,* trans. Katherine Hanson, Nancy Sipe, and Barbara Wilson (University Park: Pennsylvania State University Press, 1992), 65.

15. Ibid., 63.
16. For a discussion of the prostitution contract, see Carole Patemen, *The Sexual Contract* (Stanford, Calif.: Stanford University Press, 1988), 198–218.
17. See Hanna Olsson, *Prostitution: Beskriving Analys Forslogtill Atgarder* (Stockholm: Liber, 1981), a study on prostitution commissioned by the Swedish government.
18. Hoigard and Finstad, 51.
19. Hoigard and Finstad, 55.
20. Council For Prostitution Alternatives Annual Report, Portland, Oregon, July 1990–June 1991.
21. Evelina Giobbe, "Juvenile Prostitution: Profile of Recruitment," in Ann Wolbert Burgess, ed., *Child Trauma: Issues and Research* (New York: Garland Press, 1992), 125.
22. Mimi Silbert and Ayala Pines, "Pornography and Sexual Abuse of Women," *Sex Roles* 10, nos. 11–12 (1984): 864.
23. Evelina Giobbe, "Prostitution: Buying the Right to Rape," in Ann Wolbert Burgess, ed., *Rape and Sexual Assault III: A Research Handbook* (New York: Garland Press, 1991), 144.
24. Alice Schwarzer, "Domenica Prostituierte," in *Warum gerade sie? Weibliche Rebellen Begegnung mit beuhmten Frauen* (Frankfurt: Fischer, 1991), 25–44.
25. Ibid.
26. Lisa Maher and R. Curtis, "Women on the Edge of Crime: Crack Cocaine and the Changing Contexts of Street-Level Sex Work in New York City," *Crime, Law, and Social Change* 18, no. 3 (1992): 227.
27. *Detroit News,* July 31, 1992.
28. Maher and Curtis, 225.
29. Hoigard and Finstad, 41.
30. Ibid., 42.
31. Maher and Curtis, 230.
32. Ibid., 250.
33. Homicide Analysis, Office of Management, Analysis of Crime Section, New York, 1976.
34. Maher and Curtis, 243.
35. Colin Nickerson, "A Death Brings Harsh Light to Japan's Dark Side," *Boston Globe,* October 29, 1991.
36. Phyllis Chesler, "Sex, Death and the Double Standard," *On the Issues* (Summer 1992): 31.
37. Phyllis Chesler, "A Woman's Right to Self-Defense: The Case of

Aileen Carol Wuornos," *St. John's Law Review* 66, no. 4 (Fall–Winter 1993): 946.

38. Ibid., 947.
39. Ibid., 967.
40. *New York Times,* November 15, 1992.
41. *Detroit News,* July 31, 1992.
42. Margaret Baldwin, "Split at the Root: Prostitution and Feminist Discourses of Law Reform," *Yale Journal of Law and Feminism* 5 (Fall 1992): 88.
43. Jane Caputi, *The Age of Sex Crime* (Bowling Green, Ohio: Bowling Green State University Popular Press, 1987), 3.

Notes to Chapter 2

1. Pasuk Phongpaichit, *From Peasant Girls to Bangkok Masseuses* (Geneva: International Labour Office, 1982), 22.
2. Gabriella Women's Coalition, "Highlights of the Court Decision," Manila, March 25, 1991. Decision of the Manila Regional Trial Court, Case of Nestorio Placer, 12, 14.
3. The sexualization of women cannot be relegated to cultural production, as if sexual subordination were not economic and political. Either to homogenize the complexity of sexual politics globally or to reduce sexual politics to cultural production is to reduce the significance of the power of male domination and the global sexual exploitation of women. See Thanh-Dam Truong, *Sex, Money and Morality: Prostitution and Tourism in South-East Asia* (London: Zed, 1990), 48, which represents patriarchy as a cultural force building on the traditional socialist feminist reduction of radical feminism to cultural feminism.
4. Patricia Hill Collins, *Black Feminist Thought: Knowledge, Consciousness, and the Politics of Empowerment* (New York: Routledge, 1990), 167.
5. Christine Delphy, *Close to Home,* trans. Diana Leonard (Amherst: University of Massachusetts Press, 1984), 144.
6. Michel Foucault, *History of Sexuality, vol. 1* (New York: Vintage, 1980), 70–71.
7. Ibid., 107.
8. Sheila Jeffreys, *Anticlimax* (New York: New York University Press, 1990), 143.
9. Stephen Heath, *The Sexual Fix* (New York: Schocken, 1982), 65.
10. Richard Ben-Veniste, "Pornography and Sex Crime: The Danish

Experience," United States Commission on Obscenity and Pornography Technical Report, vol. 7, 245–47.

11. Andrea Dworkin and Catharine MacKinnon, *Pornography and Civil Rights: A New Day for Women's Equality* (copyrighted and published by authors, 1988), 33.

12. Ibid., 36.

13. Catharine MacKinnon, *Toward a Feminist Theory of the State* (Cambridge: Harvard University Press, 1989), 215.

14. *Boston Globe,* May 17, 1992.

15. Diane E. H. Russell, *Sexual Exploitation: Rape, Child Sexual Abuse, and Workplace Harassment* (Beverly Hills, Calif.: Sage, 1984), 125–26.

16. Philip Blumstein, Pepper Schwartz, *American Couples: Money, Work, Sex,* (New York: William Morrow, 1983) 303.

17. Andrea Dworkin, *Intercourse* (New York: Free Press, 1987), 128.

18. Ibid., 129.

19. "Teenage Sexual and Reproductive Behavior," in *Facts in Brief* (New York: Alan Guttmacher Institute, 1991).

20. Ibid.

21. Bruce Ambuel and Julian Rappaport, "Developmental Trends in Adolescents' Psychological and Legal Competence to Consent to Abortion," *Law and Human Behavior* 16, no. 2 (1992): 149, citing K. A. Moore, C. W. Nord, J. L. Peterson, "Nonvoluntary Sexual Activity among Adolescents," *Family Planning Perspectives* 21, 110–14.

22. American Association of University Women Educational Foundation, "Hostile Hallways: The AAUW Survey on Sexual Harassment in America's Schools," researched by Louis Harris and Associates, June 1993, 7, 8, 15, 16.

23. Correspondence and survey results from Ed Donnellan, 1991–92 and 1993.

24. See Arlie Russell Hochschild, *The Managed Heart: Commercialization of Human Feeling* (Berkeley: University of California Press, 1983).

25. Richard Sennett, *The Fall of Public Man: On the Social Psychology of Capitalism* (New York: Vintage, 1978), 27.

26. Janice G. Raymond, *Women as Wombs: Reproductive Technologies and the Battle Over Women's Freedom* (San Francisco: Harper Collins, 1993).

27. Carol Vance, *Pleasure and Danger: Exploring Female Sexuality* (Boston: Routledge & Kegan Paul, 1984).

28. Erich Goode, *Deviant Behavior: An Interactionist Approach* (New York: Prentice-Hall, 1978), 72. Based on Gresham M. Sykes and David Matza, "Techniques of Neutralization: A Theory of Delinquency," *American Sociological Review* 22 (Dec. 1957): 664–70.

29. Ibid., 664–70.

30. Foucault, 93.

31. Ibid., 92.

32. Ibid., 103.

33. Nancy Hartsock, "Foucault on Power: A Theory for Women?" in Linda Nickolson, ed., *Feminism/Postmodernism* (New York: Routledge, Chapman & Hall, 1990), 157–75, points out how Foucault writes from the perspective of the dominator. Hartsock points out how he loses track of social structures to focus on individuals on pages 168–69.

34. See Alain Corbain, "The Secret of the Individual" and "Intimate Relations," in Michelle Perot, ed., Arthur Goldhammer, trans., *A History of the Private Life, Vol. IV* (Cambridge, Mass.: Harvard University Press, 1990), 457–614.

35. Katie Roiphe, "Date Rape's Other Victim," *New York Times,* June 13, 1993, 40.

36. *New York Times,* September 19, 1993.

37. Janice G. Raymond, "Sexual and Reproductive Liberalism," in Dorchen Leidholdt and Janice G. Raymond, eds., *Sexual Liberals and the Attack on Feminism* (Elmsford, N.Y.: Pergamon Press, 1990), 103.

38. Dorchen Leidholdt, "Introduction," in Leidholdt and Raymond, ix.

Notes to Chapter 3

1. Vern Bullough, *The History of Prostitution* (New Hyde Park, N.Y.: University Books, 1964), 167.

2. Josephine E. Butler, *Personal Reminiscences of a Great Crusade* (Westport, Conn.: Hyperion, 1976), 2.

3. Judith Walkowitz, "The Making of an Outcast Group," in Martha Vicinus, ed., *A Widening Sphere: Changing Roles of Victorian Women* (Bloomington: Indiana University Press, 1977), 82.

4. Butler, 13.

5. Ibid., 112–13.

6. In Glen Petrie, *A Singular Iniquity: The Campaign of Josephine Butler* (New York: Viking, 1971), 16–17.

7. Josephine E. Butler, *Some Thoughts on the Present Aspect of the Crusade against the State Regulation of Vice* (Liverpool: Brakell, 1874), 18.

8. Josephine E. Butler, "Sursum Corda: Annual Address to the Ladies National Association" (Liverpool: Brakell, 1871), 7.

9. Ibid., 35.

10. Timothy J. Gilfoyle, *City of Eros: New York City, Prostitution, and the Commercialization of Sex, 1790–1920* (New York: Norton, 1992), 29.

11. Alain Corbain, *Women for Hire: Prostitution and Sexuality in France after 1850* (Cambridge, Mass.: Harvard University Press, 1990), 205.

12. Gilfoyle, 60.

13. Howard Davidson and Gregory Loken, *Child Pornography and Prostitution: Background and Legal Analysis,* National Center for Missing and Exploited Children, National Obscenity Enforcement Unit, U.S. Department of Justice, 48.

14. Gilfoyle, 248.

15. Ibid., 119.

16. Corbain, 39.

17. Ibid., 193.

18. Walkowitz, 73.

19. Ibid., 85.

20. Ibid., 86–87.

21. Josephine E. Butler, "State Regulation of Vice," 1898 (British Committee, Leaflet No. 108b, July 1910), 3.

22. Josephine E. Butler, "Address Delivered at Croyden," Ladies National Association, 1871, 10.

23. Petrie, 102–4.

24. Charles Terrot, *Traffic in Innocents* (New York: Dutton, 1960), 35–36.

25. Edward J. Bristow, *Vice and Vigilance: Purity Movements in Britain since 1700* (Totowa, N.J.: Rowman and Littlefield, 1977), 80.

26. Alfred S. Dyer, *The European Slave Trade in English Girls* (London: Dyer, 1880), 7.

27. Bristow, 88.

28. Gilfoyle, 287.

29. Maurice Gregory, *The Suppression of the White Slave Traffic* (London: Friends Association for Abolishing State Regulation of Vice, 1908), 9.

30. Petrie, 22.

31. Ibid., 235–41.
32. Ann Stafford, *The Age of Consent* (London: Hodder and Stoughton, 1964), 134–35.
33. Josephine E. Butler, *Rebecca Jarrett* (London: Morgan and Scott, 1886), 28–29.
34. Terrot, 160.
35. Ibid.
36. Ibid., 168.
37. Ibid., 171.
38. Bristow, 110.
39. Stafford, 214.
40. Butler, *Rebecca Jarrett*, 54–55.
41. Butler, *Sursum Corda*, 12.
42. David J. Pivar, *Purity Crusade: Sexual Morality and Social Control, 1868–1900* (Westport, Conn.: Greenwood, 1973), 158.
43. Walkowitz, 90–91.
44. Ibid., 73, 91.
45. Petrie, 228.
46. Spending and containment are discussed by G. J. Barker-Benfield in "The Spermatic Economy: A Nineteenth-Century View of Sexuality," *Feminist Studies* (Summer 1972): 45–74, and are developed more fully by him in *Horrors of the Half-Known Life* (New York: Harper & Row, 1976); and by Steven Marcus in *The Other Victorians* (New York: Basic, 1964), chapter 1.
47. Corbain, 27.
48. Sofie Lazarsfeld, *Women's Experience of the Male* (London: Encyclopedic, 1938), 437.
49. *International Agreement for the Suppression of the White Slave Traffic,* May 18, 1904, London, Her Majesty's Stationery Office, 1905.
50. Teresa Billington-Grieg, "The Truth about White Slavery," *English Review*, June 1913.
51. Ibid., 445.
52. Ibid., 445–46.
53. Ernst A. Bell, *Fighting the Traffic in Young Girls* (Chicago: Bell, 1911), 160.
54. Maude Miner, *Slavery of Prostitution* (New York: Macmillan, 1916), 116.
55. Ibid., 104.
56. Carol Green Wilson, *Chinatown Quest* (San Francisco: California Historical Society, 1974).

57. Bristow, 179.
58. Christabel Pankhurst, "The Government and White Slavery," pamphlet reprinted from the *Suffragette*, April 18, April 25, 1913.
59. Emma Goldman, *The Traffic in Women* (Washington, N.J.: Times Change Press, 1970), 20.
60. Ibid., 26.
61. Pankhurst, 7, 8.
62. Goldman, 27.
63. Pankhurst, 11.

Notes to Chapter 4

1. "Violation of Children's Rights in El Salvador, 1989–91," *Children's Rights International*, 1991, 26.
2. Adrianne Aron, Shawn Corne, Anthea Fursland, Barbara Zelwer, "The Gender-Specific Terror of El Salvador and Guatemala: Post-Traumatic Stress Disorder in Central American Refugee Women," *Women's Studies International Forum* 14, Nos. 1–2: 41.
3. Ibid., 40.
4. Ibid., 38.
5. From Petition against the Japanese Government by the Korean Council for the Women Drafted for Sexual Service by Japan, 16.
6. Ibid., 14.
7. Speech of President of Japan Federation of Bar Associations, UN World Conference on Human Rights, Vienna, Austria, June 14–25, 1993.
8. Ibid., 23.
9. "Story of Song Siin Do, Korean Former 'Comfort Woman' Resident in Japan," statement prepared for the UN World Conference on Human Rights, Vienna, Austria, June 14–25, 1993.
10. *New York Times,* January 14, 1992.
11. *New York Times*, August 9, 1992.
12. Yayori Matsui, "Sexual Slavery in Korea," *Frontiers: A Journal of Women's Studies* 2, no. 1 (Spring 1977): 27–28.
13. Le Ly Hayslip, with Jay Warts, *When Heaven and Earth Changed Places* (New York: Doubleday, 1989), 224.
14. Alan Dawson, *Patpong: Bangkok's Big Little Street* (Bangkok: Thai Watana Panick Press, 1988), 39.
15. Mohamed Awad, *Report on Slavery* (New York: United Nations, 1966), 198.

16. Susan Brownmiller, *Against Our Will* (New York: Simon and Schuster, 1975), 93–95.
17. Roland-Pierre Paringaus, "Vietnam, Consequence de la guerre," *Le Monde,* June 2, 1977.
18. Neil Jamieson, *Understanding Vietnam* (Berkeley: University of California Press, 1993) 333.
19. Alan Dawson, *Fifty-five Days* (Englewood Cliffs, N.J.: Prentice-Hall, 1977), 267.
20. Hayslip, 224.
21. Ibid., 223–24.
22. Ibid., 224.
23. Ibid.
24. Ibid.
25. *Le Monde,* June 2, 1977.
26. "La rehabilitation des anciennes prostituees au Sud Vietnam," *Femmes et Mondes* (Clichy, France), no. 36 (1977).
27. Le Thi Quy, "Social Policy on Prevention and Restriction of Prostitution in Vietnam," Vietnamese country paper prepared for Coalition Against the Trafficking in Women–Asia Conference, Manila, Philippines, April 2–4, 1993, 3.
28. Walden Bello, "From American Lake to a People's Pacific," in Sandra Pollock Sturdevant and Brenda Stoltzfus, *Let the Good Times Roll: Prostitution and the U.S. Military in Asia* (New York: New Press, 1992), 14–21.
29. Yayori Matsui, "Trafficking in Women and Prostitution in Japan," Japanese country paper prepared for the Coalition Against the Traffic in Women–Asia Conference, Manila, Philippines, April 2–4, 1993, 5.
30. "Trafficking in Women: Prostitution and Sexual Violence: The Situation of Sexual Exploitation in Korea," Korean country paper prepared for the Coalition Against the Trafficking in Women–Asia Conference, Manila, Philippines, April 2–4, 1993, 5.
31. "Organized Crime in Pennsylvania: A Decade of Change, 1990 Report" (Harrisburg: Pennsylvania Crime Commission, 1990), 304.
32. Yayori Matsui, "Why I Oppose Kisaeng Tours," in Kathleen Barry, Charlotte Bunch, and Shirley Castley, eds., *International Feminism: Networking against Female Sexual Slavery* (New York, 1984), 67. Report of the Global Feminist Conference, Rotterdam, Netherlands, April 6–15, 1983.
33. Ibid., 66.
34. Kim Hae Won, "The Realities of Kisaeng Tourism in Cheju Island,"

in *Exploitation of Women and Children: Its Causes and Effects* (New Delhi, India: Vishwa Yuvak Kendra, 1988), 147–49.

35. Matsui, "Why I Oppose Kisaeng Tours," 71.

36. *Depthnews,* September 17, 1981.

37. See *Boston Globe,* November 25, 1991; and Lillian S. Robinson, "Touring Thailand's Sex Industry," *Nation,* November 1, 1993, 494.

38. Lloyd Shearer, "Intelligence Report," *Parade,* November 11, 1977, 12.

39. Brian Eads, "Package Tours That Provide a Wife," reprinted from *London Observer* in *San Francisco Chronicle,* June 9, 1977.

40. Tom Weber, *San Francisco Chronicle,* April 20, 1976.

41. Dawson, *Patpong: Bangkok's Big Little Street,* 40.

42. Ibid., 68.

43. Pasuk Phongpaichit, *From Peasant Girls to Bangkok Masseuses* (Geneva: International Labour Office, 1982), 9.

44. Steven Erlanger, "A Plague Awaits," *New York Times Magazine,* July 14, 1991.

45. Linda K. Richter, *The Politics of Tourism in Asia* (Honolulu: University of Hawaii Press, 1989), 99.

46. Cynthia Enloe, *Making Feminist Sense of International Politics: Bananas, Beaches, and Bases* (Berkeley: University of California Press, 1989), 37.

47. *New York Times,* March 25, 1991.

48. EMPOWER, "The Trafficking of Women and Girls for Prostitution," Thai country paper prepared for the Coalition Against the Trafficking in Women–Asia Conference, Manila, Philippines, April 2–4, 1993, 4.

49. *Nation* (Bangkok), January 18, 1993.

50. *Bangkok Post,* December 31, 1992.

51. Joint study of Research and Development Division of the Police Department and the Population Institute of Chulalongkorn University. *Bangkok Post,* January 3, 93.

52. Virginia Miralao, Celia Carlos, and Aida Fulleros Santos, *Women Entertainers in Angles and Olongapo: A Survey Report* (Manila: Women's Education Development, Productivity, and Research Organization and KALAYAAN, 1990), 35.

53. Enloe, 87.

54. Aurora Javate DeDios, "Struggle against Sexual Exploitation and Prostitution: A Philippine Perspective," paper prepared for International Meeting of Experts: "Protecting Women's Human Rights

from Sexual Exploitation, Violence, and Prostitution," State College, Pennsylvania, April 8–10, 1991, 4.

55. Ibid.

56. *Daily Globe* (Manila), 1991.

57. *New York Times,* March 25, 1991.

58. Letter to Kathleen Barry from Aurora DeDios, October 22, 1992.

59. Philippines Development Plan for Women, 1989–92, 139.

60. Aurora Javate DeDios, "Sexual Violence and Exploitation in a Crisis Situation: The Philippine Case," paper prepared for International Meeting of Experts: "Protecting Women's Human Rights from Sexual Exploitation, Violence, and Prostitution," State College, Pennsylvania, April 8–10, 1991, 5.

61. Lynn Lee, "Alternative Employment, Economic Livelihood, and Human Resource Development for Women in the Entertainment Industry," report by Women's Education Development, Productivity, and Research Organization (WEDPRO), Manila, June 1992.

62. *Manila Bulletin,* March 31, 1993.

63. Miralao, Carlos, and Santos, 35.

64. Ibid.

65. Ibid.

66. Jamieson, 339.

67. Siriporn Skrobanek, "In Pursuit of an Illusion: Thai Women in Europe," *South East Asia Chronicle* 96: 7–13.

68. Thanh-Dam Truong, *Sex, Money, and Morality: Prostitution and Tourism in South-East Asia* (London: Zed, 1990), 187.

69. Eads.

70. *San Francisco Chronicle,* December 8, 1975.

71. *New Women's Times,* January 5–18, 1979.

72. Siriporn Skrobanek, "Voices of Thai Women," April 1990.

73. Chat Garcia, "A Report on Australia," Australian country paper prepared for the Coalition Against the Trafficking in Women–Asia Conference, Manila, Philippines, April 2–4, 1993, 5.

74. *Wall Street Journal,* January 25, 1984.

75. DeDios, "Struggle against Sexual Exploitation and Prostitution: A Philippine Perspective," 125.

76. *Bangkok Post,* January 22, 1991.

77. *Washington Post,* January 2, 1991.

78. Guido de bruin, Interpress service feature, appearing on Women's Studies List, BITNET, June 20, 1992.

79. John Krich, "The Blossoming Business of Imported Love: Here Come the Brides," *Mother Jones* (Feb.–March 1986): 37.

80. *Liberator,* November 1991, 5.
81. Socialist Republic of Vietnam, Section I, Republic Act. No. 6955.
82. *Los Angeles Times,* November 12, 1991.
83. *San Francisco Chronicle,* July 2, 1988.
84. *Atlanta Journal & Constitution,* July 12, 1990.
85. *New York Times,* May 12, 1990.
86. *New York Times,* June 13, 1991.
87. *New York Times,* May 12, 1990.
88. Katherine Marton, *Multinationals, Technology, and Industrialization* (Lexington, Mass.: Lexington, 1986), 42.
89. Hnin Hnin Pyne, "AIDS and Prostitution in Thailand: Case Study of Burmese Prostitutes in Ranong," Thesis May 1992.
90. Mattanimojdara Rutnin, "Prostitution and Economic Empowerment of Women in Thailand: A Case Study of Alternatives in A Chiengmai Village in Northern Thailand," paper presented at the Association of Women in Development Conference, Washington, D.C., November 1989, 3.
91. Phongpaichit, 22.
92. Ibid., 24.
93. *Bangkok Post,* January 1991.

Notes to Chapter 5

1. Report of a regional seminar, "Criminal Law and Women in Latin America and the Caribbean," *Women: Watched and Punished,* (CLADEM, Latin American Committee for the Defense of Women's Rights, Lima, Peru, 1993), 12.
2. M. Islam, "Economic Backwardness along with Ignorance and Superstition Are Causes for Prostitution in Bangladesh," in *Exploitation of Women and Children: Its Causes and Effects,* Asian Regional Conference (New Delhi, India: Vishwa Yuvak Kendra, 1988), 39.
3. Khaleda Salahuddin and Ishrat Shamim, *Women in the Urban Informal Sector: Employment Pattern Activity Types and Problems* (Dhaka, Bangladesh: Women for Women, 1992), 135.
4. Ishrat Shamim and Quamrul Ahsan Chowdhury, *Homeless and Powerless: Child Victims of Sexual Exploitation* (Dhaka, Bangladesh: Bangladesh Sociology Association, January 1993), 34.
5. Ishrat Shamin, "Rural and Urban Prostitution in Bangladesh: Its Causes and Suggestions for Remedies," in *Exploitation of Women*

and Children: Its Causes and Effects, Asian Regional Conference (New Delhi, India: Vishwa Yuvak Kendra, 1988), 79; Ittefaq, *Bangladesh Daily,* January 9, 1991.

6. Ishrat Shamim, "Slavery and the International Trafficking of Women and Children: Its Nature and Impact," Bangladesh country paper prepared for the Coalition Against the Trafficking in Women–Asia Conference, Manila, Philippines, April 2–4, 1993, 6.

7. Based on report from Alamgir Rahman and Shamsur Raham, "Traffic in Women," *Weekly Bichitra* (Dhaka, Bangladesh), March 4, 1983.

8. International Abolitionist Federation, 29th International Congress Proceedings, Vienna, Austria, September 1987, 57. From Ishrat Shamin, associate professor of sociology, University of Dhaka.

9. Ibid., 58.

10. *Bangkok Post,* January 2, 1993.

11. *Newsday,* July 21, 1992.

12. International Abolitionist Federation, 60, from *Daily Ittefaq,* April 4, 1985.

13. Zia Awan, *Mag,* August 16–22, 1990, 19.

14. *Daily News,* April 3, 1991.

15. *New Nation,* August 30, 1991.

16. *Wall Street Journal,* October 30, 1990.

17. Jyoti Sanghera, "Trafficking and Sexploitation of Nepali Children and Women in the Sex Industry," statement to UN working group on "Contemporary Forms of Slavery," July 29–August 2, 1991.

18. Robin Morgan, ed., *Sisterhood Is Global* (New York: Doubleday, 1984), 455.

19. Ibid., 461. Paper prepared by Bina Pradhan and Lynn Bennett on "Rural Women's Participation in the Nepali Household Economy," for the seminar on Appropriate Technology for the Hill Farming Systems, June 1981.

20. "Nepal, Human Rights in the Himalayas," special report of Nepal National Coordination Committee, INHURED International, June 1993.

21. Robert Ankerson, Jr., "Every Young Girl's Nightmare," *Independent,* September 9, 1992.

22. Jyoti Sanghera, "Poverty and Prostitution in Asia: Redefining Some Categories," *Diva* (Sept.–Dec. 1992): 48.

23. Ankerson, 11.

24. *Female Sexual Slavery,* 93.

25. Ankerson, 11.

26. *Human Development Report* (New York: United Nations, 1992), 34.
27. Ibid., 1.
28. The factors, which include life expectancy, adult literacy, and purchasing power to buy commodities for satisfying basic needs, are reflected in a computation based on the gross national product (GNP). The Human Development Index is a measure of deprivation based on targets of 100% for each of the areas that are meant to fulfill human choice. In measuring poverty, this index "focus[es] on the access, or lack of access, that people have to various options for human development." One approach to measuring poverty is to identify the minimum calorie intake required and convert it into foodstuffs necessary to meet that level, which is culture specific and is adjusted for gender, age, type of activity, and health status. This measurement also includes necessary nonfood items.
29. See Kathleen Barry, *Susan B. Anthony: A Biography of a Singular Feminist* (New York: New York University Press, 1988).
30. Ishrat Shamim, "Rural and Urban Prostitution in Bangladesh: Its Causes and Suggestions for Remedies," in *Exploitation of Women and Children: Its Causes and Effects,* Asian Regional Conference (New Delhi, India: Vishwa Yuvak Kendra, 1988), 80.
31. Edward Gargan, *New York Times,* November 15, 1992.
32. Nepal Human Rights, for the United Nations World Conference on Human Rights.
33. Bhubaneshwari Satyal, "Causes of Prostitution in Nepal," in *Exploitation of Women and Children: Its Causes and Effects,* Asian Regional Conference (New Delhi, India: Vishwa Yuvak Kendra, 1988), 217.
34. I. S. Gilada and Vijay Thakur, "Devadasi: A Study of Sociocultural Factors and Sexual Exploitation," in *Exploitation of Women and Children: Its Causes and Effects,* Asian Regional Conference (New Delhi, India: Vishwa Yuvak Kendra, 1988), 71.
35. Ibid., 73.
36. Asha Ramesh and Philomena H. P., "The Devadasi Problem," in Kathleen Barry, Charlotte Bunch, Shirley Castley, eds., *International Feminism: Networking Against Female Sexual Slavery* (New York: International Women's Center, 1984), 84; and Asha Ramesh, "The Devadasi Practice," in *Exploitation of Women and Children: Its Causes and Effects,* Asian Regional Conference (New Delhi, India: Vishwa Yuvak Kendra, 1988), 84.
37. Gilada and Thakur, 73.

38. Ramesh, 120.
39. Ibid., 122.
40. Thanh-Dam Truong, *Sex, Money, and Morality: Prostitution and Tourism in South-East Asia* (London: Zed, 1990), 134.
41. Ibid.
42. Mattanimojdara Rutnin, "Prostitution and Economic Empowerment of Women in Thailand: A Case Study of Alternatives in a Chiengmei Village in Northern Thailand," paper presented at the Association of Women in Development Conference, Washington, D.C., 3.
43. Dr. Aruna Upreti, "There are at least 5,000 Prostitutes in Kathmandu," *Independent*, September 2, 1992.
44. Laxmi Maskey, "Poverty and Prostitution in Nepal," in *Exploitation of Women and Children: Its Causes and Effects*, Asian Regional Conference (New Delhi, India: Vishwa Yuvak Kendra, 1988), 48.
45. Rosy Win, "Trafficking and Forced Prostitution of Chinese and Burmese Women in Thailand," Burmese country paper prepared for the Coalition against the Trafficking in Women–Asia Conference, Manila, Philippines, April 2–4, 1993, 6. Based on her interviews with Relief Organization officials who visited the camps during the time that the abovementioned deportation took place.
46. BITNET, Women's Studies List, August 14, 1992.
47. *Independent*, March 9, 1992.
48. *The Nation* (Bangkok), June 11, 1992; Win, 7.
49. A. Rosy Win, "Trafficking and Forced Prostitution of Chinese and Burmese Women in Thailand," 7; derived from a thesis on "AIDS and Prostitution in Thailand: A Case Study of Burmese Prostitutes in Ranong," by Hnin Hnin Pyne, May 1992.
50. Ibid.
51. Edith Mirante, Terre des Femmes, Tubingen.
52. Ibid.
53. United Press International, April 2, 1992.
54. Ibid.
55. Win, 9.
56. Ann Scott Tyson, "Chinese 'People Mongers' Prey on Women and Children," *Christian Science Monitor*, March 29, 1990.
57. Ibid.
58. Win, 13–14.
59. Leonora Angeles and the Philippine Organizing Team, "Between the Devil and the Deep Blue Sea: Transnational Issues and Trends

in Trafficking of Filipino Women," Philippines country paper prepared for the Coalition against the Trafficking in Women–Asia Conference, Manila, Philippines, April 2–4, 1993, 3. Figures from the Asia Migrant Center, Philippines.

60. Ibid.

61. Ibid., 13–14; based on figures presented in Kanlungan Center Foundation, "Overseas Filipina Domestic Helpers: Issues and Problems," in Palma-Beltran and Aurora DeDios, eds., *Filipina Overseas Contract Workers: At What Cost?* (Manila: Goodwill, 1993), 33.

62. Findings reported from two hearings on P.S. Res. 555 and P.S. No. 556, July 7, 1989 and August 9, 1989.

63. Denis MacShane, "Gulf Migrant Labor: Working in Virtual Slavery," *Nation*, March 8, 1991.

64. Chris Hedges, "Foreign Women Lured into Bondage in Kuwait," *New York Times*, January 3, 1992.

65. Jack Kelley, " 'Help Me': Tales of Torment in Kuwait," *USA Today*, March 5, 1992.

66. Yayori Matsui, "Trafficking in Women and Prostitution in Japan," Japanese country paper prepared for the Coalition Against the Traffic in Women–Asia Conference, Manila, Philippines, April 2–4, 1993, 7. Angeles and the Philippine Organizing Team, 4.

67. "Wir sind die Erben der Samurai," *Der Spiegel* (Hamburg), June 25, 1990, 108–21.

68. Matsui, 3.

69. *Chicago Tribune*, November 19, 1991.

70. *New York Times*, January 11, 1992.

71. *New York Times*, January 30, 1992.

72. Salahuddin and Shamim, 13.

73. Ibid, 14, citing World Bank, *Bangladesh: Strategies for Enhancing the Role of Women in Economic Development* (Washington, D.C., 1990).

Notes to Chapter 6

1. Evelina Giobbe, WHISPER Oral History Project, Minneapolis, Minnesota, 1987.

2. Testimony to the New York State Select Committee on Crime, public hearing on Children, Pornography, and the Illicit Sex Industry, November 14, 1977.

3. Testimony before the Grand Jury of the City and County of San

Francisco, State of California, Investigation of _____, April 19, 1976.

4. Council for Prostitution Alternatives Annual Report, July 1990–June 1991, Portland, Oregon.

5. Mimi Silbert, *Sexual Assault of Prostitutes: Phase One* (Washington, D.C.: National Center for the Prevention and Control of Rape, National Institute of Mental Health, 1980), 51.

6. Iceberg Slim, *Pimp: The Story of My Life* (Los Angeles: Holloway, 1969), 11–12.

7. Ibid., 74–75.

8. From papers confiscated from a pimp in 1977 in a San Francisco police raid.

9. This and following quotes between pimps and Mary Christenson are derived from transcripts of tape recordings made while Mary was working undercover, usually at the San Francisco bus station, May 1977.

10. Testimony to the New York State Select Committee on Crime, public hearing on Children, Pornography, and the Illicit Sex Industry, November 14, 1977.

11. The Council for Prostitution Alternatives Annual Report, July 1990–June 1991, Portland, Oregon.

12. Mark Schorr, "Blood Stewart's End," *New York*, March 27, 1978.

13. Ibid., 56.

14. Linda Lovelace with Mike McGrady, *Ordeal* (Secaucus, N.J.: Citadel, 1980).

15. Ibid., 40–41.

16. Christina Milner and Richard Milner, *Black Players* (Boston: Little, Brown, 1972), 90.

17. Ibid., 94.

18. Ibid.

19. Ibid., 95.

20. Eleanor Miller, *Street Woman* (Philadelphia: Temple University Press, 1986), 38.

21. Bernard Cohen, *Deviant Street Networks: Prostitution in New York* (Lexington, Mass.: Lexington, 1980).

22. Ibid., 55–59.

23. Miller, 39.

24. Ibid.

25. Cecilie Howard and Liv Finstad, *Backstreets: Prostitution, Money and Love,* trans. Katherine Hanson, Nancy Sipe, and Barbara Wil-

son (University Park: Pennsylvania State University Press, 1992), 135.

26. Ibid.

Notes to Chapter 7

1. Testimony to the New York State Select Committee on Crime, public hearing on Children, Pornography, and the Illicit Sex Industry, November 14, 1977.
2. D. Kelly Weisburg, *Children of the Night* (Lexington, Mass.: Heath, 1985), 172.
3. Theresa Lynch and Marily Neckes, "The Cost-Effectiveness of Enforcing Prostitution Laws," unpublished report, San Francisco, December 1978, chapter 3, 29.
4. Florida Legislation, PCB/HB 597.
5. Barbara Yondorf, "Prostitution as a Legal Activity: A Policy Analysis of the West German Experience," unpublished paper, Seattle: University of Washington, School of Public Affairs, 1977.
6. Ibid., table 1.
7. Ibid., 16.
8. Alice Schwarzer, "Domenica Prostituerte," *Warum gerade sie? Weibliche Rebellen Begebnung mit Beruhmten Frauen* (Frankfurt: Fischer, 1991), 24–44.
9. Sam Janus and Barbara Bess, *A Sexual Profile of Men in Power* (Englewood Cliffs, N.J.: Prentice-Hall, 1977), 96–97.
10. *Die Tageszeitung,* October 26, 1991.
11. *Los Angeles Times,* July 29, 1991.
12. United Nations, UNE/1990/13, 7.
13. Ibid, 10.
14. Cornelia Flitner, *Emma,* March, April, 1993.
15. Frank Bovenkerk and Sivander Poel, "Prostitution and Crime: A Comparative Research Project in the Netherlands and the U.S.A.," working paper 1, Utrecht Willem Pompe Institute for Criminal Sciences, University of Utrecht, 1992, 6.
16. *Boston Globe,* May 27, 1992.
17. "International Prostitution Files," *Review of the International Abolitionist Federation,* Paris, 1989, 5.
18. Interview with staff of *Equipe d'Action,* Paris, March 1978.
19. *France-Soir,* November 1974.

20. Dallayrac, *Le Nouveau Visage de la Prostitution* (Paris: Laffant, 1976), 92–93.
21. Kathleen Barry, "International Politics of Female Sexual Slavery," in Kathleen Barry, Charlotte Bunch, and Shirley Castley, eds., *International Feminism: Networking against Female Sexual Slavery* (New York, 1984), 26. Report of a Global Feminist Conference, Rotterdam, Netherlands, April 6–15, 1983.
22. "The Madrid Report," UNESCO Meeting of Experts, Madrid, Spain, 1986. (See also *Penn State Report,* April 1991.)
23. Jean D'Cunha, "Prostitution in a Patriarchal Society: A Critical Review of the SIT Act," *Economic and Political Weekly,* November 7, 1987, 1919–26.
24. Ibid., 1920.
25. "Position Paper on Prostitution: The Sexual Exploitation of Women in Prostitution in the Philippines," position paper of WEDPRO, Kalayaan, Women's Crisis Center, Gabriella Commission on Violence against Women, CONSPECTUS Foundation and Women's Legal Bureau, presented at the Coalition against the Trafficking in Women–Asia Conference, Manila, Philippines, April 2–4, 1993.
26. Thanh-Dam Truong, *Sex, Money, and Morality: Prostitution and Tourism in South-East Asia,* 2d. ed. (London: Zed, 1990), 160.
27. Ibid., 177.
28. *Bangkok Post,* December 31, 1992.
29. April 1991, "Current and Future Dimensions of the HIV/AIDS Pandemic," WHO/GPA/SF1/91.4.
30. *U.S. News and World Report,* July 22, 1992, 54–58.
31. *American Health,* May 1991, 39.
32. William Masters and Virginia Johnson, *Crisis: Heterosexual Behavior in the Age of AIDS* (New York: Grove, 1988), 133.
33. United Nations Focus, U.N. Department of Public Information, February 1991.
34. *New York Times,* December 28, 1990.
35. *New York Times,* November 18, 1991.
36. Bob Drogin, "HIV Spreading 'Out of Control' in India's Red-Light District," *San Francisco Chronicle,* November 27, 1992.
37. *Bangkok Post,* January 17, 1991.
38. Seven Erlanger, "A Plague Awaits," *New York Times Magazine,* July 14, 1991, 24.
39. *Economist,* February 8, 1992, 33.
40. "Thailand Moves to Stanch the Virus: Catch If Catch Can," *Far Eastern Review,* February 13, 1992, 29.

41. *HIV/AIDS Surveillance Report* (Atlanta: Centers for Disease Control and Prevention, October, 1993), 8. *U.S. News and World Report*, February 16, 1987.
42. Masters and Johnson, 132.
43. Ibid., 114.
44. New York State Department of Health, "A Guide to HIV Counseling and Testing," February 1990, 5.
45. "Thailand Moves to Stanch the Virus: Catch If Catch Can," *Far Eastern Review*, February 13, 1992, 29–30.
46. *AIDS Action*, September 1991, 2.
47. Cecilie Hoigard and Liv Finstad, *Backstreets: Prostitution, Money and Love*, trans. Katherine Hanson, Nancy Sipe, and Barbara Wilson, (University Park: Pennsylvania State University Press, 1992), 191.

Notes to Chapter 8

1. *The Trial of Patricia Hearst* (transcript) (San Francisco: Great Fidelity Press, 1976), 163.
2. Fred Soltysik, *In Search of a Sister* (New York: Bantam, 1976), 230.
3. Transcript, 62.
4. Ibid., 257.
5. Ibid., 257–58.
6. Joseph Gabel, *False Consciousness* (New York: Harper, 1978), 231.
7. Transcript, 256.
8. Gabel, 226.

Notes to Chapter 9

1. See Andrea Dworkin, *Intercourse* (New York: Free Press, 1987), for a discussion of intercourse as sexual exploitation.
2. Originally organized with Filipina women by Brenda Stoltzfus, a member of the Mennonite Central Committee who lived in the Philippines for 5 years and worked closely with the bar women in Olongapo.
3. Brenda Stoltzfus, Karla Rowlins, and Sarah Williams, "Hospitality—What Price? The U.S. Navy at Subic Bay . . . and the Women's Response," pamphlet (Olongapo, Philippines: Evan and Sochce, 1989.)

4. Council for Prostitution Alternatives, Participation Agreement and Grievance Procedure, Portland, Oregon.
5. Maria Lourdes Barreto, "Everybody Shuts Up, We Speak Up," in *Women: Watched and Punished* (Lima, Peru: Latin American Committee for the Defense of Women's Rights, 1993), 285.
6. *Independent* (Kathmandu, Nepal), September 2, 1992.
7. Yayori Matsui, "Trafficking in Women and Prostitution in Japan," Japanese country paper prepared for the Coalition Against the Traffic in Women–Asia Conference, Manila, Philippines, April 2–4, 1993, 6.
8. Judith Herman, *Trauma and Recovery: The Aftermath of Violence, from Domestic Abuse to Political Terror* (New York: Basic, 1992), 156.
9. Ibid., 175.
10. Ibid., 183.
11. Ibid., 178.
12. Ibid., 196.
13. Ibid., 202.
14. Herman, 207.
15. Ibid., 215.
16. Council for Prostitution Alternatives Annual Report, July 1990–June 1991, Portland, Oregon, 5.
17. Council for Prostitution Alternatives Handbook, Portland Oregon, 29.
18. Le Thi Quy, "Social Policy on Prevention and Restriction of Prostitution in Vietnam," Vietnamese country paper prepared for Coalition Against the Trafficking in Women–Asia Conference, Manila, Philippines, April 2–4, 1993, 5–6.
19. A Swedish seminar in Hanoi introduced gender theory in 1991. Penn State Seminar on Women and the Family, 1993.
20. Hector Gros Espiell, "Human Rights and International Humanitarian Law," *Bulletin of Human Rights* 91, no. 1 (New York: United Nations, 1992), 16.
21. Ibid.
22. Erica-Irene Daes, "Freedom of the Individual under Law: An Analysis of Article 29 of the Universal Declaration of Human Rights" (New York: United Nations, 1990), 3.
23. *Penn State Report, International Meeting of Experts on Sexual Exploitation, Violence, and Prostitution,* (State College, Pennsylvania, April 1991), Report published by UNESCO and the Coalition against Trafficking in Women, 7.

24. Ibid.
25. "Perspectives on Violence Against Women," background paper prepared by the Division for the Advancement of Women, Department for Policy Coordination and Sustainable Development, United Nations MAV/1993/BP.1, 29 September, 1993, 8.
26. Ibid., 9.

Index